# Beyond East and West
## Problems in Liturgical Understanding

by

## Robert Taft, SJ

The Pastoral Press
Washington, D.C.

ISBN: 0-912405-13-9

The Pastoral Press
225 Sheridan Street, NW
Washington, D.C. 20011
(202) 723-5800

The Pastoral Press is the publications division of the National Association of
Pastoral Musicians, a membership organization of musicians and clergy
dedicated to fostering the art of musical liturgy.

Printed in the United States of America

*For my brothers and sisters*
Jim, Eleanor, Dave and Kathie

# ACKNOWLEDGEMENTS

It was my friend and confrère Michael A. Fahey, S.J., President of the Catholic Theological Society of America, who first encouraged me to prepare an anthology of my publications, and helped in their selection. His enthusiastic interest in my work has been a source of constant support, for which I am deeply grateful. Thanks also to Edward Foley, O.F.M. Cap. who seconded the idea, and contacted Virgil C. Funk, founder and president of The National Association of Pastoral Musicians, about the possibility of publishing this collection under its auspices. Thanks to Virgil's immediate and positive reply, the project has become a reality.

I also acknowledge with gratitude the permission granted by the editors of the following publications to use again materials for which they hold copyright: *Studia Liturgica* (Rotterdam) for chapter 2; *Concilium* (Nijmegen) for chapter 5; *Diakonia* (John XXIII Center, Fordham University, New York) for chapters 8 and 9; *Orientalia Christiana Periodica* (Pontifical Oriental Institute, Rome) for chapter 11; The Liturgical Press (Collegeville, MN) for sections of "The Liturgical Year: Studies, Prospects, Reflections," *Worship* 55 (1981) 2–23, used in the Foreword and in chapter 1; for "Sunday in the Eastern Tradition," from Mark Searle (ed.), *Sunday Morning: A Time for Worship* (Liturgical Press 1982) 49–74, part of which comprises chapter 3; for "Lent: A Meditation," *Worship* 57 (1983) 123–134, reprinted in chapter 4; and for "Receiving Communion—a Forgotten Symbol," *Worship* 57 (1983) 412–418, which has been revised and expanded for chapter 7; all Copyright ©, in the years of publication already noted, by the Order of St. Benedict, Inc. Published by The Liturgical Press, Collegeville, Minnesota. Used with permission.

# CONTENTS

# LIST OF ABBREVIATIONS

AAS = *Acta Apostolicae Sedis*
AC = *Antike und Christentum*
ALW = *Archiv für Liturgiewissenschaft*
BELS = Bibliotheca *Ephemerides Liturgicae,* Subsidia
CCL = Corpus Christianorum Latinorum
CSCO = Corpus scriptorum Christianorum orientalium
CSEL = Corpus scriptorum ecclesiasticorum Latinorum
DOP = *Dumbarton Oaks Papers*
GCS = Griechische christliche Schriftsteller
JTS = *The Journal of Theological Studies*
LF = Liturgiegeschichtliche Forschungen
LMD = *La Maison-Dieu*
LQF = Liturgiewissenschaftliche Quellen und Forschungen
Mansi = J. D. Mansi, *Sacrorum conciliorum nova et amplissima collectio . . .*
OC = *Oriens Christianus*
OCA = Orientalia Christiana Analecta
OCP = *Orientalia Christiana Periodica*
PG = Migne, *Patrologia Graeca*
PIO = Pontificio Istituto Orientale, Rome
PL = Migne, *Patrologia Latina*
PO = *Patrologia orientalis*
SC = Sources chrétiennes
TU = Texte und Untersuchungen

# INTRODUCTION

It is difficult to imagine a much higher honor than to be invited to contribute a word of introduction to the work of one's teacher, but that is the honor that Father Taft has accorded me. I first met him at a historic gathering in Scottsdale, Arizona, a gathering that gave rise the following year to the creation of the North American Academy of Liturgy. There was occasion then for little more than to introduce myself as one who intended to do post-doctoral study during the following semester at the Pontifical Oriental Institute where Father Taft was then (as he is now) a professor.

It was during those six months in Rome, and especially at the Oriental Institute, that I really came to know Father Taft and to know so very much more through him. I went there to come to a deeper and more scientifically grounded appreciation of the liturgical traditions of the eastern churches. That I received abundantly from Father Taft, and from other members of that distinguished faculty. More importantly, however, I learned from Father Taft a style of pedagogy and an ascesis in scholarly method, both of which are richly evident in this collection of essays.

These, however, are not only technical essays exemplifying that ascesis, but also (and more specifically) the garnering of the spiritual yield of that discipline. As he himself has commented in his preface to this volume, "nothing is more relevant than knowledge." Here he demonstrates that principle.

Our current discussions of pastoral praxis, of theological meaning, of spirituality, and of much more rest finally on the assumption that we know what we are talking about; and to know what we are talking about demands knowing much more than can be generated by a mere creativity operating upon data drawn only from the experience of itself. As will become clear from the careful reading of these pages, access to a broad spectrum of data regarding not only our past, but also the present of a wide range of Christian living beyond our often limited experience, needs to be available to any who would speak with authority of the tradition of Christian worship. What will also be clear, I hope, is that the perception of the authentic tradition truly liberates, whereas attempts to declare our own freedom from that discipline of knowing have, in fact, and again and again, merely tightened our enslavement to the limited vision that is our malaise.

Here the reader will encounter significant examples of the spiritual and practical relevance of careful, technical liturgical study. The conclusions drawn from that study are valuable in themselves, but these essays will have achieved their purpose fully only if they engender in the reader a deeper appreciation of the process by which one arrives at such conclusions and a hunger to participate in that process.

The Rev. Thomas J. Talley
Professor of Liturgics
The General Theological Seminary of the Episcopal Church
New York, New York

# FOREWORD

This anthology is not just a reprint of articles that first appeared elsewhere. With the exception of chapters 2 and 4 the material has been updated and revised, in some instances substantially. Furthermore, an attempt has been made to unify the material by suppressing repetitions, and by the addition of an index.

The title represents, perhaps, the author's wishful thinking. As an orientalist specializing in the history of Eastern Christian liturgy, most of my original research publications have been highly technical studies of little or no interest to the non-specialist. None of that material is reproduced here. But amidst all the contemporary talk of "relevance" in matters liturgical it remains my firm conviction that nothing is so relevant as knowledge, nothing so irrelevant as ignorance. So I think that in matters of pastoral relevance there is still something we can learn from comparative historical scholarship across a broad range of traditions, and I have tried to show that in several of my less technical publications. It is they that have provided the essays for this book.

They deal with liturgy, both Eastern and Western, from the standpoint of history, theology, and pastoral practice. I treat questions of Eastern liturgy not only because it is my specialty, but because liturgiology, like linguistics, is a comparative discipline: one can no more be a liturgiologist by studying one tradition than one can develop a theory of linguistics knowing only one language. As one who is basically an historian in method, my point of departure is usually the *history* of the tradition. This step precedes *theology*, which is a reflection on the tradition in its intersection with contemporary experience. *Pastoral practice* should be in continuity with this tradition, and both mirror and shape our reflection on it.

Note that last point: practice is determined not by the past, but by tradition, which encompasses not only past and present, but theological reflection on both. That is why the Catholic Church has never been guided by a retrospective ideology. Tradition is not the past; it is the Church's self-consciousness *now* of that which has been handed on to her not as an inert treasure but as a dynamic inner life.

Theology must be reflection on the whole of that reality, the whole of tradition, not on just its present manifestation. One of the great contemporary illusions is that one can construct a liturgical theology without a profound knowledge of the liturgical tradition. So in spite of the (to me) rather perplexing discomfort that many Americans seem to have with history, there can be no theology without it.

Perhaps that discomfort arises from a misconception of the nature of history and its uses in theological understanding. People tend to think that history is the past, and they are quite rightly more concerned with the present. But history is not the past. Rather, it is a contemporary understanding of life in terms of its origins and evolution as seen through the prism of our present concerns. In theology we use the methods of history because we are interested in tradition, and tradition is not the past, but the present understood genetically, in continuity with that which produced it.

So we study the history of the liturgical tradition for the same reason that a psychiatrist seeks to uncover the childhood traumas of patients: not to understand their childhood, their past, but their present adult personality that was formed by those childhood experiences and can be understood only in relation to them. I think it important to insist on this. Christian liturgy is a given, an object, an already existing reality like English literature. One discovers what English literature is only by reading Chaucer and Shakespeare and Eliot and Shaw and the contemporaries. So too with liturgy. If we want to know what Christmas and Chrismation, Eucharist and Easter mean, we shall not get far by studying anthropology or game-theory, or by asking ourselves what we *think* they mean. We must plunge into the enormous stream of liturgical and patristic evidence and wade through it piece by piece, age by age, ever alert to pick up shifts in the current as each generation reaches for its own understanding of what it is we are about.

That, for better or worse, is the philosophy behind most of what is said in the essays reproduced in this book.

# Beyond East and West

Chapter One

# TOWARD A THEOLOGY OF THE CHRISTIAN FEAST

In his excellent study of the Gospel accounts of Jesus' earthly beginnings,[1] as well as in his briefer summary of the same material,[2] Raymond Brown demonstrates that the aim of the Infancy Narratives is not biographical; they do not attempt to provide a history of Jesus' earthly origins. Rather, they present a message, that of the whole Gospel in miniature: the announcing of the Good News, its acceptance by the disciples but rejection by most of Israel, its extension to the gentile world. It is not the story of baby Jesus in Bethlehem, but the meaning of Christ for humankind in the era of the post-pentecostal Church, that is behind the narratives.

Now I think one can apply an analogous hermeneutic to the feasts of the Christian calendar as a means of uncovering its theological sense, and hence its liturgical or pastoral purpose, while at the same time resolving the numerous antinomies that surface in any discussion of the church year: eschatology vs. history, dominical cycle vs. yearly, *kairos* vs. *chronos*. I do not wish to imply that these tensions are not real. But I think they arose, in germ at least, not in fourth-century Jerusalem as one usually hears, but in New Testament times. And I think that the New Testament itself provides us with the elements of a balanced theology that can lead to their resolution. This brings us to our reflections.

The basic question on every level—historical, theological, pastoral—is the problem of *meaning*: just what are we doing when we celebrate a Christian feast? Since the problem of any feast rooted not in myth but in sacred history is the problem of time and event, that is, the relationship between past unrepeatable event and present celebration, much ink has been spilt trying to uncover some special Semitic philosophy of time at the root of the whole business. This has

Originally published as the final section of "The Liturgical Year: Studies, Prospects, Reflections," *Worship* 55 (1981) 2–23.

not been very fruitful. Recent studies of Greek and Hebrew semantics and the relevant Old Testament material have concluded that there is no firm evidence for positing a peculiar sense of time in Hebrew thought, and that nothing in New Testament statements about time and eternity provides an adequate basis for a distinct Christian concept of time.[3]

What is true, however, is [1] that the Bible presents an historical teleology, a strong sense of the sequence of historical events as purposeful movement toward a goal, [2] that it uses this sequence as a medium for presenting the story of an encounter with God,[4] [3] that it presents later cultic memorial celebrations of this encounter as a means of overcoming the separation in time and space from the actual saving event.[5] The salvation manifested in the past lives on now as an active force in our lives if we encounter it anew and respond to it in faith, and we cannot do that unless we remember it. In the Old Testament, cultic memorial is one of the ways in which Israel remembered, making present the past saving events as a means of encountering in every generation the saving work of God.

That *present* encounter is the point of it all. In memorial we do not take a mythic trip into the past, nor do we drag the past into the present by repeating the primordial event in mythic drama.[6] For the events we are dealing with are not myths but history. As such they are *ephapax*, once and for all. There was one exodus from Egypt and one resurrection of Christ, and we can neither repeat them nor return to them. But that is not to say they are dead, static, over and done with. They created and manifested and remain the bearers of a new and permanent quality of existence called salvation, initiating a permanent dialectic of call and response between God and his people. The events that began and first signaled this divine wooing of humankind may be past, but the reality is ever present, for the promises were made "to you and to your descendants, forever" (Gen 13:15). The liturgy presents this challenge to each new generation, that it too may respond in faith and love to the call.

So in memorializing the past event we do not return to it nor recreate it in the present. The past event is the efficacious sign of God's eternal saving activity, and as past it is contingent. The reality it initiates and signifies, however, is neither past nor contingent but ever present in God, and through faith to us, at every moment of our lives. And if the past event is both permanent cause and contingent historical sign of salvation, the ritual memorial is the present efficacious sign of the same eternal reality. The ritual moment, then, is a synthesis of past, present, and future, as is always true in "God's time."

What the New Testament adds to this is the startling message that "God's time" has been fulfilled in Christ. So New Testament time is not some distinctive theory of time, but the fullness of time. What distinguishes it is its completeness, its *pleroma*; what is inaugurated is not some new philosophy of time, but a new quality of life. The eschaton is not so much a new age as a new existence. "New age" is but one of its metaphors, and it is important not to mistake the sign for the signified, not to be distracted from the work at hand by lofty disquisitions on kinds of time. Since our *pleroma* is in God, what we are confronted with is not the *past* made present, or even the *future* present, but the *end* present, not in the sense of the *finish* but of *completion*: God himself present to us.

This presence is fulfilled in Jesus, and that is what we mean by the "eschatological" nature of the New Age. Patrick Regan has said it better than I:

> The death and resurrection of Jesus are eschatological in that they bring the history of faith and the history of the divine presence to a close by bringing them to fulfillment. In the death of Jesus faith finds full expression; in his resurrection the divine presence is fully given.... But they come to a close as history only because they have reached that condition of fullness (*pleroma*) toward which their respective histories were ordered.
>
> The goal toward which all faith tended, and from which it derived its saving power, was the death of Christ. And the goal toward which all of God's gifts tended was the gift of himself to Christ in the Spirit. Thus the entire history of man's faith and God's self-gift are destined to find their eschatological perfection in the glorification of the crucified One. Consequently, neither faith nor the divine presence cease to exist. Rather do they remain everlastingly actual precisely because they have attained definitive and final form in the Spirit-filled Christ. Hence the eschaton is really not a thing (*eschaton*), but a person (*eschatos*). It is the Lord Jesus himself—the last man, the spiritual man—the one in whom God and man have fully and finally met in the Spirit.
>
> The death and resurrection of Jesus bring to fulfillment not only history but creation as well.... In him, man and the world have, for the first time, come to be what they were meant to be. Hence the eschatological 'last days' join the protohistorical 'first days.' The

kingdom is the garden. Christ is Adam. The eschaton is the Sabbath; the day on which God rests from his work and delights in its perfection.[7]

In other words the New Testament does two things. First, as Cullmann said, it divides time anew.[8] No longer do we await salvation. It is here in Christ, though the denouement of his parousia still lies ahead. Secondly, the New Testament recapitulates and "personalizes" all of salvation history in Christ. Nothing is clearer in the New Testament than the fact that everything in sacred history— event, object, sacred place, theophany, cult—has quite simply been assumed into the person of the incarnate Christ. He is God's eternal Word (Jn 1:1, 14); his new creation (2 Cor 5:17, Gal 6:15, Rom 8:19ff, Apoc 21–22) and the new Adam (1 Cor 15:45, Rom 5:14); the new Pasch and its lamb (1 Cor 5:7, Jn 1:29, 36; 19:36, 1 Pet 1:19, Apoc 5ff *passim*); the new covenant (Mt 26:28, Mk 14:24, Lk 22:20, Heb 8–13 *passim*), the new circumcision (Col 2:11–12), and the heavenly manna (Jn 6:30–58, Apoc 2:17); God's temple (Jn 2:19–27), the new sacrifice, and its priest (Eph 5:2, Heb 2:17–3:2; 4:14–10:14); the fulfillment of the Sabbath rest (Col 2:16–17, Mt 11:28–12:8, Heb 3:7– 4:11) and the Messianic Age that was to come (Lk 4:16–21, Acts 2:14–36). Neither the list nor the references are exhaustive. He is quite simply "all in all" (Col 3:11), "the alpha and the omega, the first and the last, the beginning and the end" (Apoc 1:8; 21:6; 22:13). All that went before is fulfilled in him: "For the law has but a shadow of the good things to come instead of the true form of these realities" (Heb 10:1); and that includes cultic realities: "Let no one pass judgment on you in questions of food and drink or with regard to a festival or a new moon or a sabbath. These are only a shadow of what is to come; but the substance belongs to Christ" (Col 2:16–17).

This is seminal for any understanding of Christian worship. The Old Testament temple and altar with their rituals and sacrifices are replaced not by a new set of rituals and shrines, but by the self-giving of a person, the very Son of God. Henceforth, true worship pleasing to the Father is none other than the saving life, death and resurrection of Christ: "iam Pascha nostrum Christus est, paschalis idem victima!"[9] And our worship is this same sacrificial existence in us.[10] Paul tells us, "Just as surely as we have borne the image of the man of dust, we shall also bear the image of the man of heaven" (1 Cor 15:49; cf. Phil 2:7–11; 3:20–21, Eph 4:22–24), the Risen Christ, "image of the invisible God, the first-born of all creation" (Col 1:15; cf. 2 Cor 4:4), who conforms us to his image through the gift of his Spirit (2 Cor 3:15, Rom 8:11ff, 29). For St. Paul, "to live is Christ" (Phil 1:21), and to be saved is to be conformed to Christ by dying to self and rising to new life in him (2 Cor 4:10ff; 13:4, Rom 6:3ff, Col 2:12–13, 20; 3:1–3, Gal 2:20; Eph 2:1ff, Phil 2:5ff, 3:10–11, 18–21) who, as the "last Adam" (1 Cor 15:45), is the definitive form of redeemed human nature (1 Cor 15:21–22, Rom 5:12–21, Col 3:9–11, Eph 4:22–24). Until this pattern is so repeated in each of us that Christ is indeed "all in all" (Col 3:11) we shall not yet have "filled up what is lacking in Christ's afflictions for the sake of his body, that is, the church" (Col 1:24). For we know "the power of his resurrection" only if we "share his sufferings, becoming like him in his death" (Phil 3:10).[11]

To express this spiritual identity, Paul uses several compound verbs that begin with the preposition *syn* (with): I suffer with Christ, am crucified with Christ, die with Christ, am buried with Christ, am raised and live with Christ, am carried off to heaven and sit at the right hand of the Father with Christ (Rom 6:3–11, Gal 2:20, 2 Cor 1:5; 4:7ff, Col 2:20, Eph 2:5–6).[12] This is one of Paul's ways of underscoring the necessity of my personal participation in redemption. I must "'put on Christ" (Gal 13:27), assimilate him, somehow experience with God's grace and repeat in the pattern of my own life the principal events by which Christ has saved me, for by undergoing them he has transformed the basic human experiences into a new creation. How do I experience these events? In him, by so entering into the mystery of his life that I can affirm with Paul: "I have been crucified with Christ; it is no longer I who live, but Christ who lives in me" (Gal 2:20).

This seems to be what Christian liturgy is for St. Paul. Never once does he use cultic nomenclature (liturgy, sacrifice, priest, offering) for anything but a life of self-giving, lived after the pattern of Christ.[13] When he does speak of what we call liturgy, as in 1 Cor 10–14, Eph 4, or Gal 3:27–28, he makes it clear that its purpose is to contribute to this "liturgy of life," literally to edify, to build up the Body of Christ into that new temple and liturgy and priesthood in which sanctuary and offerer and offered are one. For it is in the liturgy of the Church, in the ministry of word and sacrament, that the biblical pattern of recapitulation of all in Christ is returned to the collectivity and applied to the community of faith that will live in him.

So to return to where we began and borrow a term from the biblical scholars, the liturgy is the ongoing *Sitz im Leben* of Christ's saving pattern in every age, and what we do in the liturgy is exactly what the New Testament itself did with Christ: it applied him and what he was and is to the present. For the *Sitz im Leben* of the Gospels is the historical setting not of the original event, but of its telling during the early years of the primitive Church. It is this, I think, that gives the lie to the notion that the celebration of any feast but Sunday and, perhaps, Easter, is "historicism." For if feasts "historicize," then so do the Gospels. Do not both New Testament and liturgy tell us this holy history again and again as a perpetual anamnesis?

> Therefore I intend always to *remind* you of these things, though you know them and are established in the truth that you have. I think it is right . . . to arouse you by way of *reminder* . . . And I will see to it that after my departure you may be able at any time to *recall* these things. For we did not follow cleverly devised myths when we made known to you the power and coming of our Lord Jesus Christ, but we were eyewitnesses of his majesty (2 Pet 1:12–16).

Note that this is not kerygma, as it is almost always mistakenly called, but anamnesis. Preaching the Good News to awaken the response of faith in the new message is kerygma. But the kerygma written down and proclaimed repeatedly in the liturgical assembly to recall us to our commitment to the Good News already heard and accepted in faith, even though "we know them and are established in the truth," is anamnesis, and that is what liturgy is all about.

Is the problem of sacred history in the Christian calendar so different from the problem of meditating on sacred history in the Bible and proclaiming it day in and day out in the liturgy of the word? But note well how the New Testament proclaims this message. What Brown says of the infancy accounts is true of the Gospels *tout court*. They are not just a history of what Jesus did, but a *post factum* theological interpretation, for the Apostolic Church, of the meaning of what he said and did and was in the light of the resurrection and post-resurrection events. So the Gospels, "passion stories with a long introduction" in the famous phrase of Kähler,[14] were written backwards, and their *Sitz im Leben* is the later life of the Church when the accounts were written.

Thus when the account of the mission of the twelve in Mt 10:18 refers to being dragged before governors and kings, and witnessing before the gentiles, it is bending the account to a new situation that had nothing to do with the original historical setting.[15] The Acts of the Apostles show that it took the Apostolic Church a long time to realize there was to be a time of mission, a time of the Church between ascension and parousia. That is why there was such resistance to receiving outsiders into the Jewish-Christian Church (Acts 10–11, 15). But once it was understood, there was no hesitation in rewriting the account of the call of the twelve to reflect this new situation. Just as the Book of Deuteronomy applied the early experience of the exodus to the later Israel, so too the New Testament applied Christ to its life-situation, its *Sitz im Leben*. And when we preach and meditate on the same apostolic call and mission, and apply it to the demands of our vocation and mission today, we are using the Gospels as the Apostolic Church did, and as they were meant to be used: not as a history of the past, but as "the power of God unto salvation for everyone who has faith, first for the Jew, then for the Greek" (Rom 1:16).

The Gospel, then, is not a story but a power (Paul wrote this before the Gospel had become the Gospels). It is God's Spirit in us now, in the age of the Church, calling us to himself. And so Matthew is not "historicizing" when he recounts the call of the twelve, nor is St. Ignatius of Loyola when he proposes in his *Spiritual Exercises* meditations on the saving actions of Jesus in the Gospels, nor is the Church when it presents the same saving mysteries to us in word and rite and feast. For the focus is not on the story, not on the past, but on Paul's "power of God unto salvation, first for the Jew, then for the Greek," and right now for you and me.

This is what we do in liturgy. We make anamnesis, memorial, of this dynamic saving power in our lives, to make it penetrate ever more into the depths of our being, for the building up of the Body of Christ.

That which was from the beginning, which we have heard, which we have seen with our eyes, which we have looked upon and touched with our hands, concerning the word of life—the life was made manifest and we saw it, and testify to it, and proclaim to you the eternal life which was with the Father and was made manifest to us—that which we have seen and heard we proclaim to you, so that you may have communion with us; and our communion is with the Father and with his son Jesus Christ. And we are writing this that our joy may be complete (1 Jn 1:1–4).

It seems to me, then, that the eschatological/historical problem arose and was solved by the Apostolic Church. But it was not solved by abandoning New Testament eschatology, which sees Christ as inaugurating the age of salvation. What was abandoned was the mistaken belief that this implied an imminent parousia. But that does not modify the main point of Christian eschatology, that the endtime is not in the future but *now*. And it is operative now, though not exclusively, through the anamnesis in word and sacrament of the dynamic present reality of Emmanuel, "God-with-us," through the power of his Spirit in every age.

In the Gospels the transition to this new age of salvation history is portrayed in the accounts of the post-resurrection appearances of Jesus.[16] They introduce us to a new mode of his presence, a presence that is real and experienced, yet quite different from the former presence before his passover. When he appears he is not recognized immediately (Lk 24:16, 37, Jn 21:4, 7, 12). There is a strange aura about him; the disciples are uncertain, afraid; Jesus must reassure them (Lk 24:36ff). At Emmaus they recognize him only in the breaking of the bread—and then he vanishes (Lk 24:16, 30–31, 35). Like his presence among us now, it is accessible only through faith.

What these post-resurrection accounts seem to be telling us is that Jesus is with us, but not as he was before.[17] He is with us and not with us, real presence and real absence. He is the one whom "heaven must receive until the time for establishing all that God spoke by the mouth of his holy prophets from of old" (Acts 3:21), but who also said "I am with you always, until the close of the age" (Mt 28:20). It is simply this reality that we live in the liturgy, believing from Matthew 18:20 that "where two or three are gathered in my name, there am I in the midst of them,"[18] yet celebrating the Lord's Supper to "proclaim the Lord's death until he comes" (1 Cor 11:26) in the spirit of the early Christians, with their liturgical cry of hope: "Marana-tha! Amen. Come Lord Jesus!" (Apoc 22:20).

So the Jesus of the Apostolic Church is not the historical Jesus of the past, but the Heavenly Priest interceding for us constantly before the throne of the Father (Rom 8:34, Heb 9:11–28), and actively directing the life of his Church (Apoc 1:17–3:22 and *passim*).[19] The vision of the men that produced these documents was not directed backwards, to the "good old days" when Jesus was with them on earth. We see such nostalgia only after Jesus' death, before the resurrection appearances give birth to Christian faith.

The Church did keep a record of the historical events, but they were reinterpreted in the light of the resurrection, and were meant to assist Christians to grasp the significance of Jesus in their lives.[20] That this was the chief interest of the New Testament Church, the contemporary, active, risen Christ present in the Church through his Spirit, can be seen in the earliest writings, the epistles of St. Paul, which say next to nothing about the historical details of Jesus' life.

It is this consciousness of Jesus as the Lord not of the past but of contemporary history that is the aim of all Christian preaching and spirituality and liturgical anamnesis. Christian vision is rooted in the gradually acquired realization of the Apostolic Church that the parousia was not imminent, and that the eschatological, definitive victory won by Christ must be repeated in each one of us, until the end of time. And since Christ is both model and source of this struggle, the New Testament presents both his victory and his cult of the Father as ours: just as we have died and risen with him (Rom 6:3–11, 2 Cor 4:10ff, Gal 2:20, Col 2:12–13, 20; 3:1–3, Eph 2:5–6), so too it is we who have become a new creation (2 Cor 5:17, Eph 4:22–24), a new circumcision (Phil 3:3), a new temple (1 Cor 3:16–17; 6:19, 2 Cor 6:16, Eph 2:19–22), a new sacrifice (Eph 5:2), and a new priesthood (1 Pet 2:5–9, Apoc 1:6; 5:10; 20:6). This is why we meditate on the pattern of his life, proclaim it, preach it, celebrate it: to make it ever more deeply our own. This is why the Apostolic Church left us a book and a rite, word and sacrament, so that what Christ did and was, we too may do and be, in him. For this reason, sacred history is never finished. It continues in us, which is why in liturgy we fête the saints, and ourselves too, as well as Christ, for God's true glorification is Christ's life that he has implanted in us. So the "communion of saints" is also a sign of sacred history, proof of the constant saving action of Christ in every age.

For Christian life, according to the several New Testament metaphors for it, is a process of conversion into Christ.[21] He is the *Ursakrament* which we have seen the New Testament present as the personalization of all that went before, and the recapitulation and completion and model and foretaste of all that will ever be. As such, he is not just the mystery of the Father's love for us, "the image of the unseen God" (Col 1:15); he is also the revelation of what we are to be (1 Cor 15:49, 2 Cor 3:18, Rom 8:29). His life is the story of entering sinful humanity and returning it to the Father through the cross, a return that was accepted and crowned in Christ's deliverance and exaltation (Phil 2:5ff). And this same story, as we have seen, is also presented as the story of everyone, the archetype of our experience of returning to God through a life of death to self lived after the pattern Christ showed us: "He died for all, that those who live might live no longer for themselves but for him who for their sake died and was raised" (2 Cor 5:15).[22]

In the New Testament, the very process of its composition reveals the growing realization of this fact: that our final passage to the Father through death and resurrection was to be preceded by a life of death to sin and new life in Christ. The whole point of the New Testament rewrite of Christ's life is to make it speak to this new awareness: that the new age was to be not a quick end but a new holy history. As Patrick Regan said in the passage already cited, the eschaton is not a time or a thing, it is a person, the new Adam, Jesus Christ (1 Cor 5:20ff, 42ff). And the new creation is a life lived in him (2 Cor 5:13–19)—or rather, his life in us (Gal 2:20).

Liturgical feasts, therefore, have the same purpose as the Gospel: to present this new reality in "anamnesis" as a continual sign to us not of a past history, but of the present reality of our lives in him. "Behold *now* is the acceptable time; behold, *now* is the day of salvation" (2 Cor 6:2). It is this vision of the mysteries of Christ's life now that we see in the festal homilies of the golden age of the Fathers, such as those of St. Leo the Great (440–461), which always stress the present salvific reality of the liturgical commemoration.[23] For salvation history does go on, but not in the sense that at Christmas Christ's birth is somehow present again. For such events are historical, and they are past, and liturgy does not fête the past. What is present is *our* being born anew in Christ, *our* entrance into new life through this coming of God to us *now*.[24] For as St. Leo says in his famous aphorism that is an entire liturgical theology, what Christ did visibly during his earthly ministry has now passed over into sacrament: "Quod itaque Redemptoris nostri conspicuum fuit, in sacramenta transivit."[25]

One pastoral conclusion from all this should be obvious: there is no ideal model of Christian feast or calendar which we must "discover" and to which we must "return." Rather, it is up to each generation to do what the Apostolic Church did in the very composition of the New Testament: apply the mystery and meaning of Christ to the *Sitz im Leben* of today. A liturgy is successful not because of its fidelity to some past ideal, but because it builds up the Body of Christ into a spiritual temple and priesthood by forwarding the aim of Christian life: the love and service of God and neighbor; death to self in order to live for others as did Christ.

And so Christmas is not just about the coming of Christ to Bethlehem, but about the coming of Christ to me, and about my going out to others. And Easter is not about the empty tomb in Jerusalem some 2000 years ago, but about the reawakening here and now of my baptismal death and resurrection in Christ. We shall see this, I think, if we put aside the folklore of the past and the modern theories of time and leisure and play, and meditate on the texts of the word of God, and of the Fathers, and of the worship of the Church. There we shall find that the festal cycle is but one facet of the life of the Church, one way of expressing and living the mystery of Christ that is radically one in all aspects of its Christian expression. As Jean Daniélou said,

> The Christian faith has only one object, the mystery of Christ dead and risen. But this unique mystery subsists under different modes: it is prefigured in the Old Testament, it is accomplished historically in the earthly life of Christ, it is contained in mystery in the sacraments, it is lived mystically in souls, it is accomplished socially in the Church, it is consummated eschatologically in the heavenly kingdom. Thus the Christian has at his disposition several registers, a multi-dimensional symbolism, to express this unique reality. The whole of Christian culture consists in grasping the links that exist between Bible and liturgy, Gospel and eschatology, mysticism and liturgy. The application of this method to scripture is called exegesis; applied to liturgy it is called mystagogy. This consists in reading in the rites the mystery of Christ, and in contemplating beneath the symbols the invisible reality.[26]

That's what the Church year, and indeed all of liturgy, is about.

NOTES

1. *The Birth of the Messiah. A Commentary on the Infancy Narratives in Matthew and Luke* (New York: Doubleday 1977).

2. *An Adult Christ at Christmas. Essays on the Three Biblical Christmas Stories* (Collegeville: Liturgical Press 1977).

3. J. Barr, *Biblical Words for Time* (Studies in Biblical Theology, London: SCM Press 1962).

4. *Ibid.* 144.

5. B. S. Childs, *Memory and Tradition in Israel* (Studies in Biblical Theology 37, Naperville, Ill.: A. R. Allenson, n.d.).

6. *Ibid.* 81ff.

7. P. Regan, "Pneumatological and Eschatological Aspects of Liturgical Celebration," *Worship* 51 (1977) 346–347.

8. O. Cullmann, *Christ and Time. The Primitive Christian Conception of Time and History* (Philadelphia: Westminister Press 1950) 82ff, esp. 84.

9. From verse four of the seventh-century Ambrosian hymn *Ad regias Agni dapes*, used in the Roman office at Sunday vespers in the Easter season.

10. All four levels—Old Testament cult, fulfilled by Christ in the liturgy of his self-giving, a pattern we emulate in our lives and in our worship, as a gauge of the future fulfillment—are expressed in Heb 13:11–16: "For the bodies of those animals whose blood is brought into the sanctuary by the high priest as a sacrifice for sin are burned outside the camp. So Jesus also suffered outside the gate in order to sanctify the people through his own blood. Therefore, let us go forth to him outside the camp, bearing abuse for him. For here we have no lasting city, but seek the city which is to come. Through him then let us continually offer up a sacrifice of praise to God, that is, the fruit of lips that acknowledge his name. Do not neglect to do good and to share what you have, for such sacrifices are pleasing to God."

11. In 1 Jn 3:14 we know this power through charity: "We know that we have passed out of death into life, because we love the brethren. He who does not love remains in death."

12. Here and in the following paragraphs I have drawn considerable inspiration from David M. Stanley, *A Modern Scriptural Approach to the Spiritual Exercises* (Chicago: Loyola University 1967). I could recommend no better book for one who wishes to learn what it means to meditate on the mysteries of Christ's life in the cycle of the church year.

13. Cf. for example Rom 1:9; 12:1; 15:16, Phil 2:17; 4:18, 2 Tim 4:6; also Heb 13:15–16 cited in note 10.

14. "Passionsgeschichten mit ausführlicher Einleitung," M. Kähler, *Der sogennante historische Jesu und der geschichtliche, biblische Christus* (Leipzig 1896[2]; Eng. tr. Philadelphia: Fortress Press 1964) 80.

15. Stanley (note 12 above) 168–175.

16. *Ibid.* 278ff.

17. *Ibid.* 280ff.

18. I am aware of the recent challenge to the liturgical interpretation of this pericope (J. Duncan M. Derrett, "Where two or three are convened in my name . . . ': a sad misunderstanding," *Expository Times* 91 no. 3 (December 1979) 83–86, but no matter; the liturgical application has become traditional regardless of the original *Sitz im Leben* of the text, and it is this traditional belief that interests us here.

19. Stanley, *op cit.* 284–285.

20. *Ibid.* 285.

21. See M. Searle, "The Journey of Conversion," *Worship* 54 (1980) 48–49, and "Liturgy as Metaphor," *Worship* 55 (1981) esp. 112ff.

22. See also 1 Jn 3:14 cited in note 11.

23. For example, *Sermo 63 (De passione 12)* 6, PL 54, 356: "Omnia igitur quae Dei filius ad reconciliationem mundi et fecit, et docuit, non in historia tantum praeteritarum actionum novimus, sed etiam in praesentium operum virtute sentimus." On Leo's liturgical theology see M. B. de Soos, *Le mystère liturgique d'après s. Léon le grand* (LQF 34, Münster: Aschendorff 1958).

24. *Sermo 36 (In epiph. 6)* 7, PL 54, 254.

25. *Sermo 74 (De ascens. 2)* 2, PL 54, 398.

26. "Le symbolisme des rites baptismaux," *Dieu vivant* 1 (1945) 17 (my translation).

# Chapter Two

# HISTORICISM REVISITED

It has become a cliché to refer to a fourth century "historicization" of the liturgy and, in particular, of the annual paschal celebration. What was once holistic and eschatological becomes fragmented and historical; what was one unitary proleptic experience of the whole mystery of redemption present and operative in our midst, decomposes into a series of commemorations recalling the successive phases of its past historical accomplishment: triumphal entry into Jerusalem, betrayal, Last Supper, passion, burial, resurrection. A parallel shift is observed in the history of Christian art, which moves from earlier symbolic forms to later narrative and didactic patterns.[1]

With regard to liturgy, at least, the change is thought to be the result of a shift in emphasis from eschatology to history. The first Christians lived in expectation of an imminent parousia. When it didn't come, disenchantment sets in, eschatology is blunted, Christianity, formerly "other worldly," becomes part of history, and the old unified Pascha, based on a sense of the immediacy of the presence of the Risen One, degenerates into an historical remembrance of things past. This, in brief, is the thesis popularized by Dix.[2] Is there really anything left to be said about all this since the caveats and qualifications so excellently presented by Thomas J. Talley in 1973?[3]

I have written elsewhere concerning the application to liturgical history of the scientific theory that knowledge in a field advances not by the accumulation of new data but by the invention of new systems; not by hypothesis verification but by hypothesis negation.[4] Now the great merit of Dix's work was to provide such a system, an intelligibility framework within which to perceive relationship and pattern in the history of Christian festive liturgy. But we must always

Reprinted from W. Vos and G. Wainwright (eds.), *Liturgical Time*. (Papers read at the 1981 Congress of Societas Liturgica [Paris, August 1981], Rotterdam: Liturgical Ecumenical Center Trust 1982) = *Studia Liturgica* 14, nos 2–4 (1982) 97–109.

test such synthetic reconstructions against the detailed analysis of each of its components, constantly seeking to reshape our framework to accommodate more precise and nuanced understanding of the data of historical research. In attempting this here, I have relied chiefly on the analytical *Wissenschaft* of the German school represented by Lohse, Huber, Strobel, to mention a few of the most recent authors.[5] The results of such an exercise do not negate the historicism thesis. But they do relativize it, and place it in a broader context than Dix's "eschatology vs. sanctification of time" antithesis, which in my opinion is shown to be an invention of the liturgists, with no foundation in history.[6]

I take the two essential components of "historicism" to be: 1) the splintering of the former integral celebration; 2) a retrospective liturgical vision that commemorates the past precisely as past history rather than as present reality—or at least puts too much weight on that side of the balance. That something new in liturgy appears at the end of the fourth century is beyond challenge. When John Chrysostom proclaims at Easter: "The day before yesterday the Lord was hanging on the cross; today he is risen,"[7] he is saying something no one would have said a century before. So there is a shift, and it can be dated. But what led to it, how "new" it really was, and what it means, are more difficult questions. Anton Baumstark once said that "die Entwicklung der Liturgie nur aus Sonderentwicklungen entsteht (the evolution of the liturgy is but the sum of particular developments),"[8] and the same is true of liturgical interpretation. So rather than begin with some preconceived idea of the Christian feast, and then look back to find it verified in the sources, let us take things piece by piece, step by step.

## 1. The First Three Centuries

The first thing the earliest sources show is that *history* is not *historicism*. The second is that *history* and *eschatology* are not mutually exclusive. The eschatological tension between the present age and the age to come is too obvious in the Early Church to need elaboration here.[9] The first Christians were convinced that they were living "at the end of the times" (1 Pet 1:20). We pray "as we wait in joyful hope for the coming of our savior Jesus Christ;"[10] the first

Christians thought they would live to see it. But to affirm, as Davies does, that "one consequence of this eschatological attitude was a complete lack of interest in all history,"[11] is completely false. Biblical faith has always been rooted in the historical event, and the fact that the New Testament chooses Salvation History as the medium to present the Good News should be enough to sound a note of caution here. But we can go further. August Strobel has shown that in the Primitive Church, "Kalender und eschatologisches Geschichtsbewusstsein gehörten . . . eng zusammen (The calendar and eschatological historical consciousness are intimately connected)."[12] Far from having no interest in history, the early Christians were intensely concerned to establish the exact chronology of Jesus' death. But this was not historicism. Eschatology and history were inseparable, for the early Christians had transformed the messianic expectation of contemporary apocalyptic Judaism (Wis 18:6–19:1ff) into an expectation of the parousia: it was at midnight on Passover that the Lord, as on the first night in Exodus 12:29, would come again.[13]

Historicism appears later among the Quartodecimans, when they exchange their original Johannine chronology for the synoptic chronology in order to justify celebrating the paschal Eucharist on the night of 14–15 Nisan, date of the Last Supper in the synoptics.[14] But this had nothing to do with their original tradition, which was anamnetic and eschatological: "to proclaim the Lord's death until he comes" (1 Cor 11:26) on the Passover, the day on which he died according to John, and on which he was supposed to come again. This is why they were so adamant in keeping their Pasch with historical accuracy, i.e. at the same time as the Jews:

> We do not observe the day carelessly, since we neither add nor subtract. For in Asia there are great luminaries who have fallen asleep, who shall rise again on the day of the Lord's parousia, when he shall come again with glory from heaven and gather in all the saints.[15]

Strobel sees the eschatological expectation of this *Urvigil* in the parable of the maidens in Mt 25,[16] and the same tradition is still alive in Jerome's (398) interpretation of this pericope:

> The tradition of the Jews is that Christ will come at midnight, in imitation of the time when the Pasch was celebrated in Egypt . . . I suppose this is why we have kept the apostolic tradition that on the day

of the paschal vigil the people awaiting the coming of Christ cannot be dismissed before midnight . . . [17]

So the original Easter was not a feast of the meta-historical, eschatological reality of the resurrection, as we like to think today, but "simply the Jewish Passover feast transcended and Christianized."[18] It was the feast of Christian redemption, just as the Jewish Passover fêted Jewish redemption. In other words it celebrated a mystery rather than an event. But the event chosen as the vehicle for the presentation of this mystery was Jesus' death in expectation of the parousia, and in both, the dying and the coming again, Jesus is the protagonist.[19] Of course there is no question in this early period of separating the death from the resurrection.[20] But it is worth noting that the scenario chosen as the historical basis for the anamnesis— the death rather than the resurrection—was not a Quartodeciman peculiarity. It was also characteristic of the earliest Easter Sunday tradition, as Christine Mohrmann has shown.[21] Neither Tertullian nor Origen were Quartodecimans, but both affirm explicitly that the Pasch commemorates the passion:

Tertullian (ca. 198–202) De bapt. 19, 1: The Passover presents a more solemn day for baptism, when also the Lord's passion in which we are baptized was fulfilled.[22]

Origen (ca. 235–245) In Is. hom 5, 2: Now there is a large crowd of people present . . . especially on Sunday, which commemorates the passion of Christ (for the resurrection of the Lord is not celebrated only once a year and not always every eighth day) . . . [23]

This reflects the earliest paschal typology—what Raniero Cantalamessa has called the "paschalization" of the Christ event—in which the slaying of the lamb was the principal type of Christ.[24] The resurrection plays no role in this imagery.

Our first evidence for this "paschalization", is 1 Cor 5:6–8:

Do you not know that a little leaven leavens the whole lump? Cleanse out the old leaven that you may be a new lump, as you really are unleavened. For Christ, our paschal lamb, has been sacrificed. Let us, therefore, celebrate the festival, not with the old leaven, the leaven of malice and evil, but with the unleavened bread of sincerity and truth.

This text, which according to Strobel gives the "Konzentrat" of an early Christian Passover Haggadah,[25] also adumbrates the second strain of early Christian paschal interpretation, which spiritualizes the paschal event and makes the Christian its protagonist.[26] Rom 6:3–23 does the same via baptism: it is the Christian who dies to sin and rises to new life in Christ.

Here the paschal mystery is not a *passion*, with *Jesus* as protagonist, but a *passage* with the *Christian* as protagonist.[27] The Pasch as passage is found already in Jn 13:1 ("Before the feast of the Pasch Jesus, knowing that his hour had come to pass from this world to the Father . . ."), and is so common in the Golden Age of patristic literature, that one is surprised to find it central neither to Easter nor to baptismal typology until it is picked up at the beginning of the third century by Clement and Origen.[28] Far from being "historicism," what we see in the Christian Alexandrines, as in Philo before them,[29] is a strong *dehistoricizing* of the Pasch (and of all liturgy, for that matter). There is a decided attenuation of the importance of Salvation History as history. The salvific *event* becomes a *type*, a symbol of an interior, spiritual reality.[30] In *Contra Celsum*, for example, Origen (*ca.* 246) spiritualizes all festivities:

> . . . to the perfect Christian, who in his thoughts is ever serving his natural Lord, God the Word, all his days are the Lord's and he is always keeping the Lord's Day. He who is unceasingly preparing himself for the true life . . . is always keeping preparation days (Friday). Again, he who considers that "Christ our Passover was sacrificed for us", and that it is his duty to keep the feast by eating the flesh of the Word, never ceases to keep the paschal feast. For pascha means "passover", and he is ever striving in all his thoughts, words and deeds to pass over from the things of this life to God, and is hastening towards His city . . . [31]

The treatise *On the Pasch* (*ca.* 245), edited by O. Guérard and P. Nautin from a papyrus discovered at Toura (Egypt) in 1941, is even bolder:

> Christ is sacrificed according to the figure of the Pasch, but He is not sacrificed by the saints, and so the Pasch is the figure of Christ, but not of His passion . . . He himself says that the Pasch is something spiritual and not sensible: "Unless you eat my flesh and drink my blood you do not have life in you". Should we then eat His flesh and drink His blood in a sensible way? But if it is in a spiritual way that He is speaking, then the Pasch is spiritual, not sensible.[32]

This third century shift from *pascha* = *passio* to *pascha* = *transitus* will eventually win out and become determinative for Christian paschal heortology.[33]

The same is true of the baptismal typology of Rom 6. With baptism a permanent component of the Easter Vigil by the third century at least,[34] the re-discovery of Paul will greatly influence the theology of Easter as the Pasch of Christians as well as of Christ. How much of this was affected by a weakened sense of eschatological expectation is impossible to determine. Obviously, by the third century it was no longer possible to sustain belief in an imminent parousia, and this surely had its effect on liturgical piety. But I doubt that this alone can explain what was happening, for eschatology was but one factor in the evolution and interpretation of the liturgy. At least two other forces are also important: the third century beginnings of a Christian mystagogy—"theology of liturgy" we would say today—and the Christological crisis provoked by Arianism.

## 2. Mystagogy[35]

A systematic Christian liturgical theology first appears in the fourth century catechetical homilies. Basically, what they do is extend to the understanding of Christian worship the method of scriptural exegesis first systematized by Origen to interpret Old Testament cult. Thenceforth all patristic interpreters of the liturgy will stress one or another aspect of this many-faceted reality.

The Alexandrines, following the Origenist exegetical penchant for the allegorical, interpreted liturgy by a process of anagogy whereby one rises from letter to spirit, from the visible rites of the liturgical mysteries to the one mystery that is God. This anagogical method is systematized by the end of the fifth century in the *Ecclesiastical Hierarchy* of Ps.-Denys.[36] Nothing could be further removed from "historicism." For Denys, the liturgy is an image of the spiritual combat and ascent, with little reference to the earthly economy of Christ, and none whatever to his divine-human mediatorship, or to his saving death and resurrection.[37] The Christian economy is simply not the model of the liturgical celebration. For that we must turn to the Antiochenes.

Antiochene exegetes, more attentive to the literal sense of scripture, were less prone than the Alexandrines to interpret the Old Testament in terms more allegorical than typological.[38] The same bias is manifest in their mystagogy, which sees the liturgical mysteries chiefly as a portrayal of the historical mysteries of salvation.[39] We see this clearly in the fourth century baptismal catecheses and other writings of Cyril of Jerusalem, John Chrysostom, and Theodore of Mopsuestia.[40] Prefigured in Old Testament types, the sacramental rites are an "imitation" (*mimesis*: Cyril) or "memorial" (*anamnesis*: Chrysostom) of the saving acts of Christ's life, and an anticipation of the heavenly liturgy.[41]

In these two systems the eschatological dimension of liturgy is not abandoned. But among the Antiochenes the emphasis shifts rather to a cultic, "realised eschatology" of the presence of the Risen One among his own as proleptic experience of the Pasch of the final days. Among the Alexandrines a moral, individual eschatology is stressed: the true Christian does not wait for the Pasch of the parousia, but is "passing continuously from the things of this life to God, hastening towards his city."[42]

## 3. THE INFLUENCE OF ARIANISM

More important for liturgical theology was the effect of the great christological disputes born of the Arian controversy.[43] This struggle shifted attention from Christ's second coming at the parousia to his first coming in the incarnation,[44] and led to renewed emphasis on the pre-existent divinity of the Logos and his consubstantial equality with the Father: Christ is mediator not as subordinate to the Father in divinity, but as man. In Alexandrine theology, this resulted in a weakening of Christ's mediatorship. Among the Antiochenes it provoked greater stress on Christ's high priesthood as pertaining to his humanity.[45] In liturgical interpretation the Alexandrine school, more concerned with the divinity of the Logos, had less to say about the historical economy of Christ's saving work. Among the Antiochenes, always more attentive to the humanity and to the literal sense in scriptural exegesis, it produced the opposite effect: a renewed emphasis on Christ's human saving work.

What happened is that the middle fell out, the risen God-man interceding for us as divine-human high priest *now*; and we are left with the two, unbridged poles of the dilemma: God and the historical Jesus. The point of intersection which is the basis for all Christian liturgical theology is precisely the divine-human mediatorship of the risen Lord, which renders actual in the present liturgical event both the past saving work and the future fulfillment. This anamnetic-eschatological, past-future tension is what worship is meant to resolve, and each school throughout the history of liturgical explanation has struggled with this problem in its own way, in response to the needs of its age. The Arian challenge led to more emphasis on the divinity among the Alexandrines. The Antiochenes, while holding to the latter, were more attentive to the humanity, but in response to the Arian attack on divine mediatorship as subordinationist, Antiochene liturgical writers elaborated their symbolism of the liturgy as a representation of the human saving work of the man Jesus.[46]

## 4. Historicism before Historicism

This does not mean that there was no liturgical "historicism" in the air. We already saw it in the later Quartodeciman use of synoptic chronology. Both the *Apostolic Tradition*[47] (*ca.* 215) and Cyprian[48] (d. 258) link the hours of prayer with events of Christ's passion. The third century Syriac *Didascalia* goes on and on about coordinating the Holy Week fast with the chronology of the passion.[49] Around 260, Dionysius of Alexandria's *Letter to Basilides*, our earliest source for a nascent Holy Week, provides an extreme case of the same thing:[50]

> You have sent to me . . . in order to inquire what is the proper hour for bringing the fast to a close at the Pasch . . . And it is your anxious desire, accordingly, to have the hour presented accurately, and determined with perfect exactness, which indeed is a matter of difficulty and uncertainty . . . But in what you have written to me you have made out very clearly, and with an intelligent understanding of the Holy Scriptures, that no very exact account seems to be offered in them of the hour at which he rose . . . But even though there may seem to be some small difficulty as to the subject of our inquiry, if they all agree that the light of the world, our Lord, rose on that one night, while they differ with respect to the hour, we may well seek with wise and faithful mind to harmonize their statements.

There follows a lengthy and tedious attempt to reconcile the various Gospel accounts of the exact time when Jesus rose, after which the author pronounces his judgement:

> As the case stands thus, we make the following statement and explanation to those who seek an exact account of the specific hour, or half-hour, or quarter of an hour, at which it is proper to begin their rejoicing over our Lord's rising from the dead. Those who are too hasty, and give up even before midnight, we reprehend as remiss and intemperate, and as almost breaking off from their course in their precipitation, for it is a wise man's word, "That is not little in life which is within a little."

That is historicism with a vengeance, 120 years before Egeria took the pilgrimage road for Jerusalem. Finally, Gabriele Winkler has demonstrated that the earliest Semitic stratum of the Syrian and Armenian initiation rites was modeled not on the eschatalogical death-resurrection motif of Rom 6, but on the messianic anointing of Jesus as his baptism in the Jordan, which was ritually re-enacted in the baptismal rites.[51]

The point I'm trying to make with these examples is that the history of liturgy and its mystagogy has not progressed in any organic evolution from "pre-Nicene eschatology" to "Constantinian historicism," but with considerably greater complexity. Alexandria shows a decidedly dehistoricizing, spiritualizing propensity in heortology. In the Syriac tradition the heart of the Pasch was the Eucharist,[52] and even today it is not Easter but Holy Thursday that bears the name "Pasch" in the Syrian Church.[53] It is in the area dominated by the more realistic Antiochene school—hellenophone Syria, Palestine, and Asia Minor—that we first see the "historicizing" fragmentation of the unitary paschal feast into a sequence of celebrations that follow the déroulement of the historical events of the passion. But this is one among several competing strains of the tradition.

## 5. EGERIA AND BEYOND

Egeria describes the results of the meeting of this Antiochene realism with the discovery of the holy places: stational liturgical services "suited to the day and place" of the celebration.[54] Is it really necessary to posit some new fourth century revolution in religious consciousness to understand this? Was it not the most normal thing in the world for pilgrims to go where Jesus did or said this or that, preferably on the anniversary of the event, and read there the scriptural account and meditate on its meaning for them?

From what Egeria's contemporary, Cyril (d. 386), has to say, such devotional practices do not necessarily imply a retrospective historicism that fragments the mystery:

> Just as we are speaking about Christ and Golgotha here on Golgotha, it was also most fitting to speak in the upper church about the Holy Spirit. For since he who descended there shares the glory of him who was crucified here, we speak here too about him who descended there. *For worship is indivisible.*[55]

Furthermore, the absence in Egeria of any Ascension Thursday feast (the one day whose chronology is unmistakable, in Acts 1) or of a Lord's Supper celebration at the Cenacle on Holy Thursday, should lead us to avoid crying "historicism" at every stational halt in the Jerusalem Holy Week processions.

John Baldovin in his new study of these Jerusalem stational services draws the following conclusions:

> ... by the end of the fourth century no effort had been made to pinpoint the site of the Last Supper or to integrate it into the Jerusalem liturgy. Rather, the "cathedral" church of the city serves as the locus of celebration for the beginning of the Pascha as a whole. This means that the whole celebration forms a sort of *inclusio* beginning and ending in the Golgotha complex. The motivation here is just as ecclesial as it is historical.
> The second aspect of the Great Week services is that the procession down the Mt. of Olives which ends at the Cross atrium on the morning of Great Friday does not really attempt a total historical mimesis of the Passion. The procession makes no detours to Caiaphas' or Pilate's but rather comes straight down the main East-West road to Golgotha. It is not unreasonable to argue on this basis that the procession itself was as important as the historical features of its stations, even though the historical character of the service as a whole cannot be denied.[56]

I have already pointed out the enormous (and much neglected) significance of stational services in the development of urban liturgy from the fourth century,[57] and I suspect they played as much a role in the evolution of Jerusalem Holy Week as did any new historicizing mentality.

I have used the Pasch as an example, because for centuries the paschal cycle was the only annual dominical celebration. But analogous forces were at work in the origins and development of the Nativity-Epiphany cycle and its theology. These feasts were introduced in the fourth century for apologetic reasons, and not because of any "historicizing" impulse to celebrate the anniversary of Jesus' birth and baptism. A scrutiny of the sources on the origins and meaning of both feasts shows that they were both celebrations of the same thing, the mystery of the appearance of God in Jesus, and not of historic events. The event was the medium through which the mystery was manifested, and served as scenario for its liturgical anamnesis.

And so the process continued. Augustine (d. 430) considered only the Pasch a "mystery;" all other feasts were "memorials."[58] Later Fathers like Leo the Great (440–461) broadened the concept "mystery" to include other commemorations of the mysteries of Our Lord.[59] Is this "the victory of the 'historicizing' view," as Huber would have it?[60] It was a poor victory at best. After all, even under Leo the Roman Church still read the whole passion at Easter.[61]

I have always felt that the real historicism in piety against which people rail today—"Baby Jesus" in the Christmas crèche, Good Friday "burial of Christ" processions, the truncated "passion piety" of the way of the Cross, etc.—has its roots long after Egeria in the historicizing piety of the type called "Franciscan," whose origins have been so well described by Jungmann.[62] But even with regard to those browbeaten old Middle Ages in the West, recent studies show that what has been said about historicism in popular piety needs a fresh look by those willing to read sources instead of repeating clichés.[63]

I am not trying to undermine the notion that there was historicism. There are signs of it everywhere: the eventual choice of Epiphany and Pentecost as baptismal feasts, the separation of Ascension Thursday from the original unitary Pentecost festivities,[64] the reduction of the Easter morning Gospel to the resurrection account in the Armenian Lectionary of Jerusalem during the fifth century,[65] etc. But historicism is only one string in a full plate of spaghetti. There are signs of it long before Egeria comes on the scene, it is far from complete long after her, and it is forced to compete with other tendencies of a decidedly dehistoricizing bent.

Furthermore, it is part of a much larger problem manifested in all
areas of patristic theology, not just in liturgy. Old Testament
foreshadowing, fulfilled in Christ, lived and celebrated in the
Church, image and gauge of the kingdom still to come; Pasch of the
Jews, Pasch of Jesus, Pasch of the Church, Pasch of the parousia;
presence and absence; fulfilled and yet not; realized eschatology and
future eschatology—these levels and the tensions among each of
them are found at the root of the whole tradition.[66] How to balance
them is the basis of all Christian exegesis and mystagogy from the
New Testament on. What we have throughout the history of
Christian theology and liturgy are various syntheses and rear-
rangements of these facets at each turn of the one kaleidoscope.
Alexandrines one way, Antiochenes another; Greek and Latin fathers
this way, Syriac and Armenian fathers that.

I think any attempt to look back in order to "recover *the* original
tradition" is futile, because it does not exist. For the New Testament
is not a history of Jesus, but a book of *interpretations* of his meaning
for the *Sitz im Leben* of its time. All the developing calendar does is
continue this process. I do not mean to imply that each step was an
organically balanced one. That is not true even of the New Testament
itself. Nor am I saying that everything is relative. For the common
basis of all orthodox Christian festivity is clear: Jesus Christ lived,
died, and rose for our salvation.

But the concrete symbolic ways chosen to express this reality are
multiple from the start. So in studying Christian heortology we must
accept diversity, not trying to homogenize everything into one
synthesis, while at the same time eschewing such excessive dis-
junctions as "dort Passah hier Ostern;"[67] here mystery, there history.
For although "the mystery is Christ among you" (Col 1:27), the
communication of that reality is inseparably linked to history.

In short, I think it is demonstrably clear that the meaning of every
feast, Sunday included, is a synthesis, the term of a process and not
its beginning. When we go back to that beginning, what we find is not
some one primitive synthesis, but several strains. To select one as
preferable is perfectly legitimate as long as one realizes that personal
taste or prejudice does not make a theology, much less a tradition.
For if one takes tradition to be *quod semper et ubique et ab omnibus*, then
as far as Christian heortology is concerned, there is no such thing.

NOTES

1. Cf. J. G. Davies, *Holy Week: a Short History* (Ecumenical Studies in Worship 11, Richmond Va.: John Knox 1963) 9ff. Of course such transformations are constantly occurring. Cf. A. Wharton Epstein, "The Problem of Provincialism: Byzantine Monasteries in Cappadocia and Monks in South Italy," *Journal of the Warburg and Courtland Institutes* 42 (1979) 28–46; T. Velmans, "Peinture et mentalité à Byzance dans la seconde moitié du XIIe siècle," *Cahiers de la civilisation médiévale* 22 (1979) 217–233.

2. G. Dix, *The Shape of the Liturgy* (London: Dacre 1945) 333ff.

3. T. J. Talley, "History and Eschatology in the Primitive Pascha", *Worship* 47 (1973) 212–221.

4. See ch. 10.

5. B. Lohse, *Das Passafest der Quartodecimaner (Beiträge zur Förderung christlicher Theologie,* II.54, Gütersloh 1953); W. Huber, *Passa und Ostern. Untersuchung zur Osterfeier der alten Kirche* (Beiheft zur *Zeitschrift für die neutest. Wiss.u. die Kunde der älteren Kirche,* 35, Berlin: A. Töpelmann 1969); A Strobel, *Ursprung und Geschichte des frühchristlichen Osterkalenders* (TU 112, Berlin: Akademie-Verlag 1977—cited hereafter as Strobel).

6. Cf. ch. 9.

7. *Hom. in sanctum Pascha,* 5, PG 52, 770. On the question of authenticity, generally accepted today, cf. J. A. De Aldama, *Repertorium pseudochrysostomicum* (Documents, études et répertoires 10, Paris: CNRS 1965) no. 144.

8. I have long since forgotten in which of B's many writings I found this expression. But it is vintage Baumstark, and has remained with me since I first read it.

9. See, however, the recent study J. Carmignac, *Le mirage de l'eschatologie* (Paris: Letouzy et Ané 1979) to counterbalance traditional exaggerations in this area.

10. Embolism after the Lord's Prayer in the Roman mass.

11. *Holy Week* 13.

12. Strobel 12.

13. *Ibid.* 12ff, 29ff.

14. *Ibid.* 22–28, 30.

15. Policrates, spokesman of the Quartodecimans in the mid-2d c. paschal dispute, cited in Eusebius (*ca.* 363) *Hist. eccl.* V. 22:4.

16. Strobel 37ff.

17. *Comm. in Mt.* 4,25,6, CCL 77, 236–237. Cf. Lactantius (*post* 313) *Div.inst.* 7, 19, 3, CSEL 19, 645, and the literature cited in Strobel 39ff.

18. G. Dix, *The Treatise on the Apostolic Tradition of St. Hippolytus of Rome* (London: SPCK 1968) 73. Cf. *Shape of the Liturgy,* 338ff, 348ff; Strobel 29; A. Baumstark, *Comparative Liturgy* (Westminster, Maryland: Newman 1958) 164–174.

19. This is stressed by R. Cantalamessa, *La pasqua nella chiesa antica* (Traditio christiana 3, Turin: Società Editrice Internazionale 1978) xviiiff (hereafter, Cantalamessa).

20. *Loc.cit.*; C. Mohrmann, "Pascha, passio, transitus", *Ephemerides Liturgicae* 66 (1952) 37–52, esp. 41–42 (hereafter, Mohrmann); B. Botte, "Pascha," *L'Orient syrien* 8 (1963) 213–226.

21. Cf. references in previous note.

22. CCL 1,293.

23. PG 13,236.

24. Cantalamessa xvii ff.

25. Strobel 19.

26. Cantalamessa xxff.

27. Loc.cit.

28. For Easter, cf. loc.cit. For baptism, see A. Benoit, Le baptême chrétien au second siècle. La théologie des Pères (Études d'hist. et de phil. rel. de Strasbourg 43, Paris: Presses Universitaires de France 1953) 227ff.; J. N. D. Kelly, Early Christian Doctrines (London: A. & C. Black 1975⁴) 194; G. W. H. Lampe, The Seal of the Spirit (London: SPCK 1967²) 149ff.; E. J. Kilmartin, "Patristic Views of Sacramental Sanctity", Proceedings of the Eighth Annual Convention of the Soc. of Cath. College Teachers of Sacred Doctrine 8 (1962) 59–82, esp. 60, 65ff, 71ff; Mohrmann, 46ff; S. G. Hall, "Paschal Baptism", Studia evangelica 6 (TU 112, Berlin: Akademie-Verlag 1973) 239–251. G. Winkler in her work on the Armenian initiation rites shows that Rom 6 did not provide the symbolism for baptism in the primitive Syriac and Armenian traditions (Das armenische Initiationsrituale, Entwicklungsgeschichtliche u. liturgievergleichende Untersuchung der Quellen des 3. bis 10. Jahrhunderts, OCA 217, Rome: P10 1982). See also E. C. Ratcliff, "The Old Syrian Baptismal Tradition and its Resettlement under the Influence of Jerusalem in the Fourth Century", Liturgical Studies, ed. A. H. Couratin and D. H. Tripp (London: SPCK 1976) 142.

29. Cf. Philo Alexandrinus, (ca. 30 BC-45 AD), De specialibus legibus II, 147, ed. R. Arnaldez et al. Les oeuvres de Philon d'Alexandrie 24 (Paris: Cerf 1975) 320–322; De congressu eruditionis gratia 106, ibid. 16 (1947) 176–178.

30. Cf. Cantalamessa, xx–xxi. For Clement (ca. 202), cf. Stromata 2, 11, 51, 2, ed. O. Stählin, Clemens 2 (GCS, Leipzig: J. C. Hinrichs 1906) 140; for Origen, cf. Contra Celsum 8, 22 cited below, and numerous other texts in Cantalamessa 62–75.

31. 8, 22, ed. P. Koetschau, Origenes 2 (GCS, Leipzig: J. C. Hinrichs 1899) 239–240; English (slightly modified) from Ante-Nicene Christian Library, vol. 23 (Edinburgh 1872) 509–510.

32. 12–13 Origène, Sur la Pâque, ed. O. Guérard, P. Nautin (Christianisme antique, Paris: Beauchesne 1979) 176ff.

33. Cf. Mohrmann, and Cantalamessa xxi–xxiii, xxv–xxix.

34. On when baptism became a permanent part of the paschal celebration, see the article of Hall (supra note 28).

35. For a full discussion of the background and development of mystagogy from the 4th century, see my article "The Liturgy of the Great Church: an Initial Synthesis of Structure and Interpretation on the Eve of Iconoclasm", DOP 34–35 (1980–81) 59–75.

36. PG 3, 369–485. On Alexandrine mystagogy and Ps.-Denys. cf. R. Bornert, Les commentaires byzantins de la Divine Liturgie du VIIᵉ au XVᵉ siècle (Archives de l'Orient chrétien 9, Paris: Inst. Français d'Études byzantines 1966) 52–72; E. Boulard, "L'Eucharistie d'après le Pseudo-Denys l'Apréopagite," Bull. de litt. ecclèsiastique 58 (1957) 193–217; 59 (1958) 129–164; R. Roques, L'univers dionysien. Structure hiérarchique du monde selon le Ps.-Denys (Théologie 29, Paris: Aubier 1954); H.-J. Schulz, Die byzantinische Liturgie (Sophia 5, Trier: Paulinus-Verlag 1980²) 51ff; "Kultsymbolik der byzantinischen Kirche," in Symbolik des orthodoxen u. orientalischen Christentums (Stuttgart: A Hiersemann 1962) 9–17.

37. Eccl. hier. III passim, PG 3, 424–45.

38. On this Antiochene school of exegetes, see C. Schäublin, Untersuchungen zur Methode und Herkunft der antiochenischen Exegese (Theophaneia 23, Cologne-Bonn: Peter Hanstein 1974).

39. Bornert, Commentaires 72–82; Schulz, Die byzantinische Liturgie 33*–38,* 36–44.

40. Cyrille de Jérusalem, *Catéchèses mystagogiques,* ed. A. Piédagnel, trad. P. Paris (SC 126, Paris: Cerf 1966); Jean Chrysostome, *Huit catéchèses baptismales inédites,* ed. A. Wenger (SC 50, Paris: Cerf 1957); R. Tonneau, R. Devreesse, *Les homélies catéchétiques de Théodore de Mopsueste* (Studi e testi 145, Vatican: Bibliotheca Apostolica Vaticana 1949).

41. Bornert, *Commentaires,* 73ff. The most extensive application of this method to the liturgy is seen in Theodore of Mopsuestia's last two homilies (15–16).

42. Origen, *Contra Celsum,* cited above. Cf. Cantalamessa, xx–xxi.

43. On the liturgical effects of these controversies, see J. A. Jungmann, "The Defeat of Teutonic Arianism and the Revolution in Religious Culture in the Early Middle Ages," *Pastoral Liturgy* (New York: Herder and Herder 1962) 1–101; *The Place of Christ in Liturgical Prayer* (New York: Alba House 1965) chaps. 11–14.

44. Cf. M. Magrassi, "Maranatha. Il clima escatologico della celebrazione primitiva," *Rivista liturgica* 53 (1966) 375.

45. Cf. J. Betz, *Die Eucharistie in der Zeit der griechischen Väter,* Bd. I, 1 (Freiburg im B.: Herder 1955) 99–105, 121ff, 125ff, 128ff, 136ff, 194.

46. H.-J. Schulz (*Die byz. Liturgie,* 34*ff, 28ff) has noted in this same period a reinforcement of the Eucharist as a memorial of salvation history via a twofold extension of the anamnesis. First the liturgical *text* itself is expanded to include mysteries other than the death and resurrection. Secondly, in liturgical *interpretation* the notion of anamnesis is extended to include not just the anaphora but the entire rite. Cf. Dix, *Shape of the Liturgy* 264ff.

47. 41, ed. B. Botte (LQF 39, Münster: Aschendorff 1963) 90–92.

48. *De orat.* 34 CCL III A, 111–112.

49. V, 10–20, ed. Funk I, 264ff = ch. 21, R. H. Connolly, *Didascalia apostolorum* (Oxford: Clarendon 1929) 178–192.

50. Ed. C. L. Feltoe, *The Letters and other Remains of Dionysius of Alexandria* (Cambridge Patr. Texts, Cambridge: University Press 1904) 94ff; English version, *The Ante-Nicene Fathers* (Grand Rapids: Eerdmans 1978) VI, 94–95.

51. *Op. cit. supra,* note 28.

52. Cf. Cantalamessa, xxiii–xxv.

53. *Breviarium juxta ritum ecclesiae antiochenae syrorum,* pars verna secunda, vol. V (in Syriac, Mosul 1892) 140.

54. "apta diei et loco" (25:10; 29:2 and 5; 31:1). Cf. Éthérie, *Journal de voyage,* ed. H. Pétré (SC 21, Paris: Cerf 1948) 65 and *passim.*

55. *Cat.* 16, 4, PG 33, 924 (emphasis added). The authenticity question has no relevance for our argument.

56. Yale University dissertation cited by permission of the author.

57. See ch. 11.

58. Cf. what is perhaps the earliest treatise on liturgical theology, Augustine, *Ep.* 55 to that troublesome layman Januarius (CSEL 34, 169ff). Cf. G. Hudon, "Le mystère de Noël dans le temps de l'église d'après s. Augustin," *LMD* 59 (1959) 60–84.

59. Cf. J. Gaillard, "Noël, memoria ou mystère?" *LMD* 59 (1959) 37–59.

60. *Passa u. Ostern* (*supra* note 5) 183ff.

61. *Sermo 59,* 1. Léon Le Grand, *Sermons* III, ed. R. Dolle (SC 74, Paris: Cerf 1961) 128ff.

62. "The Defeat of Teutonic Arianism" cited above, note 43. See also the interesting study of A. Kolping, "Amalar von Metz und Florus von Lyon, Zeugen eines Wandels im liturgischen Mysterienverständnis," *Zeitschrift für katholische Theologie* 73 (1951) 424–464.

63. Cf. J. Leclercq, "La dévotion médiévale envers le crucifié," *LMD* 75 (1963) 119–132; F. Vandenbroucke, "La dévotion au crucifié à la fin du moyen âge," *ibid.* 133–143.

64. Cf. R. Cabié, *La Pentecôte. L'évolution de la cinquantaine pascale au cours des cinq premiers siècles* (Bibliothèque de la liturgie, Tournai: Desclée 1965) 181ff.

65. It had also included the account of the burial (Mk 15:42–16:8), but was reduced to Mk 16:2–8. A. Renoux, *Le codex arménien Jérusalem 121,* I: Introduction, PO 35, 156.

66. I treat this question more fully in the article cited above, note 35.

67. C. Schmidt, *Gespräche Jesu mit seinen Jüngern nach der Auferstehung* (TU 43, Leipzig: J. C. Hinrichs 1919) 579, cited in Cantalamessa xv.

Chapter Three

# SUNDAY IN THE BYZANTINE TRADITION

There are seven Eastern Christian liturgical traditions, all of which share a common ethos, at least when contrasted with the West. I shall speak about the most representative of these traditions, the Byzantine, to which the vast majority of Eastern Christians adhere. Most of them belong to the Eastern Orthodox Churches, but there are also some eight million Byzantine Catholics, if we count those in Rumania and the Soviet Ukraine who were forcibly incorporated into the Orthodox Church in the late 1940s.

The epithets "Eastern" or "Oriental" may conjure up visions of Bangkok and the Taj Mahal. But the Christian East is the Orient in the pre-Renaissance sense. It includes Southern Italy and Sicily, much of Yugoslavia, Bulgaria, Rumania, Greece, Asia Minor, as well as what we call the Middle East—in other words, the eastern half of the Mediterranean basin, cradle of our common Greco-Roman heritage. So we are talking about the Christianity of the Eastern patristic world that is no more exotic or foreign than the Bible, which, after all, was written in Hebrew and Greek.

Like most great cultural traditions, the Byzantine Rite is a mongrel. At its basis lies the liturgical synthesis formed in the cathedral liturgy of Constantinople by the beginning of the eighth century. And in the monasteries of the capital, a new monastic synthesis was in formation under the leadership of the great Byzantine monastic reformer, St. Theodore Studites (d. 826). For the origins of the liturgy that came out of this monastic reform, we must look to Jerusalem. After the Persians destroyed the Holy City in 614, the monks of St. Sabas monastery in the wilderness near Jericho picked up the pieces and restored monastic life. As often happens after violent destruction, a remarkably creative period followed the holocaust, and a new

Revised from "Sunday in the Eastern Tradition," in : M. Searle (ed.), *Sunday Morning: A Time for Worship* (Collegeville: Liturgical Press 1982) 49–74.

monastic office was produced via a massive infusion of ecclesiastical poetry into the former staid and sober monastic psalmody. It is from this poetry that our present Byzantine liturgical anthology of Sunday propers, called the *Oktoichos*, or *Book of Eight Tones*, was formed.

To make a long story short, this Palestinian monastic synthesis was adopted by the Studite monasteries of Constantinople, and after the fall of the city to the Latins in 1204, this monastic office replaced the more elaborate cathedral rite even in the secular churches. So, for the celebration of Sunday in the Byzantine tradition, we have today a synthesis found in two sets of liturgical books: a native Constantinopolitan sacramentary (*Euchology*) and lectionaries; and a Book of Hours (*Horologion*) and its Sunday propers (*Oktoichos*), both of Jerusalem provenance.

To anyone beginning the study of Sunday in early Christian literature, the initial impression is one of confusion: Sunday is the first day, the day of creation, the day of light, the day of the new time. But it is also the last day, the eighth day, the day beyond days, the day of jubilee, the day of the end-time. It is the day of resurrection, but also the day of the post-resurrection appearances and meals. It is the day of the descent of the Spirit, day of the ascension, day of the assembly, day of the Eucharist, day of baptism, day of ordinations— until one asks, "Is there *anything* Sunday *doesn't* mean?" The answer, of course, is no. For in the Early Church, Sunday was indeed everything. It was *the* symbolic day, sign of the time of the Church between ascension and parousia, the time in which we are living now. It is the day symbolic of all days, for the purpose of all Christian liturgy is to express in a ritual moment that which should be the basic stance of every moment of our lives. Boone Porter has expressed this well in his little book on Sunday:

> All things in the Christian life are carried out in faith, hope, and charity, looking forward to the glory that is yet to be revealed. This is pre-eminently true of the Sunday gathering of the faithful. On the Eighth Day, the perpetual First Day of a new age, this view of eternity comes into focus. Then, in a particular sense, our heavenly citizenship is clearly and unequivocally affirmed . . . . Here we renew our allegiance each week to the Jerusalem that is above, here we are given some vision of the hope of our calling. On Sunday this is given to us not merely in homiletic exhortations to belief or catechetical declarations of the faith, but in the actual living experience of a full and comprehensive worship.[1]

It is this "living experience of a full and comprehensive worship" that characterizes Sunday in the Christian East. It is full because it still includes the complete cycle of cathedral services first synthesized in the Golden Age of the Fathers of the Church. It is comprehensive because it has retained the symbolic polyvalence of the pristine Lord's Day. Westerners are accustomed to thematic liturgies. Even ordinary Sundays in the Roman tradition were, until recently, feasts of the Trinity, with their proper preface. All this is foreign to the East, where such thematization, far from seeming an enrichment, would appear to limit the inexhaustible symbolic richness of the Sunday celebration to some topic of our choosing.

By and large, Eastern piety has remained free of the historical developments that in other places have led at times to the highlighting of relatively peripheral aspects of Christian devotional life. Consequently, the East's devotional storehouse has remained more or less uncluttered; its piety is still focused almost exclusively on the fundamentals of the faith. This is especially true of Sunday, which in the East has refused to be exploited for special interests not its own. It serves no purpose beyond itself. As such, it has the gratuitousness and uselessness of all symbol. It doesn't mean *something*; it simply *means*. It has no more use than art, or poetry, or a kiss. This is in radical contrast to contemporary narcissism regarding the worship of God: "I don't go to church because I don't get anything out of it." What one "*gets* out of it" is the inestimable privilege of glorifying God.

But if Sunday means everything, two of its themes stand out in the Byzantine tradition: day of light, day of the paschal mystery. The two poles of the liturgical expression of this reality in Christian antiquity were the vigil and the assembly for Word and Eucharist. Both have been preserved in the Byzantine tradition. I do not intend to concentrate on the Eucharist, because its meaning for Sunday is similar in all traditions. So, for the explication of these Sunday themes, let us turn to the vigil.

The "All-night Vigil" of the Byzantine tradition is originally a cathedral service comprising solemn vespers, the Sunday resurrection vigil, matins, and lauds, which in monasteries was drawn out through the night with long monastic psalmody. In parish worship this vigil is either split up, with vespers on Saturday evening and the rest before Sunday morning mass, or—as in the Russian usage—it is celebrated as a unit Saturday evening, but without the long monastic psalmody. In this abbreviated, parochial form it lasts at least an hour and a half, and is a service of unparalleled beauty.

It opens in a flood of light and incense, as the doors of the brilliantly illumined sanctuary are opened before the darkened church, and the celebrant proclaims in solemn chant: "Glory to the holy, consubstantial, and undivided Trinity, now and always, and unto ages of ages!" No Byzantine service begins without a blessing or glorification of the Holy Trinity, the ultimate aim of all worship. Then the deacon and priest call the congregation to prayer with verses adapted from Psalm 94:6:

> Come let us adore our God and King!
> Come let us adore Christ our God and King!
> Come let us adore and fall down before the same Lord
>   Jesus Christ our God and King!
> Yes, come let us worship and bow down to him!

After this the deacon, lighting the way with a huge candle, symbol of Christ who lights up our path, leads the celebrant through the whole church incensing—really incensing, with clouds of smoke, not just a few perfunctory swings of the thurible from the distant sanctuary.

Meanwhile, the choir is chanting the invitatory psalm of vespers, Psalm 103 (104), a psalm of creation. In the East, liturgy is not just a service. It is also the place of theophany. In the Sunday vigil, as in the Bible, the very first theophany is creation. In chanting the invitatory psalm, special emphasis is given to the christological theme of darkness and light, which forms the base-symbolism of the cathedral office. The psalm verses expressing this theme are repeated twice:

> The sun knows when to set; you bring darkness and it is night.
> How manifold are your works, O Lord! In wisdom, you wrought
>   them all!

This light theme is resumed immediately in the central rite of evensong, the *lucernarium*, which opens with Psalm 140, the heart of all Christian vesperal psalmody:

> O Lord I cry to you: hear me O Lord!
> Let my prayer rise like incense before you, my hands like the
>   evening sacrifice.

While clouds of incense once again fill the church, sign of our prayers rising to the throne of God, as the psalm says, every candle in the church is lit, and the choir chants the proper refrains with which the psalmody is farced, refrains showing how the mystery of light that transforms creation is fulfilled in the dying and rising of Christ. Here are some of the variable refrains from the Sunday service in the third tone:[2]

> Everything has been enlightened by your resurrection, O Lord, and paradise has been opened again; all creation, extolling you, offers to you the perpetual hymn of praise.

> We, who unworthily stay in your pure house, intone the evening hymn, crying from the depths: "O Christ our God, who has enlightened the world with your resurrection, free your people from your enemies, you who love humankind."

> O Christ, who through your Passion have darkened the sun, and with the light of your resurrection have illumined the universe: accept our evening hymn of praise, O you who love humankind.

> You underwent death, O Christ, so that you might free our race from death; and having risen from the dead on the third day, you raised with you those that acknowledge you as God, and you have illumined the world. O Lord, glory to you.

During the chanting of the final refrain, the priest and deacon, bearing the smoking censor, walk in procession through the church. On coming to the doors of the sanctuary, they intone the age-old Hymn of Light, the *Phos hilaron*, which for over sixteen centuries, day after day, without variation or change, has proclaimed that the light of the world is not the sun of creation by day, nor the evening lamp by night, but the eternal Son of God, "the true light that enlightens everyone," in the words of the prologue of St. John's Gospel (1:9). I must confess that I find consolation in the company I am in when I intone this immortal hymn. St. Basil the Great, who quotes it in the fourth century, says it was already so old that no one remembers who composed it,[3] and Egeria surely heard it in Jerusalem around the same time. A literal version of the original Greek text reads:

> O joyous light of the holy glory of the immortal Father, heavenly, holy, blessed Jesus Christ!

Having come to the setting of the sun, and beholding the
  evening light,
We praise God Father, Son and Holy Spirit!
It is fitting at all times that you be praised with auspicious
  voices, O Son of God, giver of life;
That is why the whole world glorifies you![4]

The collect at the end of the vesperal intercessions resumes the
themes of the service:

O great and exalted God! You alone are immortal and dwell
in unapproachable light! In your wisdom, you created the
entire universe: You separated light from darkness, giving
the sun charge of the day, and the moon and stars, the night.
At this very hour, you permit us, sinful as we are, to approach
you with our evening hymns of praise and glory. In your love
for us, direct our prayers as incense in your sight, and accept
them as a delightful fragrance. Throughout this present evening and the night that is to come, fill us with your peace.
Clothe us in the armor of light. Rescue us from the terror of
night.... Give us that sleep which you designed to soothe our
weakness.... As we lie in bed this night, fill us with compunction, and enable us to keep your name in mind. Then, glad-
dened by your joy and enlightened by your precepts, may we
rise to glorify your goodness, imploring your great tenderness
of heart, not only for our own sins, but for those of all your
people. And for the sake of the Theotokos, touch all our lives
with your mercy. For you are good and full of love for us, O
God, and we give you glory, Father, Son, and Holy Spirit: now
and forever, and unto ages of ages, amen.[5]

In spite of its great solemnity, this is liturgy at its most basic, taking
the ordinary but universal fears and needs of human life and turning
them into theophany, signs of God. The fear of darkness is a basic
fear; the light that dispels it is a need felt by all. "God is light," says
the First Letter of John (1:15), and this light shines in our world
through the transfigured face of Jesus Christ, "The true light that
enlightens everyone" (Jn 1:9).

In Byzantine Sunday worship, this theme serves as symbolic
matrix to express the unity of the Sunday mystery—the Passover of
Christ—and its sacramental symbols: baptism, which in the Early
Church was called *photismos* or "illumination," and Eucharist.

It is a theme that pervades all of Byzantine spirituality and mysticism. In a moving passage of his Sermon on the Transfiguration, Anastasius of Sinai (d. *ca.* 700) has our transfigured Lord say:

> It is thus that the just shall shine at the resurrection. It is thus
> that they shall be glorified; into my condition they shall be
> transfigured, to this form, to this image, to this imprint, to
> this light and to this beatitude they shall be configured, and
> they shall reign with me, the Son of God.[6]

This symbolism not only marks the rhythm of the hours in the Byzantine Office. It also pervades the propers. At Saturday vespers (tone 5) we chant with the vesperal psalms:

> We offer the evening worship to you, the light that never sets.
> In the fullness of time you shone on the world ... and descended
> even into hell to dispel the darkness which was there, and showed
> the light of the resurrection to the nations. O Lord the giver
> of light, glory to you!

And in the First Ode of the canon of Sunday matins, tone 2:

> O pure one, through the inaccessible door of your closed womb
> the Sun of righteousness passed and appeared to the world ...

Because Christ is the light, Mary is the lamp that bears it, a favorite theme of the refrains for the feast of the Entry of the Mother of God into the Temple on November 21. And at the feast of Theophany on January 6, John the Baptist is the candlestick of the light, the forerunner of the sun, the morning star.

There is nothing specifically Eastern or Byzantine about all of this—except that in the East it is still a living reality.

In the Sunday vigil, vespers is followed by matins, the resurrection vigil, and lauds. The invitatory of matins, Psalm 117 in the Septuagint Greek, resumes once again the theme of light and applies it to Christ:

> The Lord God is our light! Blessed is he who comes in the
> name of the Lord!

*Verse*: Give thanks to the Lord, for he is good! Everlasting is his love!

*Verse*: They surrounded me, they encircled me, but in the Lord's name I overcome them!

*Verse*: No, I will not die; I will live, and declare the works of the Lord!

*Verse*: The stone rejected by the builders has become the cornerstone; this is the Lord's doing, a marvel in our eyes![7]

In parish worship, the monastic psalmody of matins is generally omitted, and one passes immediately to the three psalms of the third nocturn, which on Saturday night is transformed into the psalmody of the resurrection vigil described by Egeria (24:9–11), the *Apostolic Constitutions* (II, 59:2–4), and other ancient sources. The elements of this service are:

1) Three psalms in remembrance of the three days in the tomb;
2) An incensation in remembrance of the aromatic spices brought by the women to anoint the body of the Lord, thus inaugurating the first watch before the tomb, model of all Christian resurrection vigils, including what we call a wake.
3) A solemn proclamation of the Gospel of the resurrection, in remembrance of the angel who stood at the rolled-back stone of the tomb announcing the resurrection.

Egeria describes this service as she saw it some 1600 years ago in the rotunda of the resurrection in Jerusalem:

But on the seventh day, the Lord's Day, there gather in the courtyard before cock-crow all the people, as many as can get in, as if it were Easter.... Soon the first cock crows, and at that the bishop enters, and goes into the cave in the Anastasis. The doors are all opened, and all the people come into the Anastasis, which is already ablaze with lamps. When they are inside, a psalm is said by one of the presbyters, with everyone responding, and it is followed by a prayer; then a psalm is said by one of the deacons, and another prayer; then a third psalm is said by one of the clergy, a third prayer, and the Commemoration of All. After these three psalms and prayers they take censers into the cave of the Anastasis, so that the whole Anastasis basilica is filled with the smell. Then the bishop, standing inside the screen, takes the Gospel book and goes to the door, where he himself reads the account of the Lord's resurrection. At the beginning of the reading the whole assembly groans and laments at all that the Lord underwent for us, and the way they weep would move even the hardest heart to tears. When the Gospel is finished, the bishop comes out, and is taken with singing to the Cross, and they all go with him. They have one psalm there and a prayer, then he blesses the people, and that is the dismissal.[8]

In the Byzantine tradition the present vigil opens with the solemn chanting of select verses from Psalms 134, 135, and 118, accompanied by refrains of the myrrh-bearing women, those who went to the tomb to anoint the body of the Lord and thus became the first witnesses of the resurrection. As soon as the choir intones "Praise the name of the Lord" from Psalm 134, the doors of the sanctuary are opened, all the lights and candles in the church are lit, and the celebrant, preceded once more by the deacon and his candle, incenses again the whole church. The refrains of the myrrhbearers give the sense of this service:

> By the tomb stood an angel radiant in light, and thus did he speak to the myrrh-bearing women: "Let not your sorrow mingle tears with precious ointment. You see the tomb before you; look for yourselves. He is not here; he has risen!"

> With the first rays of dawn they had set out for the tomb, sobbing and lamenting as they walked along. But when they reached the tomb, they were startled by an angel who said: "The time for tears and sorrow is now over. Go! Tell his friends that he has risen!"

> Your women friends had come with ointment, Lord, hoping to anoint your bruised and battered body cold in death. But the angel stood before them, saying: "Why seek the living among the dead? He is God! He has risen from the grave."

There follow the responsory and the solemn chanting of the Gospel of the resurrection, after which the Gospel book is solemnly borne in procession to the center of the church and enthroned there, while the choir sings the resurrection hymn professing faith that, having heard the paschal Gospel, we too have seen and tasted the glory of God:

> Having seen Christ's resurrection, let us adore the holy Lord Jesus Christ, who is alone without sin. We worship your

cross, O Christ, we sing and tell the glory of your holy resurrection. For you are our God, we know of no other than you,
we call on your name. Come all you faithful, let us worship
Christ's holy resurrection. For behold, through the cross
has joy come to all the world. As we continually bless the Lord,
we sing of his resurrection, for he has endured the cross and
destroyed death by death.[9]

After the intercessions, one of the eight Canons of the Resurrection is chanted according to the Sunday tone, while the faithful come up to venerate the Gospel, be anointed with aromatic oil, and receive a piece of blessed bread, signs of the fortitude needed in the true vigil, the vigil of life.

The same themes of light and paschal triumph are found throughout the rich poetry of lauds, especially in the odes of the canon, a series of refrains composed according to the themes of the biblical canticles. I do not have time to describe all this, but the same realities are proclaimed: darkness and light; the darkness of sin overcome by the illumination of the risen Christ.

Equally important liturgically is that these realities are not just affirmed *pro forma*, in a ho-hum sort of way. They are shouted and chanted and hymned. They are woven into a scenario of poetry and procession, movement and rest, darkness and light, smoke and symbol and song, so that the casual visitor is often a bit over-whelmed, and would be moved to say, "Why, they really believe all that!" And, indeed, they do. The Vatican II Constitution on the Sacred Liturgy (no. 2) calls the liturgy "the outstanding means by which the faithful can express in their lives and manifest to others the mystery of Christ and the real nature of the true Church." A concrete example of what this means can be seen on any Sunday in the Eastern tradition, where liturgy permeates the everyday lives of the people in a way that has long ceased in most other traditions.

Eastern Christians have a sense of ownership and pride in their rite. It is their church, their tradition, their community, bound up with their whole history and culture. There is no separation between piety and liturgy. It's all one thing, liturgy and personal piety, and it still marks the rhythm of daily life. I like to have my Eastern students write an essay on what their tradition means to them. Here is a typical passage from such an essay, written by a young American layman of the Ukrainian Catholic Church:

To be in the center of the crowd that pushes forward to kiss the cross on some major feast day, each waiting to have the head anointed and maybe to exchange a few words with the priest—you know you are surrounded by people that would never be satisfied with the almost furtive handshakes that are exchanged in Latin churches during the Rite of Peace. But the enthusiasm of the tradition doesn't end in the church building. In many ways it is carried into the daily lives of the people. The icons one finds in homes are one way this is done: the same saints one sees in church one also sees in the kitchen or bedroom, often with a burning candle and a decorative scarf. On great feasts there are the blessings of things we use every day—water on Theophany, fruit on Transfiguration, herbs and flowers on Dormition. These things are taken home and used: the water is drunk, the fruit is eaten, and the flowers decorate the table for several days.

So much for liturgy. I began there deliberately, because in the East that is where one always begins. There, liturgy is not one of the many things the Church does. It is its very life. One might ask, of course, what relevance all this has today. I can only refer to my own experience, and to the testimony of others who can in no way be accused of living in a romantic cloud of incense divorced from the realities of the modern world. One is Olivier Clément, contemporary French writer and lay theologian converted at the age of 27 from atheism. He chose Orthodoxy because, in his own words, "I was hungry for a Church that was above all Eucharist. For a community which professed to be the Body of Christ in the Eucharist. For a theology that flowed from the chalice. It was then that I met the Orthodox."[10] More telling, perhaps, is the witness of Tatiana Goricheva, feminist and activist of the Christian renewal movement in Leningrad, expelled from the Soviet Union in July 1980. Born in 1947 of atheist parents, she knew absolutely nothing about religion, had never even been inside a church. Then she visited an Orthodox church and discovered the liturgy:

> I was enchanted by the liturgy, by the beauty of the rite. . . . I did not want to leave church after the liturgical celebrations. It seemed like leaving paradise to fall back into hell. I was overwhelmed and won over by all that not because of any estheticism, but on the level of religious ontology, so to speak, and not on the level of sentimentality.[11]

My message is not that Western Christians should all rush out and head East. The Christian East has its bad side too. But it is presumably the good qualities that Westerners wish to learn from. What are some of the good things we have seen in the Eastern tradition of Sunday that the Western Christian could reflect on with profit?

1) Sunday is not just Eucharist. If all you have on Sunday is Eucharist, then you're offering a feast with only the main course. I think that what I have said about the vigil illustrates that clearly enough.

2) Liturgy is *liturgy*, the common service of the People of God. Let me illustrate what I mean with a couple of personal experiences. One Sunday in July 1966 I found myself in Timosoara, capital of the Banat in Western Rumania, and decided to attend the Sunday liturgy in the Orthodox cathedral. I call it *the* Sunday liturgy because there was only one. It was concelebrated by three presbyters and two deacons. Since it was not a feast day, the archbishop was not celebrating, but presided from his throne in the nave. The rest of the clergy assisted from the choir. Needless to say, this was *their* Sunday Eucharist, too, and not some sort of conventual or chapter mass at which they were obliged to be present *pro forma*, following the private celebration of *their* mass! This was it: their mass, the bishop's mass, the cathedral mass, everybody's mass. One people, one community, one church, one liturgy.

This year on Palm Sunday I was in a Catholic retreat house. I asked about Sunday mass, received a perplexed stare that said, "But aren't you a priest?" and was informed that there was a mass "for the people" at 7:30 AM. Since I entertain the illusion that I'm people, I allowed myself to attend. The celebration commenced with the celebrant announcing that there would be no sermon because of the length of the Gospel (as it turned out, the whole service lasted exactly thirty-eight minutes). I won't go into all the details. The celebrant did everything alone, including all the readings. Hosts were consecrated at the mass, but that was not for us. We were given communion from the tabernacle, after which the freshly consecrated hosts were reserved for the following week. Although the retreat house was full, very few were at this mass. During it, however, several priests were saying private (i.e., solitary) masses on both sides of the same chapel. And all day long, other groups were doing their thing. Palms were blessed at two other masses. But it was all so divisive, so fragmented. The simple "non-groupie" Christian who just wanted Palm Sunday community worship could not find it because it was not to be had. Everyone worshiped God, everyone was doing something, but they did not come together to do it; they split.

The point I'm making is that nowhere in the Eastern Church could that scene have taken place. And I know of no cathedral of the Roman Catholic Church where the Timosoara cathedral scene could have taken place. And that's part of what is wrong with Western Catholic liturgy. It's too often a private party.

3) Eastern Sunday worship is *traditional*. It is always the same familiar liturgy. Week after week the same invitatories open the services, the incensations are always done in the same place and in the same way, the Litany of Peace prays for the same basic needs. Psalm 140 and the Hymn of Light are always the heart of vespers. After the vigil Gospel, the same resurrection hymn is sung. Of course there are numerous variable parts, but that's the problem of the clergy and choir. Everything is *familiar*, it's *ours*, we *know* it. It's not boring because it is magnificent, and it is done well. So, from my experience, I am tempted to think that the contemporary Western mania for variety in liturgy is because the liturgy is often done so poorly—sometimes appallingly so—that people are scrambling to escape the impasse by forever trying something new. Someone once asked me how to plan an Easter liturgy. I suggested some old standbys, like the paschal candle. "We did that last year" was the answer I got. Well, Christians have been doing a lot of things for almost two thousand years, and I hope we keep it up until the parousia. The answer is not to replace what we do, but to do it as if we meant it. Nor do we need to go East for examples of what I'm trying to propose. At Notre Dame we have the same familiar evensong every Sunday, year in and year out, and nobody complains, because it is *good*! Indeed, one of the reasons it is good is because it is familiar, and hence viable. Variety is not the answer to trash.

4) Eastern Sunday liturgy is traditional also because it is *focused*. There is really only one basic theme: Jesus Christ died and rose for our salvation, and is with us all days even unto the end of time. But I said enough about this point above.

5) Many other characteristics could be highlighted. One final one must be mentioned, however: Eastern worship has a sense of *transcendence*. This is true not only of the liturgy itself but of the whole

atmosphere of sacredness and mystery that surrounds its every movement and communicates a sense of reverential awe. To see a Byzantine liturgy in the richly iconographic setting of a properly appointed Byzantine church is to cross the threshold to another world, for in the East, iconography and liturgy have the same quality. The liturgy is not a "ceremony"; it is an object of contemplation, an awesome vision full of mystery, before which one prostrates in reverential awe.

Worshiping in this atmosphere of profuse symbolism through which the supernatural splendor of the inaccessible divine majesty is approached, Eastern Christians witness the exaltation and sanctification of creation, the majestic appearance of God who divinizes us through the transfiguring light of his heavenly grace. It is not only a matter of receiving the sacraments, but also one of living habitually within a liturgical atmosphere which stirs us in body and soul in order to transform us before a vision of spiritual beauty and joy.

Our lowliness and unworthiness, when faced with such an intense liturgical expression of the unsearchable majesty of God, might be forbidding were it not for the deep Christianity of the Byzantine liturgical prayers. The glory of the Lord and his incomparable transcendence, our lowliness and sinfulness—these themes lead us to a deep sense of reverence and humility. "Lord have mercy!" is the congregation's incessant refrain to the diaconal petitions. These sentiments find balance, however, in another constantly repeated theme: Christ is the Ruler of All, to be sure; but he is also the divine philanthropist, the "lover of humankind" who poured himself out for our salvation.

Not only in the prayers of the priest but also in the exclamations to which the people respond with their "Amen," this balance between glorification and tender love is a constantly alternating refrain.

For You are a good God and You love humankind, and we give
    glory to You . . . .
Again and again we bow down before You and we beseech
    You, O gracious lover of humankind . . . .
To You, O Lord and lover of humankind, we commend our
    whole life and hope . . . .

So there is not just majesty and awe, but also an integrity and equilibrium, a sense of the balanced wholeness of things. The liturgy is transcendent but not distant, hieratic but not clericalized, communal but not impersonal, traditional but not formalistic.

Apart from this liturgical ethos I have been describing, several nonreligious factors on the sociological and historical level also contribute to making Sunday what it is in the Eastern traditions. For most Eastern Christians, the Church has become and remains the symbol of their national identity, especially in areas such as Serbia, Greece, Macedonia, and the Middle East, where centuries of Ottoman tyranny left the people with no other bastion of communal self-identity and self-respect apart from the Church.

A second factor is that of size. Most Eastern congregations are small, and by Western standards most Eastern church buildings are small. This has considerable impact on the dramatic and tangible aspects of liturgical prayer: its movement and staging, its choreography, and their effect. Many medieval Byzantine churches were no more than thirty feet long. Perhaps this miniaturization reflected the desire for a more intimate worship to counteract the shift from the classical openness of the early liturgy to the more remote and inaccessible cult of medieval Byzantine monasticism.[12] At any rate, this smallness helps dispel the anonymity of the modern parish community, and this is not just an old world phenomenon. On the contrary, it is even reinforced in the diaspora, where the parish often remains the last bastion of ethnic community life.

After the Sunday morning liturgy in many churches in the U.S., there is a rush to the parking lot as if someone had yelled "Fire!" This is not true in most Eastern parishes. Everyone mills around outside when the weather is good, and chats. In smaller parishes there is a coffee hour in the parish hall. This hall is an essential component of the parish plant, and the focus of all sorts of activities. Even the often unreachable young seem drawn by this togetherness. (On a recent lecture tour among the Ukrainian Catholic communities of Western Canada, I stayed at the rectory of the Ukrainian Redemptorists in Saskatoon. The place was overrun by teenagers coming for various meetings during the few days I was there.)

Another exemplary Eastern community is in nearby Chicago, at the Ukrainian Catholic Church of Saints Volodymyr and Olha. This parish in the old, inner-city Ukrainian neighborhood was chosen as the subject of a program on public television a few years ago. Not only is there a beautiful new church building completely decorated with frescoes in the traditional style, but this parish has become the nucleus of urban renewal for the whole area. People who had moved to the suburbs have been drawn back to the old neighborhood. Old buildings have been bought up, renovated, and turned into housing for the aged, for the clergy, for seminarians. In the basement of the church is the parish hall, where lectures and banquets and other social and cultural affairs are held in dizzying succession. Behind the church there is a youth center with its own building. In still another parish building there is a Ukrainian cultural center where several young men studying for the priesthood are in residence and share intimately in the life of the community. Across the street from the church is the old folks' home, also run by the parish.

And there is the liturgy. The choir is superb, and esthetically the services are some of the purest and best Eastern liturgy in the Western hemisphere. The Sunday I was there, vespers on Saturday evening lasted for about an hour. Then there was a buffet supper in the parish hall, at which I gave a lecture to the audience of about two hundred, including many families and young people. On Sunday morning, matins of the resurrection began at eight, followed immediately by the Eucharist. These morning services, done in Ukrainian with great reverence and devotion, lasted about two hours.

Of course one will immediately protest: *"One* hour Saturday evening, *two* more on Sunday morning—who will put up with that?" Some not only put up with it, they demand it. Others come for only part of it, according to their devotion, but even they would be the last to say it should be cut down or omitted. Liturgy in the East is like liturgy in a monastery. It has an indivisible quality, an objectivity which demands that the cycle of prayer be accomplished in its integrity. This *opus Dei* is primarily the work of the community as a whole, and not of its individual members. The fact that some cannot or will not participate in all of it is not an argument for its suppression. So, in Eastern churches, people drift in and out of services according to their fervor and need. In Chicago, for example, many were there throughout vespers Saturday evening, while very few were present at the start of matins early Sunday morning. But gradually people drifted in, and the church was almost full by the time the Eucharist got under way.

Furthermore, when reacting with horror at the thought of so much liturgy, we should be careful—especially in a campus setting—with our judgments of what modern Americans will or will not put up with. Teenagers will wait in line outside all night in bad weather to buy tickets to a rock concert. And, by tradition, Notre Dame students stand—stand, not sit—throughout the entire two-and-a-half to three hours of every home football game. People will give time to whatever is important to their life: rock concerts, football, or the glorification of almighty God.

Of course I have been describing an ideal. In many parishes the tradition has cracked under the customary strains of urban secular life. So we must not deceive ourselves, as some Orthodox writers do when they contrast Eastern "Eucharistic" ecclesiology, rooted in the communion of the Body of Christ, with what they call the "legalistic" ecclesiology of the West. Bishop Kallistos (Timothy) Ware, Anglican convert to Orthodoxy, writes of "Western secularism," and affirms: "We are present in the Western world above all as a celebrating community, a Eucharistic communion, a people of prayer."[13] That is all very beautiful, but one wonders what a "Eucharistic" ecclesiology can mean in churches where practically no one goes to communion more than a few times a year. Or why secularism is "Western" when—according to their own statistics—in the region of Athens, where one-third of all Greeks live, only nine percent go to church every Sunday, and even these figures can be considered generous.[14] Other statistics put Greek-Orthodox Sunday practice at about six percent in the villages and five percent in urban areas, with twice as many women in church as men.[15] Among the Orthodox Balkan Slavs, the weekly attendance is even less.[16] By contrast, in the supposedly "secular" West, in France, where religious practice is notoriously low, twelve percent of the Catholics go to church regularly.[17] And in West Germany, thirty percent attend Sunday mass.[18] So much for "Western" secularism and Orthodox witness in the West as a eucharistic community of prayer! Among Eastern Catholics the percentage of those who regularly practice and communicate is much higher. But honesty forces us to admit that although the Eastern Churches have a glorious heritage still observable in their Sunday liturgical and social observances, they could learn a thing or two from the Catholic West about getting the people to church and to communion.

So we all have something to learn from one another. That is why the ultimate answer to our problems is the one that Christ started out with in the first place: the union of all in him.

NOTES

1. H. B. Porter, *The Day of Light* (Greenwich, Conn.: Seabury 1960) 81.
2. English version adapted from *The Office of Vespers in the Byzantine Rite* (London: Darton, Longman and Todd 1965) 42–43.
3. *On the Holy Spirit* 29, 73, PG 32, 205.
4. Adapted from A. Tripolitis, "*Phos hilaron.* Ancient Hymn and Modern Enigma," *Vigiliae christianae* 24 (1970) 189.
5. *A Prayerbook* (Cambridge, N.Y.: New Skete 1976) 198–199.
6. A. Guillou, "Le Monastére de la Théotokos au Sinai. Origines; épiclese; mosaique de al Transfiguration; Homélie inédite d'Anastase le Sinaite sur la Transfiguration (étude et texte critique)," *Mélanges d'archéologie et d'histoire* 67 (1955) 253.
7. *Prayerbook* 69.
8. J. Wilkinson, *Egeria's Travels* (London: SPCK 1971) 124–125.
9. *Prayerbook* 110–111.
10. O. Clément, *L'autre soleil. Quelques notes d'autobiographie spirituelle* (Paris: Stock 1975) 142.
11. P. Modesto, "Intervista a Tat'jana Goriceva," *Russia cristiana* 2 (176) anno 6 (March–April 1981) 58.
12. See T. F. Mathews, "'Private Liturgy in Byzantine Architecture: Toward a Re-appraisal," *Cahiers archéologiques* 30 (1982) 125–138.
13. K. Ware, "The Meaning of the Great Fast," *The Lenten Triodion*, trans. Mother Mary and K. Ware (London and Boston: Faber & Faber 1978) 15. The second citation is from *Episkepsis* (Bulletin of the Orthodox Center of the Ecumenical Patriarchate, Chambésy-Geneva) no. 246 (February 15, 1981) 7.
14. *Episkepsis*, no. 240 (November 1, 1980) 8.
15. M. Rinvolucri, *The Anatomy of a Church: Greek Orthodoxy Today* (London: Burns and Oates 1966) 27.
16. *Ibid.* 177, and my own observations in Serbia and Macedonia.
17. *Informations catholiques internationales* no. 548 (March 15, 1980) 13, 15.
18. *Ibid.* no. 557 (December 15, 1980) 34.

## Chapter Four

# LENT: A MEDITATION

Much in contemporary American spirituality represents a shift away from the more eschatological orientation prevalent in the spiritual outlook of the early Christians (1 Pt 1:20). Of course Christian eschatology has always held that the final days have already arrived in Christ. But this was interpreted to mean that we have already been borne, in him, out of this present world.[1] It did not mean that the final transformation of all into Christ was to focus on this world here below. What Tertullian tells us I am sure will come as news to most: the Christian has no interest in public affairs (*Apol* 38), even desires to be taken out of this world (*Ad uxorem* 1,5), and is "a foreigner in this world, a citizen of Jerusalem, the city above" (*De corona* 13). This has traditionally been the stance of Christian monasticism, both Eastern and Western. But it is radically different from the incarnational spirituality prevalent for the past thirty years, which tells us that since God became man Christ is in our neighbor, and the real work of Christian spirituality is not to leave the world but to dive in and grab life with both hands. Justice is more important than mortification, love more important than celibacy, and so on.

One result of this contemporary spiritual ideology is that it has dealt a death blow to fasting, penance, mortification. Today among contemporary religious one hears more of gourmet cooking than of fasting—a striking countersymbol to anyone even superficially acquainted with the spiritual literature at the origins of religious life.

And yet the season of Lent is still a major part of the liturgical year. Can such a season of penance have any real meaning for us today? It is in the context of this dilemma that I would like to suggest some scriptural and liturgical themes for meditative reflection during the forty days of Lent, in order to help draw meaning from the framework of penance into which the liturgy introduces us in these

Originally published in *Worship* 57 (1983) 123–134.

days. Only by personal reflection on the tradition can we decide what this Lent should be in our lives.

The problem is a broad and complicated one. There is, first, the very problematic of penance and asceticism for modern men and women—a problem which comes from modern psychology, and the quest for meaning and sincerity in an increasingly dehumanized technological world. Modern Christians reject penance and asceticism because they often lead to the distortion or destruction of more important human values. Hard things are not necessarily good things. Growth in freedom is more important than blind conformity to a set of rules. Self-development is more important than self-repression. And from the pragmatic point of view, asceticism is often seen to be insincere—or at least useless because it doesn't work. We are not impressed by the poverty and prayer of an Athonite monk when we experience his fanatical opposition to ecumenism or his bigotry against fellow Christians not of his church.

The problem, then, is a real one. Penance does not turn people into Christians. And anyway, what is the value of self-inflicted pain for modern men and women whose whole drive is to eliminate pain, to develop in freedom the autonomous self? Escape the world? We want to plunge into it, affirm it for all the glory that it is!

To meet this problem, let us turn first to the New Testament, sole revealed source for the understanding of Christian life. The place of penance and self-abnegation in the New Testament is undeniable. The very overture to the preaching of the kingdom, its first word in fact, is *"metanoeite*, for the kingdom of heaven is at hand"* (Mt 3:2). And the life of the preacher witnessed to what he preached. The Baptist's *metanoeite* is translated in the Vulgate *"poenitentiam agite"*— historically perhaps the first distortion of the meaning of Christian penance. Our English "pain" comes from *poena* (penalty, punishment), and one could build a whole theological investigation around this confusion.

But we know better now. What John the Baptist, or better, the Precursor as he is known in the Christian East, the one who went before to prepare the way for the Messiah—what John preached was conversion, a change of mind or mentality, *meta-nous*, as is clear not only from the Greek, but from what he did. He did not drive his hearers before him into the desert to imitate his ascetic life; he invited them to change their lives and bear good fruit, lest the axe be laid to the root. And his baptism was the ritual or liturgical expression of this "change of heart." For life is a celebration of reality, and liturgy a celebration of life: we need to express what we are not just for the sake of expressing it, but to be it, because we are persons, not souls, and it is us, not our souls, that Jesus came to save. Hence New Testament repentance is accompanied by the externalization of what preceded it interiorly: the recognition and admission of the reality of what we are (cf Lk 5:8; 18:13f).

A bit later, Jesus' proclamation of the New Law in Matthew 5 (the Beatitudes) states that we are blessed, happy, enjoy the favor of God, for ill-fortune. It is good to be poor and suffer persecution; it is good to suppress self-affirmation and ambition, good to be meek. One might object that here Jesus makes a virtue of necessity. And the Church has sometimes done just that, transforming coercion into holiness, scarcity into providence. Where men and women had no choice, no option, theology came to the rescue, assuaging helplessness and elevating futility, often in the Church's own favor, so that sheer inertia before the powers that be passed for conformity to the will of God. But this is not what Christ meant. John the Baptist went right after the Sadducees and Pharisees, and Christ himself was far more of a revolutionary than many of today's church leaders dare admit.

I believe it is only the cross that provides us with a basis for a truly Christian theology of self-denial and penance. The New Testament says practically nothing about what is often understood today as penance: the infliction of self-punishment. New Testament penance is *metanoia*: the imitation of Jesus by putting off the old Adam to put on the new, dying to self so that we might rise again in Christ. And this implies asceticism: "If any man would come after me, let him deny himself, take up his cross and follow me. For whoever would save his life will lose it, and whoever loses his life for my sake will find it."[2] This asceticism is nothing more than the necessary objectivity and distance from whatever is impermanent and secondary in the human endeavor; the self-discipline necessary to maintain true freedom and make the right choices, the destruction of egoism by the honest person who has the courage to stand naked before self and God. "I have been crucified with Christ; it is no longer I who live, but Christ who lives in me" (Gal 2:20). That's the point of it all, not a turning in on self, not a concentration on self-discipline as some sort of spiritual athletics, but an openness to new life, and through it an openness to others, the end to which it is all supposed to lead. Let us not forget that there are only two commandments, and the second is the same as the first.

So New Testament penance is in the sign of the cross. It is a life face-to-face with the mystery of death as a sign of proximity to God, for Christ is "First born *from among the dead*" (Apoc 1:5). And the following of Christ on both the *operational* and *mystagogical* (or if you prefer, ontological) plane is a radical transformation into the death of Christ. We are created according to the image of God—*kat'eikona tou theou*—but according to the Greek Fathers, this image of God is logos; hence we live as the image of a God who died. The great paradox of Christian life is that the death of Jesus was the death of death. Yet we can enter this new life only by death to self, including the acceptance of physical death. David M. Stanley in his superb book *A Modern Scriptural Approach to the Spiritual Exercises*, has expressed this Pauline teaching as follows:

> By accepting his death in all its concrete reality from the hand of his Father, Jesus Christ destroyed forever the sinful solidarity which had bound humanity to the first Adam. For he freely "became obedient even to death, yes, death upon the cross" (Phil 2:8), as the one effective, redeeming representative of the whole race. By his resurrection, Christ created a new, supernatural solidarity of grace, thereby creating the possibility of an entirely new relationship for man towards God as his Father, through his union with the unique Son of God. "And he died for all, in order that the living might no longer live for themselves, but for him who died and was raised for them" (2 Cor 5:15).
>
> Yet in order that man personally might attain this salvation, he must pass through the ultimate redemptive experience, Christian death, the "new creation" that became a reality in Jesus' own death. The possibility of attaining this crucially necessary experience, Paul teaches, is initially opened to the individual human being through baptism, the sac-ramental participation in Jesus' redeeming death (Rom 6:3–4). Yet another experience, participation in Jesus' resurrection, which his baptism also makes possible, is also needed for the completion of man's salvation: and it is to occur at the parousia (1 Cor 15:23ff).
>
> Thus the emphasis in Paul's thought is not upon the vicarious nature of Jesus' redemptive work, although that element is not absent, but rather upon the efficacy of Christ's death and resurrection in involving man in a totally new human experience. For this he is prepared here below by the Christian sacraments, principally by baptism and the Eucharist. Ultimately however he is saved by being totally conformed

through death in Christ and resurrection to Christ, who exhibits in himself the definitive form of redeemed human nature as "the last Adam."[3]

This theme of death is at the very outset of Christian life, when in baptism we are baptized into the death of Christ, as Paul said (Rom 6:3–11). It is this that renders conformity to his life, his image, possible. For the Christian the following of Christ is never merely operational, but a conformity of us to him, by him, in the mystery of his Spirit now dwelling in the Church. As the mystagogic catecheses of the fourth century make clear, we not only strive to imitate the goodness of his life, but he conforms us to himself in the liturgical mystery of the Church. In the teachings of Origen this is explicitly an introduction into the history of salvation, and in this perspective the fourfold dimension of salvation history appears: the Old Testament foreshadowing, relived by Christ; re-presented to us in the life and liturgy of the Church; lived out by us in the day-to-day "liturgy" that is our life in Christ. If Christian life in essence is a configuration to the death and resurrection of Christ, the sacraments of initiation are only the radical, mystagogical initiation of a long exodus of spiritual combat, according to the teaching of Chrysostom. For as he says, the Christ present in us is a *crucified* Christ, and his life will grow only in a crucified flesh. Both Chrysostom and Cyril of Jerusalem express this process of growth in terms of a spiritual exodus which the neophyte, like the Jew in Egypt, begins in company with the whole Church. And according to Evagrius, *askesis* is an essential element of this process, because it is the only method God has given us to detach ourselves from ourselves, in his pregnant phrase.

This brings us to the practice of Lent, for we have discussed the place of penance and asceticism in personal and liturgical terms, and Lent should bring forth a union of both. As a preparation not only for Easter, but for baptism, Lent is directed not merely at life (resurrection), but at the death which preceded it: the cross, life as baptismal death in Christ, lived out in death to self.

In scriptural terms, Lent is a time of desert. In the Middle Eastern milieu of the Scriptures, the struggle for life is a struggle for water, and the desert is the place of malediction par excellence. Habitable only by wild beasts, the desert is hostile to humans; there the Evil One roams freely, unafraid and unchallenged. But it is also there that the power of Yahweh is most manifest, for in the desert there is no salvation but in God: it is there that Yahweh is the "God who saves." God's great gift to Israel was to lead them out of Egypt through the desert and across the Jordan's waters into the Promised Land. God leads us out of the desert; the devil desires to lead us into its depths in order to conquer us (cf. Lk 8:29 and the rite of the scapegoat in Lev 16:20ff). The desert is also where the devil seeks refuge when driven out (Mt 12:43).

Then why did the Baptist, and Christ, and later the monks, go into the desert? In the symbolism of Scripture, it was not to flee the world that God led his people, John the Baptist, Jesus, and later the anchorites and hermits into the desert, but rather that they might manifest there, where the battle is most difficult, his victory and his rights. If Christ retired to the desert after his miracles, it was not to escape but to encounter the power of God.[4]

Salvation history began in a garden and was vitiated by food; the Good News opens in the desert and is accompanied by fasting. This is the antinomy of salvation history posed symbolically by Lent. Only by prayer and fasting are some devils cast out (Mk 9:29). Hence the desert is the perfect type of the "world" in the New Testament sense. It is the kingdom of Satan, hostile to God. It is there that the Son of Man must preach the Good News. The "desert theme" of Lent, therefore, is not an invitation to flee the real world. Besides, in recent discussions of the "secular city" vis-à-vis the Church there has been altogether too much talk of "relevance" and "flight from the real world" and "cultural ghettoes." The world of the Christian standing in vigil before God is just as "real" as any "real," and those who have never experienced it are the ones stuck in an irrelevant and unreal ghetto.

Recall the biblical pattern of salvation history, our salvation history, and the meaning of Lent for us becomes clear. What Israel did prefigured Christ; what he did, the Church re-presents in the daily liturgical theophany of his saving action so that it can touch our lives. But what the Church actualizes in us radically through its sacramental life must be lived out by us in the exodus of our own pilgrimage. Israel crossed the desert into Israel, and so must I. Of course we do not physically withdraw to a desert. For us the desert of Lent, like all liturgy, is a spiritual stance: a re-posturing of the heart by the asceticism of withdrawal not from life, but from attention to our petty selves, and from the mass of irrelevancies with which we surround ourselves. This is not to escape life, but to begin to live by escaping the many drugs with which we ordinarily dull our spiritual sensibilities.

Just as the desert balances the lush oriental Garden of Eden, so too the forbidden fruit has its antithesis in the fast. I think that for an understanding of what fasting should image forth for us, we must recall the extraordinarily large role that food and eating play in the Bible. Revelation is immersed in the simplest routines of life. Did you ever reflect on how often Christ eats or talks of eating in the New Testament?[5] This is intimately connected with the Old Testament tradition of the messianic meal: to sit down at table and feast with the Messiah is one of the signs of the kingdom: "As my Father appointed a kingdom for me, so do I appoint for you, that you may eat and drink at my table in my kingdom."[6] These meals of Jesus show the difference between the period of John the Baptist (*fasting* in expectation of the kingdom) and the coming of Christ (a period of joy and *banqueting*). Jesus and the apostles do not fast, because, as Jesus himself says, one does not fast when the bridegroom is with us.[7] But the note struck by Christ at the end of his life, in the vow of abstinence,[8] introduces the theme of fasting into Christian life between ascension and parousia, until the fullness of the kingdom comes: "And the woman fled into the wilderness, where she has a place prepared by God, in which to be nourished for one thousand two hundred and sixty days" (Apoc 12:6).

Of course the bridegroom is always with us. Did he not say "I am with you always ... " (Mt 28:20)? But another of the innumerable antinomies in the dialectic of Christian life is that he also said he must go to the Father ("A little while and you will see me no more" (Jn 16:16). We are in this "little while" of vigil before the parousia, both in the Presence while awaiting it.

In the New Testament, then, there is an intimate connection between fasting and waiting, and the presence of the Lord is manifested in feasting, the breaking of the long fast of waiting which was the Old Testament (cf. Is 25:6). This is why Jesus ate so often, especially with sinners; this is why at Emmaus he was known only "in the breaking of the bread." But it is also why we have at the end of the New Testament the eschatological *maranatha*, for the parousia of Christ is only inchoative, not yet perfected in salvation history.

Hence the New Testament also tells us to "watch and pray" for we know not when the Master will come, like the bridegroom and his friends, like the thief in the night.[9]

Now the liturgy, like Christian life, presents these multiple tensions which are irreducible and must simply be lived: the kingdom is here and not fully here, Christ is with us yet we wait for him still. The liturgical tension is inevitable because all symbolism is a span between the expressible and the ineffable, and if all we grasp is the symbol without reaching beyond to the concrete reality through living this imaged life, then we will never know what liturgy is all about. Hence do not expect from liturgy some sort of logical resolution to the symbolized antinomies. They are all there, all at once, all as part of every minute of life, just as every moment in our total salvation history is in us now because it is basically the Passover in the literal sense of Jesus' passover from death to life, and in baptism we have already been conformed to this, we too have passed over from death to life—and yet we haven't, in another sense, until we too die and rise again in him.

But as we saw in the catecheses of the Fathers, this end symbolized in baptism is just a beginning, this death a life, and all must be lived out, expressed, in our daily existence as other Christs. Hence, too, in the liturgy of the Church, the Christ who is present to all of us must be waited for again. For obvious reasons, the liturgy at times singles out these inseparable elements to give now one, now another, a privileged moment in the year of the Church to symbolize in the true mystagogical sense of make-real-for-us, conform us in a more intense way to, what must really be an element of every day in our Christian life.

Lent, then, presents the polarity of wait and arrival, history and eschatology, and this is seen in the fasting and liturgy of Lent. First, there is what Alexander Schmemann calls the fast of the Church, for the Eucharist is the way in which the Church daily resolves its wait for the Messiah: his banquet shows the kingdom as come, and hence in many Eastern traditions the Eucharist is incompatible with the lenten fast. For the Eucharist is the Church in festival, the feast of the presence of its Lord. This is the meaning of all eucharistic fasting. It has nothing to do with asceticism: it is a vigil before the sacramental parousia, and consists not only in fast, not just in not eating; there is also the vigil before Sundays and feasts, which primitively, with Saturday, were the only days on which the full Eucharist was celebrated.

But fasting is demanded not only by the nature of the Church, but also by human nature. This is the *ascetic* fast, fast *in* the Church. Christ fasted in preparation for his ministry (Mt 4:2) and it is only by fasting that certain devils are mastered (Mt 17:21). It is by food that Satan seduced Adam and Eve. Hence ascetic fasting is the radical symbol of our lenten stance before God. It is the renunciation, the exorcising of Satan by accepting the paradox that those who do not eat die, but that only those who lose their life shall find it, for it is not by bread alone that one lives. By its very radicalness, at least in symbolic intention, it leads to freedom because it is true *mortification*, that is, death to self by the abandonment of what is considered necessary for life. The refusal of submission to necessity is freedom, which is of the essence of all true life in Christ.

Thus there is nothing unnatural or degrading about asceticism when put in the context of tradition. There is no denial of human values here for the Christians who in faith know what they are. In the words of Origen, the Christ-life is a participation in the mystery of the Church, and the mystery of the Church is a nuptial mystery, a mystery of total fidelity through uniting love. But the only ultimate proof is final fidelity throughout time, and this means death to self, to egoism; and it means patience; and it means pain. This is why for centuries the Church called "saint" and celebrated liturgically no one who was not a martyr. Martyrdom was proof of holiness not because of stoicism or because there is any value in pain, but because it was a sign of lasting love *unto the end*. As Chrysostom said, charity without martyrdom can make disciples, martyrs without charity, never.[10]

We can't all be martyrs, but we can and must all give witness to our enduring love. And so the Church began to assimilate to the martyrs and call "saint" those who through *askesis* had died to self in order to live for Christ, for the total Christ which is every man and woman. In this we see the deep human value of asceticism: openness to others is the beginning of growth, and death to self is the condition of that openness. Of course it is hard to die to self when we don't know who we are—a very special modern problem—but this should not deter us, for in opening ourselves to the Christ in others we discover who we are in the deepest sense of the word, far more deeply than by the superficial path of self-affirmation that comes from the insecurity of an undetermined self-image.

Lent, therefore, like the baptism for which it originally prepared, should bring us face to face with the mystery of death, and therefore with self, for death is the one thing we must all do alone. Just as it is an error to think of any aspect of Christian life as a static event, so too death. Death is not a door through which we shall once pass, but a passage we enter physically at birth, and mystically in Christ at baptism: "It is no longer I who live, but Christ who lives in me."

We have been meditating upon the enormously rich tradition that is ours, and for this traditionalism I do not apologize at all. For we do look to the past, to our collective memory, the memory of a saving reality rendered present by the Church now, which is the root of all that Christianity has ever meant. Harvey Cox is wrong in saying that the Church looks only to the future. Only those who have no past can afford such schizophrenia. We live by faith as well as by hope, and the true resolution of the past-future polarity is depicted in the liturgical life expressing the eternal in time and beyond: past and future become present in the Christian celebration of life, provided we accept the presupposition of this reality: that the world of this new life is a world beyond death, and here on earth that means death to self.

This, then, is what our liturgy is in the broadest sense: the Christian celebration of life, wherever the life of Christ touches ours. This does not mean that liturgy and life are always coterminous, because the Christ-bond can be dissolved. If our liturgy is not a privileged *moment* feasting a *permanent reality* in our lives, then it is a hollow show. Unless our celebrated vigil is the communal bursting forth in song and prayer of the Christian soul wakeful before God, then what can it mean? The movement is of course dialectic: liturgy is not merely expression of but also transforming source of what we must be. And this must be true of our vigil of Lent, which is why we have spoken of so many things, for they all pertain to the whole Christ-life, but we are called to celebrate them in a special way now.

What then should we do during Lent? Just that: celebrate the event by allowing the elements we have discussed, which are part of our daily lives at all times, to rise to the surface and reach expression and unity through the Church's tradition as re-presented in the liturgy of Lent, so that it in turn may, through the sacred action of the praying Church, bring the healing finger of God to bear on the wounds of our life.

The tradition will not destroy our freedom but perfect it, just as eternity does not render time absurd, but rather gives it its true weight. It is in our "typicon," our age-old usages and rites, that the Church has hidden her understanding and transformation of time. Our lenten liturgy is not a question of a "schedule of services" nor a "sanctification of time," but a sanctification of life by mediating to us the presence of Christ in our time. Only such an understanding of the liturgy does not divide life into sacred and profane but transfigures one by the other in making all of life a witness to the Lord. For he came not to "symbolize" his real presence in liturgy, but to transform and save by his real presence in you and me.

Let Lent, then, be a time of healing (*salus*, salvation), and let our fast be the "diet" of this restoration to health. Let us enter into the desert of our hearts where, removed from side issues, we can face what we are, and in compunction, *penthos*, over that reality, let us "do penance"—that is, *metanoia*—dying to self so that we may live for others, as we make vigil before the coming of the Lord.

Have I painted a grim picture, inconsistent with the paschal joy that permeates the Christian tradition? Nicholas Arseniev has written that the joy of the resurrection is the fundamental trait of the Orthodox world view. But St. Pimen said to Abbot Arsenius a long time before anyone heard of his namesake Arseniev: "Blessed are you for having wept over yourself in this lower world." The contradiction is only apparent. The joy of Tabor is at the summit of a spiritual mountain—or ladder, if you prefer Climacus—and all the Fathers concur that it is a rough climb. Perhaps Symeon the New Theologian summed up the fusion of both elements when he spoke of "a chant mingled with tears." The chant is the chant of the resurrection, and the tears are not the forbidden sadness of the unsaved—no Christian can be sad—but the *penthos* of which the Fathers speak.

In entering willingly, then, the desert of our Lent, we know that the resurrection of Christ symbolized for us in the paschal candle burns already, going before us like the pillar of fire that led the Jews through the desert to the Promised Land. It is that which gives meaning to it all.

## NOTES

1. Gal 1:4; Col 1:13; Phil 3:20; Heb 6:5.

2. Mt 16:24–25; cf Mk 8:34–35; Lk 9:23–24.

3. (Chicago: Institute of Jesuit Sources 1967) 294–295.

4. Mk 1:35; Lk 4:42; 5:16.

5. Cf Mt 9:11; 14:15–21; 15:32–38; 22:1ff; 25:10; 26:20ff; Mk 8:1–9; 14:3–25; 16:14; Lk 5:29–35; 7:33–34; 9:13–17; 10:40; 11:37ff; 13:29; 14:1–24; 22:16ff, 29–30; 24:28–35, 41; Jn 2:1–11; 6; 7:33–50; 13ff; 21:9–13; Rev 19:9, 17.

6. Lk 22:29–30; cf 13:29; Mt 22:1ff.

7. Mt. 9:15; Mk 2:18–20; Lk 5:33–35; 7:33–34.

8. Mt 26:29, Mk 14:25; Lk 22:16.

9. Mt 24:42–51; 25:1–13; Mk 13:33–37; Lk 12:35–40, 46; 2 Pt 3:10; Rev 3:3.

10. *Praise of St Roman the Martyr* I, 1.

Chapter Five

# THE FREQUENCY
# OF THE EUCHARIST
# THROUGHOUT HISTORY

The New Testament has Jesus say, "Do this in memory of me." He does not say how often, and the problem before us is the various answers given to that question throughout history. My point of departure will be the established Christian eucharistic tradition in this "command to repeat" reported by Lk 22:19 and 1 Cor 11:25–26, though not by Mk or Mt. Whether Jesus actually said it, and whether what ultimately emerged as the Eucharist goes against the original expectation of an imminent parousia, are beyond the scope of my interest here. Even with such thorny questions eliminated, there will be space only for the barest outline of the general evolution, though I recognize that one can find exceptions to any general picture.

First some distinctions. There are community Eucharists and Eucharists of a more private nature. There is the eucharistic liturgy or mass; and eucharistic communion, whether during mass or not; and the relative frequency of each. Finally, each of these "Eucharists" has its own rhythms and demands its own separate answer to the question, "How often?" Our main interest here is not the frequency of communion—i.e. with what frequency the faithful actually received the Eucharist—but rather with what frequency mass was celebrated or communion made available to communicants outside of mass.

1. The First Three Centuries

From the New Testament we can conclude nothing certain about eucharistic frequency. All were "assiduous" at the "breaking of the

Revised from *Concilium* 152 (1982) 13–24.

bread" (Acts 2:42), though how often is not indicated: the "daily" of Acts 2:46 refers with certainty only to the temple prayer. An incipient Sunday rhythm may be implied in Acts 20:7–12 and 1 Cor 16:2, and one might infer the same from the meals of the Risen Lord on the "first day", or from the parallelism between the "the Lord's Supper" and "the Lord's day" in Apoc 1:10.[1]

By the middle of the second century, however, the picture is clear: for the community synaxis, Sunday and Eucharist form a unity as the symbolic celebration of the presence of the Risen Lord amidst his own, a presence that signals the arrival of the New Age.[2] And it is generally agreed that everyone present communicated.

Although this Sunday synaxis was initially the only common Eucharist, it was customary for the faithful to take from it enough of the blessed gifts for communion during the week. The evidence for this from Tertullian on is unquestionable.[3] This practice of communion outside mass lasted among the laity until the seventh century,[4] and even longer in monastic circles, as we shall see.

In addition to these "common" uses of the Eucharist there were "occasional" eucharistic celebrations for special groups and purposes of the most varied sort: at the graveside,[5] at oratories in honor of the martyrs,[6] in prisoners' cells,[7] in private homes.[8] In North Africa these "special" Eucharists were so common that Cyprian (d. 258) refers to priests celebrating mass daily,[9] possibly to accomodate this demand. But this type of "small-group" mass must not be confused with the "private" mass that appears only later.

By the end of the second century we also see a filling out of community worship. Masses are celebrated at martyrs' tombs on the anniversary of their victory.[10] Saturday is gradually assimilated to Sunday, and by the fourth century has acquired a eucharistic celebration everywhere except Rome and Alexandria.[11] And the weekly stations or fast days on Wednesday and Friday have already become eucharistic days in North Africa in the time of Tertullian (ca. 200).[12]

## 2. THE EUCHARIST AFTER CONSTANTINE

With the Peace of Constantine (313) and the spread of the monastic movement, we must distinguish not only "community" and "occasional" or "domestic" Eucharists, but also "monastic" practice.

In both East and West the practice of "domestic" Eucharists becomes common. In Cappadocia, Basil (d. 379) refers to priests under interdict who are allowed to celebrate only in private homes.[13] Gregory Nazianzen (d. *ca.* 389) celebrates in his sister's house, and their father, also a bishop, celebrates an Easter night Eucharist in his sickroom.[14] Home liturgies are a well-entrenched practice in fifth-century Constantinople, as Patriarch Nestorius (428–431) is informed when he reproves presbyter Philip for it.[15] Ambrose (d. 397) celebrates for a Roman noblewoman in her palace in Trastevere,[16] and Melany the Younger (d. 439) has her chaplain Gerontius say mass for her daily, "as was the custom of the Roman Church."[17] Indeed, things got out of hand, for the Councils of Laodicea (*ca.* 360–390) and Seleucia-Ctesiphon (410) proscribe the practice outright, and the Second Council of Carthage (*ca.* 390) requires episcopal authorization for it.[18]

The practice continued, however. It lasted in the West in spite of all attempts to suppress it, until Session 22 of Trent (1562) finally succeeded in doing so.[19] In the Orthodox Church we still see it in the seventh century. The life of the Cypriot St. John the Almsgiver (d. *ca.* 620), Chalcedonian Patriarch of Alexandria, refers twice to the bishop celebrating privately in his domestic oratory.[20] Canon 31 of the Quinisext Council in Trullo (692) demands episcopal approval for the practice—a sure sign that it was still alive.[21] Indeed, house chapels or *eukteria oikoi* were so common that they are provided a special category in Byzantine property law.[22]

In the community or "cathedral" usage there is clear evidence for daily mass in Milan,[23] Aquileia,[24] Spain[25] and North Africa[26] by the end of the fourth century. Augustine (d. 430) tells us things were different in the East,[27] but that does not mean daily Eucharist was a purely Western phenomenon. Eastern evidence is more disparate, and it is not always clear what sort of liturgy is referred to, but the process of filling in the eucharistic week had clearly begun there too.

In Alexandria, Athanasius (*ca.* 340) and Socrates (*ca.* 380) both limit the Eucharist to Sunday,[28] but the *Responsa canonica* attributed to Patriach Timothy of Alexandria (381–385) speak of Eucharist on Saturday as well as Sunday,[29] and according to Cassian the Egyptian monks *ca.* 400 had the same usage.[30] Not long after, Cyril of Alexandria (d. 444) refers to daily Eucharist.[31]

In spite of the extraordinarily full liturgical day in the cathedral usage of Jerusalem in the time of Egeria (*ca.* 384), there was weekday mass only on Wednesdays and Fridays outside of Lent, on Saturdays during Lent, and of course on certain feast days too.[32] Severian of Gabala (d. 408) concords with Egeria.[33] Eusebius (d. 339), on the other hand, speaks of "a daily memorial of the body and blood of Christ" in Palestine,[34] although elsewhere he refers to the common synaxis only on Sunday.[35]

The *Testamentum Domini* I, 22, a fifth-century Syriac document from somewhere in the Syriac-speaking hinterlands of the Mediterranean littoral, indicates Eucharist on Saturdays, Sundays, and fast days.[36] And the *Oratio de sacra synaxi* attributed to Anastasius of Sinai, who died sometime after 700, refers to the eucharistic liturgy as a daily affair.[37]

Epiphanius (d. 403) of Salamis in Cyprus, writes *ca.* 377 of mass there on Sunday, Wednesday, and Friday, as in Jerusalem.[38] The hagiopolite usage is also found in the East-Syrian Church *ca.* 400, in a letter of Bishop Marutha of Maipherkat and in other Mesopotamiam sources.[39]

In the environs of Antioch, the *Apostolic Constitutions* (*ca.* 380) mentions the Wednesday and Friday fast, but only Saturday, Sunday and feast-day Eucharist.[40] In Antioch itself, however, Chrysostom (*ante* 397) testifies that Friday, Saturday, and Sunday were the normal eucharistic days outside of Lent.[41] So if one adds the feasts and martyrs' memorials to which Chrysostom also refers, then his claim of "almost daily" Eucharist is accurate enough.[42]

The Council of Laodicea (*ca.* 360–390),[43] and Chrysostom in Constantinople (397–404),[44] concur that the practice in Asia Minor and Constantinople was Saturday-Sunday Eucharist—i.e. the same usage as North Syria beyond Antioch, according to the *Apostolic Constitutions*. Of course there was also Eucharist for feasts and memorials.

Around 372, Basil in Caesarea recommends daily communion, and says that the practice there was to receive Wednesday, Friday, Saturday, and Sunday.[45] This must refer to mass and not to communion at home; otherwise why not communicate daily? He also speaks of solitaries giving themselves communion from the reserved species, and says that in Egypt even the laity did so.

So we see the Eucharist spreading from Sunday, to Saturday and Sunday in Alexandria, North Syria, Asia Minor and Constantinople;

to Wednesday, Friday, Sunday in Palestine (including Jerusalem), Cyprus and Mesopotamia; to Friday, Saturday, Sunday in Antioch; to Wednesday, Friday, Saturday, Sunday in Caesarea; and finally to "every day" in fifth-century Alexandria. But daily mass does not appear in Rome or Constantinople until later.

The Roman system can be traced in the development of the sacramentary and lectionary. Initially there are weekday propers only for a non-eucharistic synaxis on Wednesdays and Fridays in Lent. Monday, Tuesday, and Saturday are added from the fourth century. By the sixth, all these synaxes have become eucharistic, Gregory II (715–731) rounds off the week with a Thursday mass, and Lent becomes the first and only Roman season with a proper mass and station for each ferial day.[46]

Note that the traditional fast days, Wednesday and Friday, become the *first* eucharistic ferias in some areas—Africa, Rome, Jerusalem and Palestine, Cyprus, Mesopotamia—whereas in Constantinople and Asia Minor, fast days and Eucharist were considered mutually inimical.

In Constantinople we see a more or less complete yearly cycle by the beginning of the ninth century.[47] A century later, the Typicon of the Great Church gives a complete picture of the cathedral liturgy of the capital.[48] The Eucharist is celebrated on Saturdays and Sundays throughout the year, daily from Easter to Whitsunday, on feasts of Our Lord, and on some Marian and sanctoral commemorations. In the latter two instances, however, it is not a question of masses in every church, but of one stational service in a designated shrine.

However, no mass does not mean no communion. On fast days in Constantinople there was generally no mass, but the fast was broken in the evening at a Liturgy of the Presanctified Gifts. Though the Typicon is not explicit, apparently this service was celebrated Wednesday and Friday of the week before Lent, Monday through Friday during Lent, and Monday to Wednesday of Holy Week.[49] In addition, the Presanctified Liturgy could be celebrated on Wednesdays and Fridays throughout the year, though by the time of the Typicon, mass was also allowed on those days. Much of this is contrary to present Byzantine usage, which stems from Palestinian monasticism. We shall return to this question of Eucharist on fast days.

According to Cedrenus' *Historiarum compendium*, in 1044 Emperor

Constantine IX Monomachus (1042–1055) assigned revenues to have the Eucharist celebrated in Hagia Sophia daily, and not just on Saturday and Sunday as had been the custom.[50] So eucharistic multiplicity was by no means a medieval Latin monopoly. The same is true of eucharistic excess. The synaxary of the Coptic Church tells of seventh-century heretics who communicated twenty times a day.[51] And a ninth-century Byzantine *tomos synodikos* decrees that "The priest should celebrate only once a day, not more"[52]—a sure sign that the abuse existed. The reprobation of this practice is repeated in mid-eleventh century Byzantine sources such as the *Protheoria*.[53] And Thomas Mathews has noted the multiplication of small eucharistic chapels in Middle and Late Byzantine Churches, provoked perhaps by the need to reconcile multiple Eucharists with the prohibition against celebrating more than one mass a day on any one altar.[54]

The later history in the West involves the question of private mass. This has been well-treated elsewhere.[55] Besides, the principle of daily Eucharist had already been established before the spread of this novelty. But before we turn to the modern period, let us return to the question of Eucharist on fast days, and to monastic usage.

### 3. EUCHARIST AND FASTING

We have observed that the gradual spread of the Eucharist from Sunday to other days did not spring from the inner dynamic of the Eucharist itself. It depended on some other factor in the liturgical life of the local church: the assimilation of Saturday to Sunday, a station, a feast, a memorial. Community mass was not celebrated just because it is a good thing in itself, but because its celebration was required to solemnize the day.[56] In other words the spread of the Eucharist followed the development of the calendar. And in this development, it was thought necessary not only to celebrate the Eucharist on some days, but to forbid it on others. So the Eucharist did not have an absolute value; its celebration was not self-justifying, as it is seen to be today. In all this we are speaking of the community synaxis. The rhythm of "occasional" Eucharists was more flexible, but even there it was the "occasion" that called for Eucharist, not the Eucharist that created the occasion.

Still, one cannot not spin a theological thesis out of the reasons for having or not having Eucharist on certain days, for the question of fast-day Eucharist now divides Rome and Alexandria from the rest of the East. By the sixth century, the Roman fast-day synaxes had become eucharistic, and a similar evolution can be observed in Egypt. The original Alexandrine usage as recounted in the fifth century by Socrates was a synaxis followed by communion from the pre-sanctified gifts on Wednesdays, Fridays, and Saturdays.[57] But, as in Rome, these days eventually acquire a mass, and today the Coptic Church is the only Eastern tradition with daily Eucharist during periods of fast.

This is the exact opposite of what we see in Asia Minor, where mass is forbidden on Lenten ferias and on some other fast days during the year, except when there is a feast. This dates at least from the fourth century, when canons 49 and 51 of the Council of Laodicea (*ca.* 360–390) prohibit martyrs' memorials and mass in Lent except on Saturday and Sunday.[58] The two go together: one cannot celebrate a feast, because to do so requires a Eucharist. Canon 52 of the Quinisext Council in Trullo (692) repeats the prohibition but ordains that the Presanctified Liturgy be celebrated on all days of Lent except Saturday, Sunday, and Annunciation.[59]

This has become more or less the attitude in the non-Egyptian East: the eucharistic liturgy is festive, and hence unsuitable for times of penance. This does *not* mean, however, that there was no opportunity to receive communion on non-eucharistic days, though this was totally dependent on local usage, and one finds diversity from place to place and from age to age even within the same tradition.

In contemporary Byzantine usage, which has not followed the old cathedral rite of Hagia Sophia since the monastic Typicon of St. Sabas took over the field after the fall of Constantinople to the Latins in 1204,[60] the Divine Liturgy is prohibited on Lenten ferias and on some other fast days, but Presanctified is celebrated only in Lent on Wednesdays, Fridays, and certain feasts.

The Maronites once had Presanctified on ferias throughout Lent, but they have abandoned their tradition in favor of the Latin usage of mass during Lent except on Good Friday.[61] Among the Syrian Orthodox, the Nomocanon of Bar Hebraeus (d. 1286) refers to the suppression of Eucharist in Lent and to the Presanctified, which he attributes to Severus of Antioch (d. 537).[62] And indeed such a liturgy is found in the liturgical mss, and is referred to in other Syrian sources.[63] The Syrian Orthodox have abandoned this rite, though the Syrian Catholic Missal of Sharfeh (1922) still has it.[64] Among the East Syrians there is similar evidence in the anonymous ninth-century *Expositio officiorum*,[65] and some later liturgical mss contain a parochial Presanctified Liturgy.[66]

In the Armenian tradition, during the first week of the three-week pre-lenten "Fast of the Catechumens" and during the whole of Lent proper, there is no mass allowed except Saturdays and Sundays.[67] Several Armenian liturgical mss contain a Presanctified Liturgy, though it is no longer in use.[68]

The broad outline emerges clearly enough: apart from Egypt and the West, no mass on weekdays in Lent. From the sixth century, however, provision is made for presanctified communion on these days, though this practice has been abandoned or at least greatly reduced in all traditions.


4. MONASTIC USAGE

Those brought up on the heady Benedictine-revival literature of the liturgical movement will recall references to the daily conventual mass as "the summit of the divine office".[69] This view owes more to nineteenth-century romanticism than to reality. Daily Eucharist has nothing whatever to do with the daily office.

Here, too, there is considerable variety from place to place and from age to age, but in general one can say that daily mass played no part in monastic life in East or West in the early period. In cenobitic communities there was often no priest, and the monks went to the local church for Sunday mass. Certain monastic legislators even banned priests from the community. And where priests were admitted, it is not certain that they were allowed to continue the exercise of their orders.[70] It was customary to ordain solitaries, but only so they could have the Eucharist without being obliged to leave their seclusion: they were forbidden to celebrate publicly.[71] So opposition to monastic priests had nothing to do with the Eucharist. The problem was how to keep the monks segregated from the laity, and at the same time protect them from the pride, ambition, envy, and challenge to the lay-abbot's authority that could ensue from introducing priests into the ranks.[72]

According to the *Historia monachorum in Aegypto* (*ca.* 394–395) there was daily communion in cenobitic communities in the Thebaid of Upper Egypt, but there is no evidence of daily mass.[73] In the early sixth-century pre-Benedictine *Rule of the Master,*[74] the lay-abbot distributed daily communion. Mass was only on Sundays, the patronal feast of the monastic oratory, and on the occasion of the blessing of an abbot. There were no priest-monks in the brother-hood, and so the monks went to the local church for Sunday Eucharist, or perhaps occasionally made use of priest-guests.

Benedict admitted priests, but his *Rule* (*ca.* 530–560), like others,[75] barely mentions the Eucharist, and beyond Sunday mass in the monastery oratory it is not clear that there was even daily com-munion.[76] At any rate there was certainly no daily conventual mass in Benedict's or in other Western monasteries at this time.[77] For that, we have to wait until the Carolingian period.

In later Byzantine monasticism, the ninth-century Studite *Hypotyposis* makes provision for daily mass except on non-eucharistic days.[78] Even on days when there was no mass, some typica provide for daily communion.[79] But the Palestinian usage found in the Sabaitic typica later adopted throughout the Orthodox East was more restrictive regarding presanctified communion, as we have already seen.[80] According to Leo Allatius (d. 1669), in Greek monastic usage the Divine Liturgy was sometimes celebrated daily, but not by the whole community:

> In some monasteries there are as many parealesia as there are days in the week. In these, except on Sundays and on the feast-days of saints when it is required of all monks to attend the services, one of the monks to whom the duty falls, and who is called the *hebdomadarios,* celebrates the rite—one day in one pareclesium, the next day in another. In this way by the time a week has passed, he has celebrated in as many pareclesia. Then the duty of celebrating falls to another hebdomadary and he starts anew. When the liturgy is celebrated in one pareclesium, the others are silent.[81]

I wonder if we have here a process parallel to what Häussling observed in the great romanesque monasteries of northern Europe: a transfer of the stational system of the cathedral city to the microcosm of the monastic enclosure?[82]

At any rate as far as the frequency of mass was concerned, monks initially did what everyone else did: went to mass on Sundays and some feasts, maybe also on Saturdays, but certainly no oftener unless, in Egypt at least, a monk was being waked.[83] This was true of hermits as well: they left their seclusion for the Sunday synaxis[84]—in Lower Egypt there was a synaxis on Saturday too[85]—and, in some times and places, the anchorites took communion to their hermitages for reception during the rest of the week.[86] We see this especially in Syria. Later in the West—except at Camaldoli—this problem was solved by admitting only priests to the solitary life.[87]

One even finds evidence of recluses refusing to come out for the Sunday Eucharist. Dadisho Qatraya, a Nestorian writer at the end of the sixth century, says that those observing total seclusion during the seven-week fast before certain feasts should not leave their cells at all, not even for the Sunday synaxis.[88] But abstention from the Sunday gathering, though not unknown, was an exception even for anchorites.[89] There were other abuses and exaggerations too. Some monks abstained from the Eucharist or received only once a year.[90] Others lived on the Eucharist alone, and so demanded a larger than normal portion.[91] The spread of "private mass" in Western monasteries from the eighth century is well known.[92] Less well known is the fact that similar practices once existed in the East. Syriac canons attributed to James of Edessa (d. 708) forbid stylites to celebrate on their columns—which surely means they did—but permit recluses to do so in their hermitages if they have no one to bring them communion[93] (stylites, whose columns were not in the wilderness, could not plead the same excuse). And in Byzantine sources there is a reference in the Life of St. John the Almsgiver (d. ca. 620) to monks celebrating the Eucharist privately in their cells.[94] But all this is peripheral, and one cannot build a theory around the peripheral—except perhaps in the West, where one notices a tendency to make the peripheral central.

One should not imagine that this diversity of monastic usage, or the absence of daily mass, sprang from any primitive "freedom of spirit." The Rule of the Master makes it clear that the whole community had to assist and communicate at the daily communion service.[95]

## 5. THE MODERN PERIOD AND THE RESTORATION OF FREQUENT COMMUNION

The decline in lay communion is complained of already by Chrysostom in Antioch at the end of the fourth century, and from then on things move downhill.[96] This disjunction between ever more mass and ever fewer communions is one of the things the sixteenth century reformers sought to correct: their basic principle was no Lord's Supper without the community present and communicating.

But the Reformation was not successful in restoring the ancient eucharistic discipline. Numerous Protestant bodies have no Lord's Supper at all, and among those that do, not all celebrate it every Sunday, though surely nothing less than that reflects the practice of the Primitive Church.

As for contemporary Catholic practice, among the more informed clergy there has been a retreat from the eucharistic narcissism ("my mass") prevalent before Vatican II. Concelebration has provided a partial solution to this problem, but has brought on a host of new ones, such as those overly clerical mob-concelebrations.[97] Among the faithful there has been enormous progress. The greatest and most successful liturgical reform in Catholic history is surely the movement for the restoration of frequent communion, sanctioned by Pius X in 1906. There are still pockets of resistance, and there are abuses, but nothing can detract from this great pastoral victory that has turned around fifteen centuries of devotional history in fifty years.

In the Orthodox Churches, the general parish custom is to celebrate Eucharist only on Sundays and feast days, but there is no fixed rule. Many Russian Orthodox urban parishes have daily Eucharist, and daily liturgy is common in Orthodox monasteries and shrines, though daily communion is not usual even for monks and nuns. The Eastern Churches generally eschew multiple Eucharists in any one community on the same day. But when circumstances demand more than one liturgy daily, then more than one is celebrated. "Private mass" is non-existent, though personal devotion to daily celebration is not entirely unknown among the clergy. St. Avraam of Smolensk (d. 1221) is said to have celebrated the Divine Liturgy every day,[98] as did John of Kronstadt in our own century (d. 1908), and Orthodox writers speak of this not in reproval, but as a mark of piety.[99]

In the matter of frequent communion, however, Orthodox practice is less than ideal. As late as the writings of the Byzantine canonist Theodore Balsamon (d. 1214), daily communion is still envisaged for those who are worthy and prepared.[100] And in Middle Byzantine monasticism, celebration of the liturgy daily or at least several times a week was not uncommon, and daily communion was the ideal. As we saw above, even when there was no Divine Liturgy, communion was available from the presanctified gifts. But monastic typica from the twelfth to the fourteenth centuries reveal the growth of a more restrictive policy. Monks may communicate once a week, or less often—every two weeks, monthly, every other month, or only three or four times a year—depending on the judgement of superiors. By the fifteenth century one still finds instances of daily communion, but they are noted exceptions even in monasticism.

At present there is a movement underway to reverse all this, especially in the renewed cenobitic monasteries on Mt. Athos[101] and in some diaspora communities among the laity. But the vast majority of Eastern Orthodox laity still receive at most once or a few times a year, and only after long (and wholly admirable) preparation that includes fasting, prayer, and confession of sins.[102]

Among the Oriental (i.e. non-Chalcedonian) Orthodox, the situation is much the same. The Syrian Orthodox must receive yearly, and are advised to do so every forty days. In India the names of those who do not receive at least at Easter time—usually on Holy Thursday—are read out in church, and they are excluded from the other sacraments.[103]

In the Armenian Church, even in monasteries the eucharistic liturgy is normally held only on Sundays and feasts.[104] Frequency of communion varies from parish to parish. Much depends on the zeal and good sense of the pastor. In some U.S. parishes, thirty percent receive every Sunday; in others, only the celebrant. In the United States there is a movement toward frequent communion, especially among the young.

The Coptic Orthodox celebrate Eucharist on Wednesdays, Fridays, and Sundays; nineteen feast days; and daily during Lent.[105] Very few laity receive communion more than once a year. Here too there is a growing movement among the educated classes for more frequent reception. Formerly daily mass was by and large unknown even in monasteries. More recently it has become common—though by no means universal—in renewed monasteries. This renaissance began under Coptic Orthodox Patriarch Pope Cyril VI (1959–1971), who is said to have celebrated mass daily for over thirty years, and there are other examples of Coptic Orthodox priests with great devotion to the service of the altar.[106]

The Ethiopians celebrate only on Sundays and feasts, though there is daily Eucharist in some monasteries. The only ones that receive communion with relative frequency are monks, the clergy, pre-adolescent children and, among the adult laity, those who are canonically married. Since canonically regular unions are rare except among the clergy; and since among the unmarried, incontinence is simply presumed unless time shows the contrary to be true; the majority of the laity never communicate after puberty.[107]

In the ancient "Church of the East," the East-Syrian or Nestorian Church, however, there is general communion of the people at the eucharistic synaxis on Sundays and feasts.

## 6. CONCLUSION

From the second century we see an evolution from Sunday community mass plus daily communion at home, to mass on some weekdays. The *reason* for this development, however, has nothing to do with "eucharistic devotion," but follows the growth of the liturgical cycle. When on a particular day something is going on liturgically, then mass comes to be celebrated as part of the festivities. We see this for Saturday, then the Wednesday and Friday stations, martyrs' anniversaries, etc. Eventually we arrive at the possibility, at least, of daily community mass except in certain penitential seasons, though in actual practice this opportunity is taken advantage of in only a few traditions. Ironically, this increase in the frequency of communion services is followed by a decrease in the frequency of communion.

Can one base any value judgements on such shifting sands? I think some constants do emerge:

1. Eucharistic frequency has varied, but in the earliest times daily communion seems to have been the ideal, and daily mass was

known in some churches as early as the fourth century. Hence to look on such frequency as "medieval," or "recent," or "Western," is simply false.

2. The Eucharist was a church affair under church control, and not at the mercy of what someone's "devotion" dictated. The expression of this common ecclesial life was a totality involving more than just the Eucharist. Its rhythm was never self-determining, but depended on other factors, such as the growth of the liturgical cycle.

3. Within this cycle there were times when not to have mass was considered preferable to having it, and abstention from it could be and was imposed. Eucharistic excess was condemned. Hence even the Eucharist has a *relative* value. It is possible to have too much of it, and sometimes it is better not to have it at all.

4. How much is too much or too little has varied. The extremes are clear: less than every Sunday can lay no claim to be traditional; more than once a day is excessive except in particular circumstances.

5. The variety found between these two extremes is due to several factors: pastoral need, the vagaries of eucharistic theology, the various symbol-systems in use at different times and places, etc.

6. These systems can be mutually contradictory: the Copts have daily Eucharist *only in Lent*; the Byzantines hold eucharistic festivity *incompatible with Lent*. This does not mean that one system is "right" and the other "wrong". It does mean that neither can be absolutized. The same must be said of contemporary attempts to construct symbol-systems, and then use them to control liturgical usage. I am thinking of the current cliché that only Sunday is "eschatological" and hence suitable for the "eschatological" eucharistic celebration; weekdays, dedicated to the "sanctification of time," should be devoted to celebrating the Liturgy of the Hours. This is ideology, not theology, and one can construct an ideology to back up almost anything.

Does this mean that everything is relative? Hardly, for there is a common tradition underneath all this. It shows, I think, that only the sacrifice of Christ has absolute value. Attempts to assign the same value to its sacrament are vain. Furthermore, this sacrament is an ecclesial, not a private matter, and the celebration of this ecclesial communion involves more than just the Eucharist itself, which cannot be considered in isolation. Purely devotional or individual norms that do not take into account this whole context have no legitimacy.

As for the question of frequency, if tradition is *"quod semper, quod ubique, quod ab omnibus"*, then for *communion* the older norm is daily availability. For *mass*, the only general norm between the two extremes of "daily" or "only on Sundays and feasts," is that of adaptation to the pastoral needs of time and place within each tradition. All attempts to construct ideologies that absolutize one or another usage; to say that all "good priests" say mass daily; or that only "eschatological Sunday" is a suitable eucharistic day; are simply clichés, products of the unhistorical mind.

I would also reject the notion that a priest should celebrate mass as often as will procure him a perceptible increase in faith and devotion, a perceptible existential participation in the Cross of Christ. This, if taken in isolation, is too individualistic to square with my understanding of the relation between Church, Eucharist, and the whole liturgical cycle. The same must be said for the supposed "right" of presbyters to concelebrate at any mass. Such issues should be determined by the pastoral needs of the celebrating community and the nature of the particular celebration, and not by the individual devotional requirements of the clergy, who have no special "rights" that take precedence over such broader ecclesial and pastoral demands.[108] Eucharist is not just participation in the Cross of Christ. It is also an epiphany of the Church within the context of a total liturgical tradition, requiring far more nuanced pastoral judgement for its celebration than any individual's "devotion".

What that judgement should be today is not for the historian to say. For history shows the past to be always instructive, but never normative. What is normative, is tradition. But tradition, unlike the past, is a living force whose contingent expressions, in liturgy or elsewhere, can change.

NOTES

1. See W. Rordorf, *Sunday* (Philadelphia: Westminster 1968) 205ff.
2. See Justin, *Apol.* I, 67:3–7, PG 6, 429–432.

3. Tertullian, *Ad uxorem* 2, 5:2ff, CCL 1, 389ff; Cyprian, *De lapsis* 26, CCL 3, 235; Basil (d. 379), *Ep. 93*, S. Basile, *Lettres*, ed. Y. Courtonne (Paris: Société d'édition "Les Belles Lettres" 1957) I, 203–204; J. Moschus (d. 619), *Prat. spir.* 30, PG 87, 2877; further references in O. Nussbaum, *Die Aufbewahrung der Eucharistie* (Theophaneia 29, Bonn: P. Hanstein 1979) 266ff.

4. Nussbaum, *Die Aufbewahrung* 269, 274.

5. Apocryphal Acts of John (*ca.* 170) 72, 85–86.

6. H. Delehaye, *Les origines du culte des martyrs* (Subsidia hagiographica 20, Brussels: Société des Bollandistes 1933²) 31ff.

7. Cyprian, *Ep. 5*, 2, CSEL 3, 479.

8. Cyprian, *Ep. 63*, 16, CSEL 3, 714: see also notes 13–22 below.

9. Cyprian, *Ep. 57*, 3, CSEL 3, 652.

10. See note 6 above.

11. Rordorf, *Sunday* 142–153.

12. *De oratione* 19, CCL 1, 267–268. Regarding Eucharist on stational days, see J. Schümmer, *Die altchristliche Fastenpraxis* (LQF 27, Münster: Aschendorff 1933) 105ff.

13. *Ep. 199*, ed. Courtonne II, 155.

14. *Or. 8*, 18, PG 35, 809ff; *Or. 18*, 29, PG 35, 1020–1021. See F. van de Paverd, "A Text of Gregory of Nazianzus Misinterpreted by F. E. Brightman," *OCP* 42 (1976) 197–206.

15. J. Hardouin, *Acta conciliorum* (Paris: Typographia Regia 1715) I, 1322.

16. Paulinus, *Vita Ambrosii* 10, PL 14, 30.

17. R. Raabe (ed.), *Petrus der Iberer* (Leipzig: J. Hinrichs 1895) 36.

18. Mansi 2, 574 and 3, 695; J. B. Chabot, *Synodicon orientale* (Paris: Imprimerie nationale 1902) 267. On this question see J. A. Jungmann, *Missarum sollemnia* I, part II.5.

19. Jungmann, *loc. cit.* note 22.

20. Ch. 39, 42, H. Gelzer (ed.), *Leontios' von Neapolis Leben des hl. Iohannes von Alexandrien* (Freiburg/B.-Leipzig: J. C. B. Mohr 1893) 77–78, 84; translated in E. Dawes and N. H. Baynes, *Three Byzantine Saints* (Oxford: B. Blackwell 1948) 247, 250. I am indebted to T. Mathews for this reference and those in notes 22, 81.

21. Mansi 11, 956.

22. *Codex Iustinianus* I, 2:25, P. Krueger (ed.), *Corpus iuris civilis* II (Berlin: Weidmann 1900) 18.

23. J. Schmitz, *Gottesdienst im altchristlichen Mailand* (Theophaneia 25, Bonn: P. Hanstein 1975) 233–240. Of course the existence of daily mass tells us nothing about who attended it. Jungmann claims it is only in the late Carolingian period that we see the faithful in the West assisting at mass daily (*Miss. sollemnia* I, pt. II.7).

24. Chromatius, *Tract. 14 in Mt.* 6, 5, PL 20, 361.

25. Toledo I (397–400), canon 5, Mansi 3, 999.

26. Augustine, *Dei. serm. in monte* II, 7:6, CCL 35, 114–115; *Tract. in Ioh* 26, 15, CCL 36, 267; *Ep. 228*, 6, CSEL 57, 489.

27. *De serm. in monte* (*loc. cit.*); cf. *Ep. 54*, CSEL 34, 161.

28. Athanasius, *Apol. contra Arianos* 11, PG 25, 268: there is no Eucharist except Sunday because "the day does not require it;" Socrates, *Hist. eccl.* V, 22, PG 67, 636–637.

29. PG 33, 1305. On the spread of eucharistic frequency in the Egyptian tradition see H. Quecke, *Untersuchungen zum koptischen Stundengebet* (Publications de l'Institut orientaliste de Louvain 3, Louvain: Université catholique de Louvain 1970) 9 note 52.

30. *Inst.* III, 2, ed. J.-C. Guy (SC 109, Paris: Cerf 1965) 92–94. See also *Historia monachorum in Aegypto* (*ca.* 394–5) XX, 7–8, trans. N. Russell, *The Lives of the Desert Fathers* (Cistercian Studies Series 34, Kalamazoo MI: Cistercian Publications 1980) 106. For complete information on the *cursus* of the Egyptian monks, see R. Taft, "Praise in the Desert: The Coptic Monastic Office Yesterday and Today," *Worship* 56 (1982) 517–527.

31. *In Lc.* 2, 8, PG 72, 489; *De ador.* 10, PG 68, 708. Daily liturgy is also implied in the Arabic canons of Athanasius, W. Riedel and W. E. Crum (eds.), *The Canons of Athanasius of Alexandria* (London: Williams and Norgate 1904) 25. For later Coptic sources, see J. Muyser, "Le samedi et le dimanche dans l'Eglise et la littérature coptes," T. Mina, *Le martyre d'Apa Epima* (Cairo: Imprimerie nationale, Boulâq 1937) 89–111.

32. Ch. 27, ed. H. Pétré (SC 21, Paris: Cerf 1948) 210ff.

33. J. B. Aucher (ed.), *Severiani sive Seberiani Gabalorum Episcopi Emensis homiliae* (Venice: Mechitarists 1827) 187.

34. *Demonstratio evang.* I, 10, I. A. Heikel (ed.), *Eusebius Werke* 6 (GCS, Leipzig: J. C. Hinrichs 1913) 46.

35. *In ps. 21*:30–31, PG 23, 213; *In ps. 91*:2–3, PG 23, 1169–1172; *De sol. pasch.* 7, PG 24, 701.

36. Ed. I. E. Rahmani (Mainz: F. Kirchheim 1899) 34–35.

37. PG 89, 841.

38. *Panarion* II, 2:22, PG 42, 825.

39. Cited in F. van de Paverd, *Zur Geschichte der Messliturgie in Antiocheia und Konstantinopel gegen Ende des vierten Jahrhunderts* (OCA 187, Rome: PIO 1970) 67 note 2. I owe several of the above references to *ibid.* 64ff.

40. II, 59:3; V, 20:19; VII, 23:2–3 (cf. 36); VIII, 33:2, ed. Funk I, 171–173, 301, 408, 432ff, 538.

41. Van de Paverd, *Zur Geschichte der Messliturgie* 61–79, gives an analysis of all the pertinent texts.

42. *In. Mt. hom 50/51*, 3, PG 58, 508.

43. Canons 16, 49, 51, Mansi 2, 567, 571: Other Asia Minor references in van de Paverd, *Zur Geschichte der Messliturgie* 65 note 1.

44. *Ibid.* 422–424.

45. *Ep. 93*, ed. Courtonne I, 203–204.

46. A. G. Martimort *et al. L'Eglise en prière* (Paris: Desclée 1961) 702ff.

47. P.-M. Gy, "La question du système des lectures de la liturgie byzantine," *Miscellanea liturgica in onore di S. E. G. Lercaro* II (Rome: Desclée 1967) 251–261.

48. J. Mateos (ed.), *Le typicon de la Grande Eglise* (OCA 165–166, Rome: PIO 1962–1963) II, 302.

49. *Ibid.* II, 189, 315–316.

50. PG 122, 340.

51. R. Basset (ed.), *Le synaxaire arabe-jacobite (rédaction copte)*, PO 3, 488.

52. V. Grumel (ed.), *Les regestes des actes du Patriarcat de Constantinople* I, fasc. 2 (Kadiköy: Socii Assumptionistae Chalcedonenses 1936) no. 588.

53. PG 140, 465. Other sources in J. Darrouzès, "Nicolas d'Andida et les azymes," *Revue des études byzantines* 32 (1974) 200–201.

54. " 'Private Liturgy' in Byzantine Architecture: Toward a Re-appraisal," *Cahiers archéologiques* 30 (1982) 125–138. The prohibition has existed since at least the 5th century. Leo the Great refers to it when writing to Dioscorus of Alexandria on June 21, 445 (*Ep. 9*, PL 54, 626–627). It was in force in some Western Churches too: see canon 10 of the Council of Auxerre (578), Mansi 9, 913.

55. The major recent studies are O. Nussbaum, *Kloster, Priestermönch und Privatmesse* (Theophaneia 14, Bonn: P. Hanstein 1961); A. Häussling, *Mönchskonvent und Eucharistiefeier* (LQF 58, Münster: Aschendorff 1973); C. Vogel, "Une mutation cultuelle inexpliquée: le passage de l'eucharistie communautaire à la messe privée," *Revue des sciences religieuses* 54 (1980) 231–250, and "La vie quotidienne du moine en occident à l'époque de la floraison des messes privées," *Liturgie, spiritualité, cultures* (BELS 29, Rome: Edizioni liturgiche 1983) 341–360.

56. See note 28.

57. *Hist. eccl.* V, 22, PG 67, 636–637. Only one liturgical ms refers to an Alexandrine Presanctified Liturgy. See E. Renaudot, *Liturgiarum orientalium collectio* (Frankfurt: J. Baer 1847) I, 76, 321–322; J.-M. Hanssens, *Institutiones liturgicae de ritibus orientalibus* (Rome: Pontifical Gregorian University 1930) II, 92–93. In the 10th century there was still presanctified communion on Tuesday of Holy Week in the Coptic Rite. See G. Viaud, *La liturgie des coptes d'Egypte* (Paris: A. Maisonneuve 1978) 52.

58. Mansi 2, 572. Orthodox canon law in the *Pedalion* gives this explanation: "The days of holy Lent are days of mourning and of contrition and of penance. But for a perfect sacrifice to be offered to God . . . is deemed by the majority of people to be a matter of heyday, and of joy and of festivity." Trans. D. Cummings, *The Rudder* (Chicago: The Orthodox Christian Educational Society 1957) 351.

59. Mansi 11, 967.

60. See Symeon of Thessalonica (d. 1429), *De sacra precatione* 301, 347, PG 155, 553, 625.

61. See synod of Mt. Lebanon (1736) XIII, 17, Mansi 38, 125; H. W. Codrington, "The Syrian Liturgies of the Presanctified," JTS 4 (1903) 71; Hanssens, *Institutiones* II, 92; III, 554–555.

62. Codrington, "Syrian Liturgies of the Presanctified," JTS 5 (1904) 371. Further evidence in Nussbaum, *Die Aufbewahrung* 40–41; P. Hindo, *Disciplina antiochena antica*, Siri III (Fonti codif. canon. orient. ser. II, fasc. 27, Rome: Typis polyglottis Vaticanis 1941) 164ff.

63. Codrington, "Syrian Liturgies of the Presanctified," JTS 4 (1903) 69ff, and "Liturgia praesanctificatorum syriaca S. Ioannis Chrysostomi," *XPYCOCTOMIKA* (Rome: Pustet 1908) 719–729; M. Rajji, "Un anaphore syriaque de Sévère d'Antioche pour la messe des présanctifiés," *Revue de l'Orient chrétien* 21 (1918–1919) 25–39; Hanssens, *Institutiones* II, 615–616.

64. Hanssens, *Institutiones* II, 552ff.

65. R. H. Connolly (ed.), *Anonymi auctoris Expositio officiorum ecclesiae Georgio Arbelensi vulgo adscripta* I (CSCO 71 = scr. syri 28, ser. 2, tom. 91, Rome: C. de Luigi 1913) 52, 153.

66. Codrington, "Syrian Liturgies of the Presanctified," JTS 5 (1904) 535–537; Hanssens, *Institutiones* II, 91–92, 627. On its use, see J. Mateos, "Les 'semaines des mystères' du carême chaldéen," *L'Orient syrien* 4 (1959) 449–458. The East-Syrian evidence, not easy to interpret, is discussed more fully in T. Parayady, *A Communion Service in the East Syrian Church* (unpublished dissertation, Rome: PIO 1980).

67. C. Tondini de Quarenghi, "Notice sur le calendrier liturgique de la nation arménien," *Bessarione* 11 (1906) fasc. 91–92, pp. 77ff; N. Nilles, *Kalendarium manuale utriusque ecclesiae órientalils et occidentalis* (Vienna: F. Rauch 1897[2]) II, 560.

68. J. Catergian, *Die Liturgien bei den Armeniern. Fünfzehn Texte und Untersuchungen*, ed. J. Dashian (Vienna: Druck und Verlag der Mechitharisten-Congregation 1897) 412–429 (in Armenian); Hanssens, *Institutiones* III, 585.

69. See J. Dubois, "Office des heures et messe dans la tradition monastique," *LMD* 135 (1978) 62ff; A. de Vogüé, *La Règle de s. Benoît*, VII: *Commentaire* (SC hors série, Paris: Cerf 1977) 240ff.

70. A. de Vogüé, "Le prêtre et la communauté monastique dans l'antiquité," *LMD* 115 (1973) 61–69.

71. J. Leclerq, "On Monastic Priesthood according to the Ancient Medieval Tradition," *Studia monastica* 3 (1961) 137–156. On the ordination of hermits see also P. Canivet, "Théodoret et le monachisme syrien avant le Concile de Chalcédoine," *Théologie de la vie monastique* (Théologie 49, Paris: Aubier 1961) 278ff.

72. de Vogüé, "Le prêtre et la communauté monastique" 64–65; A. Veilleux, *La liturgie dans le cénobitisme pachômien au quatrième siècle* (Studia anselmiana 57, Rome: Herder 1968) 232.

73. II, 7–8; VIII, 50, 56, trans. Russell (note 30 above) 64, 77–78, and cf. 131 note 12 concerning the correct translation.

74. Ch. 21–22, 45, 75, 80, 83, 93, A. de Vogüé (ed.), *La Règle du maître* II (SC 106, Paris: Cerf 1964) 102–106, 208–209, 314, 328–330, 342ff, 424–426.

75. See the references in de Vogüé, *Règle de s. Benoît* VII: *Commentaire* 240 note 157.

76. J. Neufville and A. de Vogüé, *Règle de s. Benoît* II (SC 182, Paris: Cerf 1972) 572–574.

77. de Vogüé, *Règle de s. Benoît* VII: *Commentaire* 242.

78. PG 99, 1713.

79. A. Dmitrievskij, *Opisanie liturgicheskikh rukopisej khranjashchikhsja v bibliotekakh pravoslavnago vostoka* I (Kiev: Tipografia G. T. Korchak-Novitskago 1895) 515. On this question see the references in the following note.

80. See E. Herman, "Die häufige und tägliche Kommunion in den byzantinischen Klöstern," *Mémorial L. Pétit* (Archives de l'Orient chrétien 1, Bucharest: Institut Français d'Études byzantines 1948) 203–217; V. Janeras, "La partie vespérale de la Liturgie byzantine des Présanctifiés," *OCP* 30 (1964) 210ff.

81. L. Allatios, *The Newer Temples of the Greeks*, trans. A. Cutler (University Park and London: Penn. State University 1969) 34–35.

82. See his work cited above, note 55.

83. Veilleux, *Liturgie* 373ff and D. Chitty, JTS 21 (1970) 199.

84. See Canivet, *loc. cit.* in note 71 above; Veilleux, *Liturgie* 226ff; D. Chitty, *The Desert a City* (Crestwood N. Y.: St. Vladimir's Seminary Press n. d.) 31, 33, 90, 96, 151; Muyser, "Samedi et dimanche" (above note 31); O. Hendriks, "La vie quotidienne du moine syrien," *L'Orient syrien* 5 (1960) 324–325, 418–420; I. Peña, P. Castellana, R. Fernandez, *Les reclus syriens* (Studia biblica franciscana, Collectio minor 23, Jerusalem: Franciscan Printing Press 1980) 122–128. I am grateful to V. Poggi for this and other references concerning Syrian monasticism.

85. See note 30 above.

86. On monastic communion see Mateos, "Semaines des mystères" 453–456; Hendriks, "La vie quotidienne" 419; Peña *et al. Les reclus syriens* 124ff; Parayady, *Communion Service* 57ff, 113ff; Veilleux, *Liturgie* 235, says there is no evidence of this custom in Pachomian monasticism, *pace* Basil (above, note 45) and others (cf. Peña *et al. loc cit.*).

87. Leclerq, art. cited in note 71.

88. A. Guillaumont, report on Sorbonne seminar, in Ecole pratique des Hautes Etudes, V^e section: Sciences religieuses, *Annuaire* 86 (1977–1978) 347.

89. *Hist. monachorum in Aegypto* XXV, 2 (trans. Russell 116); Canivet (note 71 above); L. Leloir, "La prière des pères du désert d'après les collections arméniennes des apophtegmes," *Mélanges liturgiques B. Botte* (Louvain: Mt. César 1972) 317–318.

90. Leloir, *loc. cit.*; Peña *et al., Les reclus syriens* 123; Veilleux, *Liturgie* 227; Canivet (note 71 above).

91. A. Vööbus, *Syriac and Arabic Documents regarding Legislation relative to Syrian*

80    FIVE: THE FREQUENCY OF THE EUCHARIST THROUGHOUT HISTORY

*Asceticism* (Papers of the Esthonian Theological Society in Exile 11, Stockholm: ETSE 1960) 61.

92. See note 55 above.

93. A. Vööbus, *The Synodicon in the West Syrian Tradition* I (CSCO 367 = scr. syri 161, Louvain: Secrétariat du CSCO 1975) 227, 245–246. For a Eucharist of Symeon Stylites (d. 459) see Evagrius Scholasticus, *Hist. eccl.* I, 13, PG $82^2$, 2453.

94. Ch. 42, ed. cited above, note 20: Gelzer 85; trans. 251.

95. Ch. 22, ed. de Vogüé (SC 106) 106.

96. *In Heb. 10 hom. 17*, 4, PG 63, 131; further references and precisions in Herman, "Die häufige und tägliche Kommunion" 204ff. See also H. Bohl, *Kommunionempfang der Gläubigen* (Disputationes theologicae 9, Frankfurt: P. Lang 1980); P. Browne, *De frequenti communione in ecclesia occidentali, usque ad annum c. 1000, documenta varia* (Textus et documenta, series theologica 5, Rome: Pontifical Gregorian University 1932).

97. I discuss these problems in chapter 6, section 3.

98. I. Kologrivof, *Essai sur la sainteté en Russie* (Bruges: Beyaert 1953) 66.

99. See Bishop Alexander (Semenoff-Tian-Chansky), *Father John of Kronstadt. A Life* (Crestwood N.Y.: St. Vladimir's Seminary Press 1979) 34ff, 179ff.

100. Here I am following Herman, "Die häufige u. tägliche Kommunion" (above, note 80).

101. See Kallistos of Diokleia (Timothy Ware), "Wolves and Monks: Life on the Holy Mountain Today," *Sobornost* 5 (1983) 63.

102. See *Journal of the Moscow Patriarchate* (1980) no. 10, 76–77.

103. Information from Rev. Mathai Mattathil of the Syrian Orthodox Church in India.

104. Z. Aznavourian, "Situazione attuale del monachesimo nella Chiesa armena," *Studi francescani* 67 (1970) 246. Eucharist is also celebrated on Saturday in major churches such as the Cathedral of St. James in Jerusalem and some of the larger churches of Istanbul, and daily in the holy places (Anastasis, Gethsemane, Bethlehem). I am grateful to my student Fr. Khajag Barsamian of the Brotherhood of St. James, Jerusalem, for this information.

105. M. Hanna, "Le rôle de la divine liturgie eucharistique dans la vie de l'Eglise Copte hier et aujourd'hui," *Proche-orient chrétien* 23 (1973) 269.

106. O. F. A. Meinardus, *Monks and Monasteries of the Egyptian Deserts* (Cairo: American University at Cairo Press 1961) 393.

107. Information obtained from Abuna Yesehaq, Archbishop of the Diocese of the Ethiopian Orthodox Church in the Western Hemisphere; and from Dr. William F. Macomber through the kind offices of Prof. Gabriele Winkler of St. John's University, Collegeville.

108. For a fuller discussion of this issue see chapter 6, section 3.

# Chapter Six

# EX ORIENTE LUX?
# SOME REFLECTIONS ON
# EUCHARISTIC CONCELEBRATION

The following notes on concelebration do not pretend to offer a complete study of the Eastern tradition, nor definitive solutions to the growing dissatisfaction with the restored Roman rite of eucharistic concelebration. But they may help to clarify the *status quaestionis*, rectify misinterpretations of early eucharistic discipline, and dispel misconceptions concerning the antiquity and normative value of Eastern usage. I'll begin with the latter and work backwards.

It has long been a theological device to turn eastwards in search of supporting liturgical evidence for what one has already decided to do anyway. Something like this was at work in certain pre-Vatican II discussions on the possibility of restoring concelebration in the Roman rite. The underlying presupposition seems to be that Eastern practice will reflect a more ancient—indeed *the* ancient—tradition of the undivided Church. Let's review the evidence.

1. CONCELEBRATION IN THE CHRISTIAN EAST TODAY

The information on contemporary Eastern forms of eucharistic concelebration given by McGowan and King[1] is generally accurate, with a few exceptions that will be corrected here.

The *Armenians* practice eucharistic concelebration only at episcopal and presbyteral ordinations, a custom they may have borrowed from the Latins.[2]

The *Maronites*, also influenced by the Latins, probably owe their practice of verbal co-consecration to scholastic theology of the

---

Revised from *Worship* 54 (1980) 308–325, with additional material from my commentary referred to in note 44 below.

Eucharist. Before the seventeenth century, concelebration without co-consecration was in use.[3]

In the *Coptic Orthodox* Church several presbyters participate in the common Eucharist vested, in the sanctuary. Only the main celebrant (who is not the *presiding* celebrant if a bishop is present) stands at the altar, but the prayers are shared among the several priests. Some prayers, but not necessarily the "consecratory" part of the anaphora, are the preserve of the main celebrant at the altar.[4] *Catholic Copts*, like the Maronites, have adopted a type of verbal co-consecration. This could represent the revival of an older usage. In several ancient Alexandrine manuscripts, diaconal admonitions at the words of institution exhort the concelebrants to join with the main celebrant at this solemn moment of the anaphora.[5] Though not necessarily a proof of *verbal* co-consecration, this certainly implies "concelebration" even in the narrow modern sense of the term.

Among the *Syrian Orthodox* it is customary for several presbyters to join with the bishop in the celebration of the liturgy. Only the bishop is fully vested. The assisting presbyters wear just the stole over their clerical gown, a garment similar to the Byzantine *rason*, but at the beginning of the anaphora one of them puts on the *phaino* (Greek *phainolion*, the principal outer vestment) and joins the bishop at the altar for the anaphora. Though the bishop shares the various prayers of the anaphora with the presbyters, he alone recites the words of institution and the epiclesis up to and including the blessing of the gifts,[6] at which point he retires to his throne while the presbyter in the *phaino* takes over at the altar to complete the epicletic prayer and share the rest of the anaphora with the other presbyters. At the end of the anaphora the bishop again takes his place at the altar, and the assisting priest retires to remove the *phaino*. It is necessary only for the bishop to communicate, but of course the concelebrants may if properly disposed. Though this form of concelebration is not mentioned in most descriptions of the *West-Syrian* rite,[7] I have assisted at such a celebration and, on inquiring, was assured that it is common usage. In addition, both Orthodox and Catholic Syrians practice a rite of "synchronized masses," each celebrant having his own bread and cup.[8]

The *Ethiopians* have a similar rite of "synchronized masses," as well as a form of eucharistic celebration in which several presbyters—ideally, thirteen—take active part with various functions and prayers distributed among them, that is, not done simultaneously by all as in verbal co-consecration.⁹ Indeed, this is the normal form of Eucharist among the Ethiopian Orthodox, and at least five presbyters, and preferably seven, are considered essential if the Eucharist is to be celebrated at all. These presbyters must all communicate at the celebration.

In the traditional *East-Syrian* Eucharist, the bishop surrounded by his presbyters presides over the liturgy of the word from the bema in the middle of the nave.¹⁰ When the time for the anaphora approaches, one of the presbyters is selected to read it. He alone "consecrates." In this tradition *all* services and sacraments are "concelebrations" in which all the various orders of ministers participate according to their rank: singers singing, lectors reading, deacons proclaiming, presbyters sharing the prayers. But they do not *all* say the *same* prayers. Distribution is the principle.

Apparently the early *Byzantine* tradition followed a similar rite in which only one celebrant recited the anaphora, but later we see, as in the West, the inexorable growth in the verbalization of eucharistic concelebration, with the same prayers being said by all concelebrating ministers.¹¹ In this as in other traditions one must distinguish Orthodox from Eastern-Catholic practice. Many Eastern-Catholic priests, under Western influence, say mass daily out of devotion, even when there is no pastoral need for them to officiate, so for them concelebration is much the same as for their post-Vatican II Latin confrères: a means of satisfying their private devotion, their desire to "say mass" every day, while avoiding the dissolution of eucharistic *koinonia* represented by that curious counter-symbol of ecclesial communion, the so-called "private mass."¹²

Among the *Byzantine Orthodox*, concelebration is normally practiced only when a bishop is celebrating solemnly, or to solemnize a festive presbyteral liturgy. Thus in a monastery on an ordinary day, one priest would celebrate and the others assist *modo laico*, unvested, in the nave or in the sanctuary. On feasts a few concelebrating presbyters would join the principal celebrant. A bishop is usually joined by numerous concelebrating presbyters, and even by other bishops.

*Byzantine Catholics* and those Orthodox that follow the *Russian* usage in this matter practice verbal co-consecration. This was once thought to be the result of Western influence in the sixteenth century, but recently scholars have challenged successfully this theory.[13] Besides, A. Jacob has shown that verbal concelebration was in use in Constantinople by at least the tenth century,[14] and it is hardly possible to postulate the adoption of Latin usage there during that period of growing estrangement and ritual dispute between the Byzantine and Latin Churches.[15]

Among the *Greek Orthodox*, however, there appear to be conflicting usages coexisting in peaceful competition. One priest whom I questioned assured me that all concelebrants should say all the priestly prayers, including the words of institution and epiclesis; another informed me that only the main celebrant consecrates. The 1951 Athens *Hieratikon* contains a rubric for the beginning of the anaphora that "all the priests read the eucharistic prayer,"[16] but the same edition gives the impression later in the text that only the main celebrant says the institution narrative and epiclesis.[17] H. Brakmann, however, has shown that these rubrics refer to the main celebrant's role, and cannot be interpreted restrictively as excluding the recitation of the consecratory prayers by the concelebrating presbyters.[18] Nevertheless, the 1962 *Apostolikē Diakonia* edition of the *Hieratikon* makes it quite clear that only the first priest consecrates.[19] Here we seem to have a case where verbal concelebration is in use *except for* the consecration! But we must not immediately conclude that this practice is in direct continuity with ancient tradition. It may be the result of the teaching of Nicodemus the Hagiorite (1749–1809), who held that in order to preserve the unity of the offering, only one priest should say the prayers.[20] But it is obvious from Nicodemus's polemic against "certain concelebrants . . . each of whom has his separate book of the Divine Liturgy and recites the prayers privately" that he was arguing against an existing practice.[21]

It is worth noting that in the Byzantine, as in other traditions, concelebration is not limited to the Eucharist. The same norms apply to other services. When a bishop celebrates vespers, a vigil, a requiem, he always has concelebrants, and the same is true of more solemn services even when there is no bishop celebrating. In such concelebrations, various parts are reserved to the main celebrant, others parceled out. The anointing of the sick is done (ideally) by seven presbyters. But except for the blessing of the oil in this rite, and the prayers of the eucharistic liturgy, the concelebrants do not all recite the *same* prayers in these services. Rather, *distribution* is the norm. But the anointing of the sick is a real "sacramental" concelebration, since even the anointings are shared. A similar rite is found among the Copts and Armenians.[22]

We do not yet have the studies at our disposal to evaluate the reasons for the appearance and spread of verbal concelebration in the East. But it does not represent the practice of the primitive Church.

2. Eucharistic Celebration in the Ancient Church:
Celebration or Concelebration?

In 1 Corinthians, our earliest witness to the Eucharist, Saint Paul presents the ideal form of this service as one fraternal banquet which the whole community "celebrates" together (11:17–34; cf. 10:16–17). I presume that one community leader presided over the celebration and said the prayer of table blessing, after the manner of Jewish repasts.[23] Paul seems to imply this in 1 Corinthians 14:16–17: " . . . if you bless with the spirit, how can any one in the position of an outsider say the 'Amen' to your thanksgiving when he does not know what you are saying? For you may give thanks well enough, but the other man is not edified." And his insistence on unity in 1 Corinthians 11 would seem to demand one blessing of the shared food.

To speak of "concelebration" in this context would of course be tautological, implying a clergy-laity division that had not hardened so early. Paul does speak of a variety of roles and ministries at the common services (1 Cor 12 and 14), and of the need for order in the community (1 Cor 12:27–30) and in its assemblies (1 Cor 14, esp. 26–40). But one certainly does not get the impression of a community divided into "celebrants" and "congregation." Rather, the whole problem in 1 Corinthians 12 and 14 is that everyone got into the act without due regard for one another, thereby provoking disorder and disunity in the (ideally) one celebration.

This same concern with unity runs through the Last Supper discourse in John (13:4–16, 34–35; 15:1–12; 17:11, 20–23) and descriptions of the primitive ecclesial assembly in Acts (1:14; 2:1, 42–47; 4:32–35; 20:7). And it is uppermost in the mind of the Apostolic

Fathers. Ignatius of Antioch at the beginning of the second century is the classic witness:

> Take care, then, to use one eucharist, for there is one flesh of our Lord Jesus Christ, and one cup of union in His blood, one altar just as there is one bishop together with the presbytery and the deacons, my fellow servants . . . (*Philadelphians* 4; cf. 6.2).
> . . . All of you to a man . . . come together in one faith and in Jesus Christ . . . to show obedience to the bishop and presbytery with undivided mind, breaking one bread . . . (*Ephesians* 20.2; cf. 5.1–3).
> . . . Strive to do all things in harmony with God, with the bishop presiding in the place of God, the presbyters in the place of the council of the apostles, and the deacons . . . entrusted with the ministry of Jesus Christ. . . . Love one another at all times in Jesus Christ, let there be nothing among you that could divide you, but be united with the bishop and those presiding. . . . Just as the Lord did nothing without the Father, being one with Him . . . so neither should you undertake anything without the bishop or presbyters. Do not try to make anything private appear reasonable to you, but at your meetings [let there be] one prayer, one supplication, one mind, one hope in love, in the blameless joy that is Jesus Christ, above whom there is nothing. Come together all of you as to one temple of God and to one altar, to one Jesus Christ . . . (*Magn.* 6–7; cf. *Smyr.* 8).

Barnabus (*Ep.* 4.10) and Clement of Rome (*Ep.* 34.7) reflect the same concern.[24] But in this literature we see more than a continuation of the Pauline preoccupation with unity at Corinth. By the end of the first century a more articulate ministerial structure has emerged to serve this unity, and is reflected in the order of services. The presiding minister or "high priest" is joined in the celebration by other ministers. They are distinguished from the "layman"—the term first appears at this time[25]—by role and seating in the assembly. If such a system cannot yet be considered general, the *Letter of Clement* testifies to it at least for Rome and Corinth by around A.D. 96:

> 40.1. . . . We should do with order (*taxis*) all that the Master has prescribed to be accomplished at set times. 2. Now He ordered that the offerings (*prosphorai*) and public services (*leitourgiai*) be done not haphazardly or irregularly, but at fixed times and hours. 3. And He has himself determined by his supreme will where and by whom He desires this to be done. . . . 4. Thus those who make their offerings (*prosphorai*) at the appointed times are accepted and blessed. . . . 5. For the High Priest (*archiereus*) are assigned the services (*leitourgiai*) proper

to him, and to the priests (*hiereis*) has been designated their proper place (*topos*), and on the levites [i.e., deacons] have been imposed their proper ministries (*diakoniai*). The lay person (*laikos anthropos*) is bound by the regulations for the laity. 41.1. Let each of us, brothers, be pleasing to God in his own order (*tagma*) . . . without infringing the prescribed rule of his service (*leitourgia*) . . . [26]

Here we see at least an adumbration of the system that emerges in documents of the third century: presbyters other than the assembly president cannot be said to have participated in the services simply "as laity." They were not just "in attendance" at the service, albeit with "reserved seats"; they also performed liturgical actions.[27] But any attempt to interpret this participation as "concelebration" in the sense of consciously exercising in common some sort of sacramental "power" proper to their order, seems to go beyond the evidence. Rather, one gets the impression of a single common assembly at which each category of laity as well as clergy had its special place and role. Indeed, most sources say far more about the role of the deacons and people in the eucharistic celebration than they do about the role of the presbyters, yet no one would think of calling them "concelebrants" in the narrow, contemporary sense of the term!

Since the fourth century, Eastern evidence generally concurs that the full-blown Eucharist involved the bishop surrounded by his presbyters, who were not merely "in attendance" in the presbyterium but actively participated in the ritual in a manner reserved to their order.[28] This is clear from canonical literature such as canon 1 of the Council of Ancyra (c. 314) or the *Second Canonical Letter* of Saint Basil (d. 379), which envisage the case of a presbyter under ecclesiastical sanction preserving his seat in the presbyterium while suspended from all ministerial functions, including the right to "offer" the Eucharist.[29] Here a clear line is drawn between presbyters in attendance at the Eucharist and those who "offer." But one cannot press the theological significance of this for concelebration. A similar situation was envisaged for laity in the final stages of penance: they were *consistentes*, allowed to "attend" the whole liturgy without, however, participating in the "offering."[30]

So it is not easy to know what theological meaning should be attached to such evidence without seeming to read history backwards. Where the evidence is clear, as in the Syrian traditions, it favors the conclusion that only the main celebrant "consecrated" the gifts.[31] But by then sacrificial theology is in bloom, and we find texts which say that concelebrating ministers of at least presbyteral rank "offer" (*prospherein, offerre*), even "as priests" (*hierourgein*) the common Eucharist.[32] Now though we must be wary of reading our later theological presuppositions into texts that seem to affirm what we hope to find, we must also avoid giving a minimalist interpretation to texts just because they do not meet modern Roman requirements for "true, sacramental" concelebration. The homilies of Theodore of Mopsuestia, for example, make it quite clear (1) that the concelebrants "offer" the Eucharist, (2) that this involves the exercise of a ministry proper to their order not shared with the laity, (3) that only the bishop says the eucharistic prayer.[33]

Two conclusions seem obvious: (1) From the fourth century we see a growing consciousness that presbyters celebrating the Eucharist together with the bishop are doing something that the laity cannot do, something only they have the mandate to perform. (2) This cannot be interpreted, without further evidence, to mean that they were "co-consecrating" verbally, that they recited in common the prayer of blessing of the gifts. Such a presumption would be anachronistic, based on the later identification in scholastic theology of the "essence" of the eucharistic sacrifice with the "consecration" of the gifts. This theory is coherent and may even be true. But it is not primitive, and that is the point at issue here.

G. Dix thought this growing consciousness that "concelebrating" presbyters "co-offer" the sacrifice with the bishop reflects the extension to presbyters of what had once been the preserve of bishops.[34] When the episcopal system of church order described by Ignatius of Antioch first appears on the scene, it seems that only the bishop presided over the eucharistic assembly, except when he would depute a presbyter to preside in his name over the assembly of some outlying community. But I would suggest that the origins of our "concelebration" are to be sought elsewhere, not in this expression of the *koinonia* of the local church, celebrated by the bishop together with the presbyters, deacons, deaconesses, widows, virgins, and so on, but rather in the "eucharistic hospitality" accorded visiting bishops as a sign of communion among sister churches. There are several clear historical instances of this in the case of visiting bishops or bishops in synod.[35] On the local level the same privilege was allowed "chorbishops" (i.e., suffragan, country bishops) by their superior, the town bishop.[36] It is precisely in the latter instance that we first see the term "concelebrants" (*syllei-tourgoi*), and it is this that canon 13 of the Council of Neocaesarea (ca. 315) explicitly forbids to country presbyters.[37] But as it became more and more common for presbyters to be assigned the eucharistic presidency, perhaps a consciousness grew that even at the bishop's liturgy they too could "co-offer," just as visiting bishops were wont to do.

What is certain is that however it happened, this consciousness did indeed grow, to the extent that a few centuries later the Eastern "*sylleitourgein*" had become, for the Latins at least, "co-consecrate,"[38] and we are on the threshold of "concelebration" identified as the verbal co-consecration of the same eucharistic elements by more than one minister of at least presbyteral rank. In the West we find it in a seventh-century passage of *Ordo romanus III*.[39] Our earliest Eastern evidence is a rubric from a tenth-century Byzantine diataxis or rubric book incorporated into Leo Tuscan's version of the Chrysostom Liturgy.[40]

Interestingly enough, this latter text witnesses to another innovation previously unheard of: a eucharistic concelebration of *presbyters alone*, without the presidency of the bishop. Just what ecclesiology such a service is meant to represent has been questioned by the late Russian-Orthodox ecclesiologist N. Afanas'ev in his slender but valuable study, *The Lord's Table*.[41]

## 3. REFLECTIONS

The above evidence reveals at least this much: that there is no one "Eastern" tradition to turn to for support, nor, as both Jungmann and Dix showed a generation ago, can one simply presume that "Eastern" equals "ancient."[42] The presbyteral, co-consecratory concelebration practiced in most Eastern-Catholic traditions has nothing to do with ancient usage, but is derived from more recent developments and is colored by later scholastic sacramental theory of individual priestly sacrifice and the "special grace" (plus stipend) accruing therefrom. And this is what was instituted for the Roman rite at Vatican II. What *is* ancient about Eastern eucharistic practice is not its various modes of concelebration, some quite admirable, others less so, but its preservation, by and large, of the ancient ideal of eucharistic unity: one community, one altar, one Eucharist. This is the crux of the matter as I see it today: the Eucharist as sacrament of the *koinonia* that is the Church. This is the real issue and it is an ecclesiological one.

The Council Fathers, in restoring concelebration at Vatican II, were aware of this issue (*Orient. eccl.* 15; *Presbyt. ordinis* 7). But they were more concerned with the (for me) secondary question of concelebration as a manifestation of the unity of the ministerial priesthood (*Sacrosanctum concilium* 57). From that standpoint the restored rite must be declared a marked success. Catholic priests have learned once more to pray together. No longer are religious communities of priests faced with the supreme irony of a community prayer-life in which everything is done in common except the one thing Christ left them as *the* sacrament of their unity in him.

It was to such largely clerical concerns that much of the pre-Vatican II preparatory literature on concelebration was dedicated. Re-reading some of this material, I was struck by how totally foreign the concerns of these authors are from those of the present. Much of their discussion is focused on whether a presbyter who does not verbally co-consecrate can be said to "offer the sacrifice" by intending to "exercise his priestly power" in gesture and intention, through the voice of the main celebrant. Even Rahner's articles, among the most sane interventions in the whole pre-Vatican II debate, are overly concerned with the celebrant and what he gets out of it.[43]

I see the present crisis as a healthy sign that, having benefited immensely from the priestly unity in prayer fostered by the restored rite of concelebration, we are now ready for a broader perspective. Excessively narrow clerical concerns are now rejected as irrrelevant, and the actual rite is more and more perceived as a celebration of division—no longer the eucharistic division among priests caused by the private mass, but the division of the community into those "celebrating" and those who "attend." I do not think that concelebration necessarily manifests *division* rather than the *hierarchic structure* of the ecclesial community. But when one thinks of those top-heavy mob concelebrations that have become common coin; of the confusion of roles created by having the laity join the concelebrants around the altar for the anaphora and even recite it with them; or worse, when one suddenly sees a hand shoot out from the pews, and a priest attending mass with the faithful begins to mumble the words of institution—when one has been subjected to such aberrations, it is difficult not to share the growing malaise.

What we are dealing with here (in addition to plain ignorance and bad taste) is a conflict of theologies. It is my own conviction that only a balanced theology of Church can be the guiding norm for the shape of our celebration, and not the "devotion" or desire or supposed "right" to "exercise one's priesthood" or to "offer sacrifice" or whatever of anyone, priest or otherwise. A 1980 commentary on "interritual concelebration"—ordained ministers concelebrating at a Eucharist celebrated in a rite other than their own—issued by the Congregation for the Eastern Churches shows, I believe, that official Catholic thinking on concelebration is beginning to move in this direction.[44] Respect for the integrity of the tradition of the local worshipping community as the concrete expression of ecclesial communion is the leitmotif of the document. The rite to be used is preferably that of the host church, contrary to previous legislation that always gave precedence to the rite of the *celebrant*.[45] And the document shows a far better sense of the basics than is usual in discussions of clerical concelebration: namely, that the Eucharist is a *communio*, a celebration of unity, not a ritualization of division; that any liturgy is the service of a local church, not a private clerical devotion; that, consequently, its norms are determined by the broader ecclesial and pastoral demands of this *communio*, not by the devotional needs of the ministers, who are there to serve the Church, not themselves.

Even more basic than ecclesiology, perhaps, is a fundamental problem in Roman Catholic liturgical theology: the classic distinction between Eucharist *ut sacramentum* and Eucharist *ut sacrificium*, with the reduction of the former to a discussion of the "real presence," and the overwhelmingly predominant role until recently of the latter in the theology of the eucharistic celebration. As sacrifice, the Eucharist is effected by the priest in the consecration. Even if done privately, it is still said to be "public," offered, like the offering of Christ on the cross, for the salvation of the whole world. The mass is the sign of this offering, and as such shares its impetratory and satisfactory value. Further, the priest offers acting *in persona Christi*, and every priestly offering involves a "separate act" of Christ the High Priest (Pius XII).[46] Since this is true of five private masses, or of one verbal co-consecration by five priests, but *not* true (again, Pius XII)[47] of mass said by one priest with four others attending or only "ceremonially concelebrating," not "sacramentally," then the conclusion for Catholic priests formed in this theory is ineluctable: everybody should "co-consecrate." Helping to sustain this is the notion that somehow "more sacrifice," "more glory," is thus offered to God, and "more grace" acquired for the co-consecrator and those for whom he offers. For someone who believes that this is what the Eucharist is all about, I see no way around the problem.

We need to return to a saner theology, such as that of Saint Thomas Aquinas, who said that the fruit of the Eucharist is the unity of the Mystical Body of Christ (*ST* III, 82, 9, ad 2), and that "the Eucharist is the sacrament of the unity of the Church, which results from the fact that many are one in Christ" (*ST* III, 82, 2, ad 3). It was this *koinonia*, and it alone, that determined the shape of the Eucharist in the early Church.[48] One community, one table, one Eucharist was the universal rule. And it remains so still in much of the Christian East. A recovery of this vision is the only way out of the devotional narcissism prevalent in Latin priestly spirituality. What is important is that the gifts *be* blessed so that all may share them. Whether or not *I* am the presbyter that says the prayer of blessing is irrelevant: to do so is a ministry, not a prerogative.

It is this sacramental manifestation of ecclesial communion, more than the choreography of who stands where and says what, that is the substance of the matter as I see it, in function of which all the other issues are to be decided. In this, history can be instructive, but not determinative, for each generation manifests its own shifts in ecclesial consciousness with corresponding adjustments in the liturgical models by which this is expressed.

What history shows us is that the external shape of the eucharistic celebration changed according to what people thought the Church and its service were all about. When the Church was a somewhat amorphous society, the Eucharist had a less structured shape. As orders and structures emerge and harden, these quite naturally find expression in the assembly: elders and deacons have special places and ceremonial roles at the worship presided over by the bishop, and visiting ministers are invited to take the place befitting their rank. Those who today are distressed by the presence of numerous vested presbyters in the sanctuary will find little comfort in history!

But somewhere along the line a turn in the road is taken, and the service begins to appear less the common celebration of all, each according to his or her rank and role, and more and more that which is done *by* the ministers *for* the rest. From high priest (bishop) presiding over a whole priestly people as the model, we have shifted to high priest/priests (presbyters)/laity.[49] I suspect that the breakup of effective eucharistic unity through the fourth-century decline in communion and division of the community into several non-communicating categories (catechumens, *energoumenoi, illuminandi,* penitents) were at the origins of this process. The Eucharist was no longer able to sustain an ideology of *koinonia* which the service in fact no longer expressed, so the ideology collapsed and the rite (ritual always outlasts theory) was forced to find ideological support elsewhere.[50]

This occurred in both East and West. The West alone, with that inexorable logical consistency with which it drives everything into the ground, took the next step of concluding (implicitly, at least) that the *laos* could be dispensed with, and private mass was off and running. But even before that, we see a growing consciousness that "concelebrating" ordained ministers "co-offer" the Eucharist in a way different from that in which the whole Church can be said to offer, a consciousness that eventually finds its liturgical expression in co-consecratory concelebration.

I doubt very much whether an *in persona Christi* theology of the eucharistic minister had anything to do with the origins of this practice in the East. But that is surely what keeps it alive in the Catholic Church today. What priest wants to give up the right to exercise this privileged role, especially when it is the basis for his whole priestly spirituality and devotion?

Let me stress that the above remarks are not to be construed as an attack on the theology of Eucharist as sacrifice. My concern is liturgical: whose sacrifice of what, offered by whom, for what purpose, and how expressed? Some years ago Aelred Tegels expressed where the answer to what should be the form of concelebration lies:

> God is worshiped in the liturgy to the extent that the worshiping people are sanctified, and they are sanctified to the extent that "conscious, active and full participation" is procured. Liturgy is essentially pastoral. The ideal form of celebration is that which will most effectively

associate this congregation, at this time and in this place, with Christ's own act of worship.[51]

Such a norm provides little justification for visiting priests who would simply use the worship of a local church as a convenient way of "saying their mass," with no concern for the wider issues. This is not to exclude the legitimate demands of clerical devotion: priests are also people, and should be able to ritualize significant realities of their religious life. But this cannot be isolated from the ecclesial norms governing concelebration and, indeed, any liturgy: *"Nisi utilitas fidelium . . . hoc impediat"*—"unless the good of the faithful stands in its way."[52] Before this norm all discussion of how this or that priest gets more or less devotion, how many "acts of Christ" or "sacrifices" are offered, who does or does not "exercise his priest-hood," whether one or more "masses are said," becomes totally secondary.

But even if one were to prescind from all ecclesial and pastoral questions and simply accept the fact that Roman Catholic priests must "exercise their priesthood," one can hardly consider the present Roman rite of concelebration ideal from a liturgical point of view. According to the present discipline of the Roman Catholic Church, no presbyter can be said to "validly" concelebrate the Eucharist unless he recites the prayer of consecration, regardless of what else he might do in gesture or symbol to show that he clearly intends to participate in—that is, concelebrate—the eucharistic liturgy according to his presbyteral rank. Though one may reject the presuppositions of medieval Latin eucharistic and sacramental theology that have led to such a conclusion, one can hardly question the right of the Roman Church to determine the concrete praxis of her ministers in the discipline of concelebration. But to raise such particular disciplinary exigencies to the level of a universal dogmatic principle, and then apply it in judging the practice of other churches or other epochs, is an unjustifiable procedure. If we approach our early and Eastern sources with such presuppositions, we are forced either to conclude that no "real" concelebration ever existed in ancient christendom, or else to invent for the ancient period a new form of concelebration, never heard of then: "ceremonial" as opposed to "sacramental" concelebration, which is the only one held to be "real."

To maintain that "verbal" concelebration is the only "real" one is also to question much of Eastern tradition.

In fact this whole problematic is foreign to a sane liturgical mentality, in which the whole body of presbyters is the moral subject of the common ministry performed by them *in solidum*. To demand that they all recite certain words together manifests an ignorance of the hierarchical and symbolic nature of sacrament expressed in presence and gesture and witness, as well as in word.[53] Concelebration even in the narrow clerical sense is the common act of a *collegium*, not the synchronization of the sum of the acts of several individuals. Hence even for one with purely "clerical" concerns, the present Roman rite of verbal co-consecration seems more a denial than a manifestation even of the collegial unity of the presbyterium.[54]

And for one with broader pastoral concerns for the liturgical expression of the unity of the whole church-*koinonia* in the eucharistic rite, presbyteral concelebration in some of the forms presently in use leaves much to be desired as a symbol of our unity, and not of what separates us.

## NOTES

1. J. McGowan, *Concelebration: Sign of the Unity of the Church* (New York: Herder and Herder 1964) 39–53; A. King, *Concelebration in the Christian Church* (London: A. R. Mowbray 1966) 102–132. The basic general study is A. Raes, "La concélébration eucharistique dans les rites orientaux," *LMD* 35 (1953) 24–47.

2. On Latin influence in Armenia, see G. Winkler, "Armenia and the Gradual Decline of its Traditional Liturgical Practices as a Result of the Expanding Influence of the Holy See from the 11th to the 14th Century," in *Liturgie de l'église particulière et liturgie de l'église universelle* (BELS 4, Rome: Edizioni Liturgiche 1976) 329–368.

3. Cf. P. Daou, "Notes sur les origines de la concélébration eucharistique dans le rite maronite," *OCP* 6 (1940) 233–239. Daou (236–239) denies that the Maronite practice arose in imitation of Latin liturgical usage, but it is certainly the result of Latin eucharistic theology, of which his very article is the perfect example.

4. Information from my colleague, Samir Khalil, professor at the Pontifical Oriental Institute and priest of the Coptic rite.

5. See R.-C. Coquin, "Vestiges de concélébration eucharistique chez les melkites égyptiens, les coptes et les éthiopiens, *Le Muséon* 80 (1967) 37–46; also J.-M. Hanssens, "Un rito di concelebrazione della messa propria della liturgia alessandrina," *Studia orientalia christiana. Collectanea* 13 (Cairo 1968–1969) 3–34, and the Coptic sources cited in ch. 7, where only one of the officiating priests is said to be the celebrant.

6. That is, up to the "Amen" in F. E. Brightman, *Liturgies Eastern and Western* (Oxford: Clarendon 1896) 89 line 11.

7. An exception is A. Cody, "L'office divin chez les Syriens Jacobites. Leurs eucharisties épiscopales et leurs rites de pénitence. Description des cérémonies, avec notes historiques," *Proche-Orient Chrétien* 19 (1969) 1–6.

8. Cf. King, *Concelebration* 121–122. Personal inquiry among Syrian Orthodox clergy has confirmed that this rite is still in use.

9. My information on Ethiopian usage is from Abba Tekle-Mariam Semharay Selim, *Règles speciales de la messe éthiopienne* (Rome: École typographique "Pie X" 1936) 10–13.

10. See W. F. Macomber, "Concelebration in the East Syrian Rite," J. Vellian (ed.), *The Malabar Church* (OCA 186, Rome: PIO 1970) 17–22; S. Y. H. Jammo, *La structure de la messe chaldéenne du début jusqu'à l'anaphore. Étude historique* (OCA 207, Rome: PIO 1979) *passim*; R. Taft, "On the Use of the Bema in the East-Syrian Liturgy," *Eastern Churches Review* 3 (1970) 30–39.

11. On the earlier form of Byzantine concelebration see R. Taft, "Byzantine Liturgical Evidence in the *Life of St. Marcian the Oeconomos*: Concelebration and the Preanaphoral Rites," *OCP* 48 (1982) 159–170. The best general study on Byzantine concelebration is H. Brakmann, "*Kai anaginôskousi pantes hoi hiereis tén eucharistérion euchén.* Zum gemeinschaftlichen Eucharistiegebet byzantinischer Konzelebranten," *OCP* 42 (1976) 319–367. Note that each concelebrant says the prayers to himself. There is no common choral recitation as in Latin usage, except among some latinized Eastern Catholics at some parts of the liturgy.

12. This discomfort with the private mass is based not on the Reformation critique of medieval eucharistic theology, but on ancient elements within the Catholic tradition of East and West. The point is not whether only two or three can constitute a Christian community to celebrate the Lord's Supper, but rather the multiplication of individual, "private masses" ("divisive mass" would be a more accurate term) *within the same community at the same time and place.* Hence the evidence sometimes advanced to demonstrate the existence of "private mass" in antiquity is beside the point. Such celebrations were what we would call "small-group masses," which are another matter entirely. The issue is not the "head count," but the weakening of *koinonia* by placing it second to the devotional desires of individual presbyters to say "their" mass. This would have been inconceivable in antiquity. Even anchorites wishing to participate in a eucharistic liturgy had to leave their solitude and come to the common synaxis. It was either that or go without mass. Relics of this traditional approach were retained by the Latin Church until recently. The absolute prohibition of private masses on Holy Thursday, at papal conclaves, at the opening of a synod (cf. McGowan, *Concelebration* 55ff) shows that when the Church wished to manifest in its fullness the eucharistic sign of ecclesial communion, eucharistic dispersion into individual masses was forbidden. If the multiplication of masses or the devotional desires of the individual celebrant to say "his" mass was truly of more spiritual value, a source of more grace and glory to God, then what possible right could the Church have had to limit God's grace and glory in this way?

13. Cf. Brakmann, "Zum gemeinschaftlichen Eucharistiegebet" 321ff, 337–367, and A. Jacob, "La concélébration de l'anaphore à Byzance d'après le témoignage de Léon Toscan," *OCP* 35 (1969) 249–256.

14. Cf. the previous note.

15. Cf. O. Rousseau, "La question des rites entre Grecs et Latins des premiers siècles au concile de Florence," *Irénikon* 22 (1949) 248ff.

16. In the appendix *"Hieratikon sylleitourgon"* 170.

17. *Ibid.* 170–171.

18. "Zum gemeinschaftlichen Eucharistiegebet" 324–334.

19. Appendix *"Hieratikon sylleitourgon"* 248–249, rubrics 15–16. The final rubric (no. 25, p. 250) could not be more explicit: if the first celebrant concedes to the concelebrants the parts that are proper to him, especially the blessings (the consecratory blessings of the epiclesis, undoubtedly), this would not be a sign of courtesy and humility on his part, but a high-handed violation of ecclesiastical discipline regardless of the pretext! Such admonitions are of course usually meant to counteract existing practice.

20. On Nicodemus, see Brakmann, "Zum gemeinschaftlichen Eucharistiegebet" 334 ff. Cf. the similar objection in Thomas Aquinas, *ST* III, 82, 2.

21. *Heortodromion étoi herméneia eis tous asmatikous kanonas tón despotikôn kai theomètorikôn heortôn* (Venice: N. Glykei 1836) 576 note 1.

22. Cf. H. Denzinger, *Ritus orientalium coptorum, syrorum et armenorum, in administrandis sacramentis* . . . vol. 2 (Würzburg: Stahel 1864) 483ff, 519ff.

23. Cf. L. Bouyer, *Eucharist. Theology and Spirituality of the Eucharistic Prayer* (Notre Dame: University of Notre Dame 1968) 80ff.

24. Barnabus, *Ep.* 4.10 PG 2, 733–734; Clément de Rome, *Epitre aux corinthiens,* ed. A. Jaubert (SC 167, Paris: Cerf 1971) 156.

25. Our first witness is the text of Clement (40.5) cited below. Cf. I. de la Potterie, "L'origine et le sens primitif du mot 'laic'," *Nouvelle Revue Théologique* 80 (1958) 840–853.

26. My translation from the edition of Jaubert, 166.

27. Cf. *Apostolic Tradition* 4, ed. B. Botte, *La tradition apostolique de s. Hippolyte. Essai de reconstitution* (LQF 39, Münster: Aschendorff 1963) 11; *Didascalia* II, 57, R. H. Connolly, *Didascalia apostolorum* (Oxford: Clarendon 1929) 119–120 = F. X. Funk, *Didascalia et Constitutiones apostolorum* (Paderborn: F. Schoeningh 1905) I, 158–166.

28. Cf. *Apostolic Constitutions* (late 4th C.) II, 57 and VIII, 11.12; 12.3–4, ed. Funk I, 159–165, 494, 496, and later related literature: *Didascalia arabica* 35, ibid. II, 124–125; *Ex constitutionibus capitula* 14, ibid. II, 139; *Constitutiones ecclesiae aegyptiacae* I (XXXI), 10, 31, ibid. II. 99, 102; Theodore of Mopsuestia (ca. 388–392), *Homily 15,* 42; *Hom. 16,* 24, ed. R. Tonneau and R. Devreesse, *Les homélies catéchétiques de Théodore de Mopsueste* (Studi e testi 145, Vatican: Bibliotheca Apostolica Vaticana 1949) 527, 569; the Synod of Mar Isaac (A.D. 410), J. Chabot, *Synodicon orientale* (Paris: Imprimerie nationale 1902) 268; *Testamentum domini nostri Iesu Christi* (5th c.) I, 23, ed. I. E. Rahmani (Mainz: F. Kirchheim 1899) 34–36; Ps.-Denys (end 5th c.) *Ecclesiastical Hierarchy* 3, 2 PG 3, 425; Narsai (d. 502) *Homily 17, The Liturgical Homilies of Narsai,* trans. R. H. Connolly (Texts and Studies 8.1, Cambridge: University Press 1909) 4–5, 9, 27; the 6th c. *Ordo quo episcopus urbem inire debet,* ed. I. E. Rahmani (Studia Syriaca, fasc. 3, Charfeh 1908) 3–4 [22], trans. G. Khouri-Sarkis, "Réception d'un évêque syrien au VI$^e$ siècle, *L'Orient syrien* 2 (1957) 160–162, R. Taft, *The Great Entrance. A History of the Transfer of Gifts and other Preanaphoral Rites of the Liturgy of St. John Chrysostom* (OCA 200, Rome: PIO 1978$^2$) 40–41; Canon 11 of the Letter of Išo'yahb I to the Bishop of Darai (A.D. 585), Chabot, *Synodicon* 430; Gabriel Qatraya bar Lipah (ca. 615), ed. Jammo, *La messe chaldéene* 33ff; and the later sources adduced in Jammo, *passim,* and Taft, *Great Entrance* 166–168, 197–198, 201–206, 210–213, 264ff, 291–310.

29. Basil, *Ep.* 199, 27 PG 32, 724; Ancyra, canon 1, Mansi 2, 514 (cf. Neo-Caesarea, canon 9, *ibid.* 542).

30. Basil, *Third Canonical Letter* (= *Ep.* 217, 56, 75, 77, PG 32, 797, 804–805).

31. Theodore of Mopsuestia, see below, note 32; Narsai, *Homily* 17, in Connolly 4, 7ff, 12ff, 18ff, but esp. 27; Ps.-Denys, *Eccles. Hier.* 3, PG 3, 425; *Test. domini* 1, 23, ed. Rahmani, 38ff.

32. Council of Neocaesarea (ca. 315) canons 13–14, Mansi 2, 542–543; Theodore of Mopsuestia, *Hom.* 15, 42, ed. Tonneau-Devreesse, 527; the letter of Presbyter Uranius describing the Eucharist celebrated on his deathbed by Paulinus of Nola (d. 431) together with two visiting bishops Symmachus and Acindynus: " . . . una cum sanctis episcopis oblato sacrificio" (*Ep.* 2, PL 53, 860); Evagrius Scholasticus' account of the visit of Bishop Damnus of Antioch to Symeon Stylites (d. 459) and the Eucharist they celebrated together: . . . *To achranton hierougésantes sôma* . . . " (*Hist. eccl.* I, 13, PG 86[2], 2453).

33. *Hom. 15 passim*, esp. 36, 41, 44, *Hom. 16*, preface and 2, 5–16, 20; ed. Tonneau-Devreesse 517–519, 525, 529, 531–535, 537–559, 563.

34. *The Shape of the Liturgy* (London: Dacre 1945) 34.

35. Several examples in McGowan, *Concelebration* 24ff, 40ff. But even in the earliest of such cases there is no evidence of "co-consecration," though the *episcopé* of the assembly was shared and this was called a "concelebration." Those texts that are clear on the matter seem to indicate that in such cases the guest bishop was "conceded" the blessing of the gifts. Cf. Eusebius, *Hist. eccles.* V, 24, 17, *Eusebius Werke* II, 1, ed. E. Schwartz (GCS, Leipzig: J. C. Hinrichs 1903) 496 = PG 20, 508; *Didascalia* II, 58, ed. Funk I, 168 = Connolly 122.

36. Neocaesarea, canon 14, Mansi 2, 542–543. "Chorbishop" is from the Greek *chôra* meaning "country" as opposed to town.

37. *Loc. cit.*

38. Cf. the letter of Pope John VIII to Photius (A.D. 879), *Ep.* 248, PL 126, 871: "tecum . . . consecrare" = "*sylleitourgesai soï*" in the Greek version in Mansi 17[1], 413 B.

39. III, 1, *Les "Ordines romani" du haut moyen-âge*, ed. M. Andrieu, vol. 2 (Spicilegium sacrum lovaniense. Etudes et documents, fasc. 23, Louvain: Université Catholique 1960) 131. On the question of dating and on the inclusion of this text in *Ordo I*, cf. *ibid.* 127.

40. Jacob, "Concélébration;" cf. Taft, *Great Entrance* 124ff.

41. *Trapeza Gospodnja* (Pravoslavie i sovremennost' 2–3, Paris: Izdanie Religiozno-Pedagogicheskogo Kabineta pri Pravoslavnom Bogoslovskom Institute v Parizhe 1952) 64ff. A. calls such a concelebration a "liturgical paradox," for the *raison d'être* of concelebration was to represent the unity of the local church: bishops, presbyters, deacons, people. Presbyters celebrated the Eucharist when sent to a segment of the local community as representative of the bishop, but they did not "concelebrate" with one another in the bishop's absence.

42. J. A. Jungmann, "The Defeat of Teutonic Arianism and the Revolution in Religious Culture in the Early Middle Ages," in his *Pastoral Liturgy* (New York: Herder and Herder 1962) 9–15; *The Place of Christ in Liturgical Prayer* (New York: Alba House 1965) part 2 *passim*, Dix, *Shape* 264ff. In fact the Roman rite has preserved important primitive elements long obscured in the East.

43. K. Rahner and A. Häussling, *The Celebration of the Eucharist* (New York: Herder and Herder 1968).

44. *Servizio informazione per le Chiese orientali* vol. 45, nos. 409–410 (Rome, July August 1980) 8–18. See R. Taft, "Interritual Concelebration," *Worship* 55 (1981) 441–444.

45. Canon 2.1 of the motu proprio *Cleri sanctitati* (1957).

46. *Magnificate dominum,* 2 November 1954, *AAS* 46 (1954) 668ff.

47. *Loc. cit.*

48. See L. Hertling, *Communio. Church and Papacy in Early Christianity* (Chicago: Loyola University 1972).

49. Dix, *Shape,* 33ff; H.-M. Legrand, "The Presidency of the Eucharist according to the Ancient Tradition," *Worship* 53 (1979) 422.

50. I discuss this in my article, "The Liturgy of the Great Church: an Initial Synthesis of Structure and Interpretation on the Eve of Iconoclasm" *DOP* 34–35 (1980–81) 68ff.

51. "Chronicle," *Worship* 44 (1970) 183.

52. *Eucharisticum mysterium,* May 25, 1967, no. 47.

53. Thus for centuries the three bishops that imposed hands at episcopal ordination were rightly considered true "co-consecrators." It would be a distortion of the whole tradition to consider them anything else, though only one said the formula of consecration. But since Pius XII all three co-consecrators have to recite the formula (*Episcopalis Consecrationis,* AAS 37 [1945] 131–132). Cf. McGowan, *Concelebration* 66–67.

54. See the concluding remarks of B. Schultze, "Das theologische Problem der Konzelebration," *Gregorianum* 36 (1955), 268–271.

Chapter 7

# RECEIVING COMMUNION—
# A FORGOTTEN SYMBOL?

In popular speech we "receive communion" or "go to communion." Some even speak of "taking communion." I think the differences are more than semantic. "To take communion," like the reflexive in certain modern languages (for example Italian:*comunicarsi*, Russian: *prichastit'sja*), places the emphasis on communion as an act of the individual believer, a personal exercise of piety; something I *do* rather than something *done to me*; something *"taken"* rather than a gift *given* and *received*, a sharing of something we have and do and receive in common and from one another—in short, a *communion*.

That this latter was the original sense of eucharistic *koinonia* in the early Church is obvious from the start. In 1 Cor 10:17 Paul tells us "Because there is one bread, we who are many are one body, for we all partake of the one bread." And he then goes on to spell out the implications of this communion. A bit later, at the beginning of the second century, Ignatius of Antioch warns: "Take care, then, to use one Eucharist, for there is one flesh of our Lord Jesus Christ, and one cup of union in His blood, one altar just as there is one bishop together with the presbytery and the deacons, my fellow servants . . ."[1]

This rule of one communion was so strict that initially presbyters— "priests" as we call them—did not "say mass" without the bishop. As a rule such sacramental ministries were celebrated by the bishop surrounded by his concelebrating church: presbyters, deacons, and people, all in the one *koinonia*. Rome, with its customary liturgical sobriety and respect for tradition, preserved this usage until at least the sixth century, according to the latest research on the topic. On Sundays the bishop of Rome celebrated the full Eucharist for the faithful. In other churches of the city a presbyter celebrated the

Expanded from *Worship* 57 (1983) 412–418.

Liturgy of the Word for the catechumens and penitents, all non-communicants, then he alone received communion from the *fermentum* or eucharistic bread consecrated at the pope's mass. This same rule of one mass is said to have been operative also at Alexandria and Carthage.[2]

Eucharistic communion, therefore, is not just the sacrament of one's personal communion with the Risen Lord. It is rather the sacrament of our communion with one another in the one Body of Christ, a body at once ecclesial and eucharistic. That this was the full meaning of eucharistic *koinonia* in the early Church has been shown clearly enough by others.[3] It is also the teaching of St. Thomas Aquinas, who says that "the Eucharist is the sacrament of the unity of the Church, which results from the fact that many are one in Christ."[4]

Contemporary liturgical reforms have once again brought into prominence the *fractio* of the one bread, a pristine ritual expression of this mystery. But historical research into other aspects of the communion rites exposes our failure to carry this thinking through to include the way in which the sacrament is administered. A detailed history of the communion rites in the various traditions would carry us beyond the purpose of these brief notes. But I keep stumbling across texts that I think reflect a more acute liturgical understanding of communion than some of the practices one sees today. The general rule in communion rites right up through the Middle Ages, in both East and West, was that communion is not just *taken*, not even by the clergy, but *given* and *received*. For communion is at once a ministry and a gift and a sharing, and as such is *administered* to the communicant through the hands of another.

## 1. LATIN SOURCES

For example, in the eighth-century *Ordines romani*, a deacon brings communion to the pope at his throne, the archdeacon or a subdeacon gives him the chalice, then the bishops and presbyters come up to receive the consecrated bread from the pope's hand. One of the bishops or presbyters gives the chalice to the other bishops, presbyters, and deacons, and a deacon in turn gives the chalice to the lesser orders. Then the people receive the bread from the pope or from the bishops and presbyters, and the deacons administer the chalice. In a word, everyone *receives* communion from someone else. No one just *takes* it.[5]

## 2. BYZANTINE SOURCES

In early Byzantine sources the only evidence I know of is the *Life of St. Marcian the Oeconomos* which describes a concelebration at Constantinople *ca.* 468–600. Marcian, though apparently only a presbyter, administers communion to all the other clergy, including, it seems, the archbishop.[6]

Similarly, the oldest (eleventh century) *diataxis* or *ordo* of the Byzantine patriarchal liturgy, which I edited a few years ago from the twelfth century codex *British Library Add. 34060*, gives this complicated set of rubrics for the communion of the patriarch:

> X.1.... [the patriarch] descends from the platform and bows three times to the east ... 2. With him bows the priest who is supposed to give him communion, and both mount the platform and kiss the holy altar. 3. And first the bishop, having stretched forth his hands, receives. 4. Then holding the bread in the last two fingers, with the other three he takes the other particle and gives it to the one that gave communion to him ... 8. And the archdeacon gives the chalice to the priest, and the bishop, after turning to him and bowing, communicates ... 10. And after kissing the holy altar, he turns, and the chalice is taken from the priest, and [the bishop] communicates him.[7]

Then the two of them go off to administer the bread and chalice to the rest of the clergy and people. Not only does the patriarch receive communion from a "priest" (*hiereus*, probably one of the concelebrating bishops: in Byzantine Greek *hiereus* is used indiscriminately for anyone in "priestly" orders). He even waits until that minister also has received the host in his hand so both can consume the holy food together. This usage was the rule of Byzantine pontifical concelebrations for as long as the rubrics of the *diataxis* of Demetrius Gemistos (*ca.* 1380) remained in force.[8] They were abandoned by the time of the *diataxis* of Patriarch Athanasius III Petelaras, composed in Moscow in 1653 for the reform of Nikon and later confirmed by Patriarchs Paisius of Alexandria and Macarius of Antioch at the

Synod of Moscow in 1667.[9] In these latter rubrics we see today's usage: the bishop gives himself communion, then administers it to the concelebrating presbyters.[10]

But the older usage was not determined by rank—that is, by whether or not the main celebrant was higher up the hierarchical ladder than his concelebrants. For we see the same thing in the rubrics of Byzantine presbyteral concelebrations. For example, the eleventh century euchology codex *Grottaferrata Gb II* (f. 20r-v) has these rubrics at communion:

> And the priest bows three times before the holy altar, and one of the concelebrating priests gives him one piece of the particles. And he in turn gives another piece to the priest. And they receive in like manner from the chalice, giving it to each other, and they kiss each other. And the second communicating priest stands to the right side of the holy altar holding the chalice, and the rest of the priests come up and receive and kiss him. Likewise the deacons, but the subdeacons and the rest of the clergy and the laity receive in the mouth and do not give the kiss. Likewise from the chalice.[11]

Leo Tuscan's version of the Chrysostom liturgy based on a Greek euchology manuscript of 1173–1178 has a like practice, though if the presbyter is celebrating alone he communicates himself, the rubrics specify:

> Then if he is alone he receives the Lord's body. But if there are several priests, the first among them, having received communion, gives it to the others, who kiss his hand and cheek. And he likewise receives the Eucharist from one of the others. And in like manner they give the chalice to one another, so that they can drink the blood of the Lord.[12]

### 3. MEDIEVAL COPTIC SOURCES

We have no evidence for early Egyptian usage in this matter, but the medieval Coptic communion rites are described by Patriarch Gabriel II ibn Turaïk (1131–1145);

> *Rules (rubrics) for the priest who celebrates the liturgy.* He receives communion first. Then he communicates the body to those priests officiating with him. But it is they who take the chalice and give it to him

to receive. Then they give the chalice to one another in communion. Then the celebrating priest gives communion to the non-officiating priests in attendance in church, and he gives them the chalice, either himself or the priests officiating with him . . . [13]

The rubrics in chapters 6–7 of the *Book of the Guide* by Patriarch Cyril III ibn Laklak (1235–1243), a sort of rubrical primer for celebrants found in codex *Vatican Arabic 117*, has the celebrating priest give communion even to bishops in attendance at the service, except in the case of the local ordinary, who precedes the celebrant in giving himself communion.[14]

## 4. EAST-SYRIAN USAGE

But as is often the case in matters liturgical, it is the East-Syrian or Nestorian Church of Persia that reflects the earliest usage and best understanding of what it is all about. Canon 2 of Catholicos Mar Išo'yahb I (518–596) prescribes the rite of communion of the ministers. The presbyter who has been chosen to consecrate the sacrament receives first, even before the bishop:[15]

> . . . The bishop, if he is present, gives it [=the consecrated bread] to him; if he is not present, the senior priest in order of precedence gives it to him. And in turn, he who consecrates gives it to the one who gave it to him. And it should be done likewise for the chalice of the Lord. He who has consecrated gives communion to the priests and deacons who are in the sanctuary . . . Then the priests distribute communion . . . [16]

The anonymous ninth-century *Commentary on the Ecclesiastical Offices* attributed to George of Arbela has the same usage, and tells us why: salvation is something mediated to us by Our Lord. So even the priest, who as the Lord's image is himself a mediator of salvation to others, must receive it from another.[17]

Most interesting of all is the following Syriac text from the end of the ninth century, in the canonical collection of the Nestorian Gabriel of Basra:

> *Question 19*: When there is only one priest and one deacon, what should they do, for in one canon it prescribes that the deacon should not give communion to the priest?

*Answer*: In this matter the Catholicos Išo'yahb has determined as follows.[18] It is not allowed that the deacon give communion to the priest, who is distinguished from the deacon by his higher rank. So if no other priest is there to give communion, but only a deacon, the situation should be handled according to a fine custom, namely: the priest takes the "coal" [=consecrated particle] from the altar and puts it in the hands of the deacon. Then he bows before the altar, takes the "coal" from the deacon's hands with the fingers of the right hand, places it on the tips of the two fingers of the left hand, and brings it back to his right palm. The deacon says only: '*The Body of our Lord.*' Likewise the chalice: he gives it into the hands of the deacon, and after he has prostrated himself and bowed, he rises and takes the chalice with both hands, while the deacon holds the foot of the chalice with one hand. When the priest receives the deacon says: '*The Blood of our Lord.*' Then the deacon puts the chalice on the altar . . . [19]

The point of the document is clear enough: if eucharistic communion, sacrament of our shared ecclesial communion in the one Mystical Body of Christ, is a food shared, a gift received from the hand of another as from Christ, with only one priest celebrating there was a real *problem*: who would give him communion? The fact that it would never cross our minds to consider this a problem is the precise point I am trying to make: there has been a decided shift in mentality, and with it a change in ritual.

A concern for preserving hierarchical precedence seems to be at least one reason for this shift. Bar Hebraeus (d. 1286), Mesopotamian Jacobite Maphrian of Tikrit in present-day Iraq, says in his *Nomocanon* IV, 5 that a deacon may not give communion to a priest, nor a priest to a bishop.[20] At any rate, rank eventually wins out over symbolism, and the older usages do not survive into the modern period except in more conservative traditions such as the Coptic and Nestorian.


## 5. Present Usage, and Some Reflections

Today in the Byzantine tradition, concelebrating or communicating presbyters give themselves communion except when the main celebrant is a bishop. But as we have seen, the earlier tradition of receiving from the hand of another was in no way dependent on such differences of rank. Other Churches have retained at least something of the original usage. In the Armenian Orthodox Church, presbyters or even a bishop communicating at the eucharistic liturgy receive the intincted host from the celebrating bishop or presbyter after he has received.[21] Among the Coptic Orthodox the chief concelebrating presbyter gives communion to the other presbyters after communicating himself. I do not know what their custom is at a pontifical liturgy. In the Ethiopian tradition the main celebrating presbyter gives the consecrated bread first to himself, then to the assisting priest, who in turn administers the chalice first to the main celebrant, then to himself.[22] In the Syrian Orthodox liturgy the celebrant takes communion first, followed by the bishop if he is in attendance and wishes to receive. Other presbyters may either take communion themselves or request the celebrant to administer it to them.[23] To the best of my knowledge only the Nestorians have preserved their ancient usage: the celebrant receives the consecrated bread from another presbyter; the chalice is handed to him by the deacon.[24]

I am not well enough acquainted with Protestant liturgical uses to comment on them. In the reformed Roman usage there are various possibilities provided by the instructions in the missal: the main celebrant communicates himself, then the other concelebrants can come up and do the same; or the bread and chalice can be brought to them at their places; or they can receive communion by intinction. One also sees less than ideal uses in the communion of the eucharistic ministers: at least for the communion of the chalice, they sometimes line up to take it rather than have it administered to them. Similar practices are not unknown in masses when the chalice is administered to the laity (as of course it should always be): the chalices are arranged on the altar at strategic points, and everyone comes up to help themselves.

Some traditions are, for the moment at least, stuck with a ritual heritage in this matter which they are at present unwilling or unable to change for a variety of reasons that need not concern us here. But that is not true of the present Roman usage, which has acquired a certain flexibility since Vatican II. What the logistics of the communion rites should be today cannot, of course, be solved by historical scholarship or by universally applicable rubrics. There are too many variables involved: the number of communicants, the liturgical disposition of the church, local traditions . . . But from the sources we have studied at least one thing is clear: the Eucharist, ideally at least, is not something one *takes*. It is a gift received, a meal shared. And since sacraments by their very nature are supposed to symbolize what they mean, then self-service, cafeteria-style communion rites just will not do.


NOTES

1. *Philadelphians* 4

2. Report of a recent Sorbonne seminar in patristics and the history of dogma, to be published fully later. See P. Nautin, "Le rite du *fermentum*," École pratique des Hautes études, Ve section—Sciences religieuses, *Annuaire* 90 (1981–1982) 338.

3. See L. Hertling, *Communion, Church and Papacy in Early Christianity* (Chicago: Loyola University 1972).

4. *ST* III, 82. 2 ad 3; cf. 82. 9 ad 2.

5. See for instance *Ordo I*, 106–121, in M. Andrieu, *Les "Ordines romani" du haut moyen âge*, vol. 2 (Spicilegium sacrum lovaniense. Études et documents, fasc. 23, Louvain: Université Catholique 1960) 101–106; *Ordo XV*, 54–65, *ibid.* vol. 3 (fasc. 24, Louvain 1961) 106–109.

6. R. Taft, "Byzantine Liturgical Evidence in the *Life of St. Marcian the Oeconomos*: Concelebration and the Preanaphoral Rites," *OCP* 48 (1982) 159–170, esp. 161–166.

7. R. Taft, "The Pontifical Liturgy of the Great Church according to a Twelfth-Century Diataxis in Codex *British Museum Add. 34060*," part I, *OCP* 45 (1979) 300–303.

8. Text in A. Dmitrievskij, *Opisanie liturgicheskikh rukopisej khranjashchikhsja v bibliotekakh pravoslavnago vostoka*, vol. 2 (Kiev: Tipografia N. T. Korchak-Novitskago 1901) 315–316. Seventeenth-century Slavonic *Trebniki* frequently have illustrations showing a bishop receiving communion from another bishop (Kiev 1646, Lvov 1682 and 1695). I am grateful to Sr. Sophia Senyk O.S.B.M. for bringing these sources to my attention.

9. On this document see Taft, "Pontifical Liturgy" (note 7 above), part II, *OCP* 46 (1980) 94.

10. *Dejanie moskovskikh soborov 1666–1667 godov*, II: *Kniga sobornykh dejanij 1667 goda* (Moscow 1893) ff. 59r ff.

11. J.-M. Hanssens, "De concelebratione missae in ritibus orientalibus," *Divinitas* 10 (1966) 512. A similar use is found in Slavonic mss from the 12–13th centuries. See A. Pétrovski, "Histoire de la rédaction slave de la liturgie de S. Jean Chrysostome, XPYCOCTOMIKA. Studi e ricerche intorno a S. Giovanni Crisostomo (Rome 1908) 870, 877.

12. A. Jacob, "La traduction de la Liturgie de s. Jean Chrysostom par Léon Toscan," *OCP* 32 (1966) 160.

13. L. Villecourt, "Les observances liturgiques et la discipline du jeûne dans l'Eglise copte," *Le Muséon* 37 (1924) 201.

14. G. Graf, "Liturgische Anweisungen des koptischen Patriarchen Kyrillos ibn Laklak," *Jahrbuch für Liturgiewissenschaft* 4 (1924) 125. The same usage is found in the *Liturgical Order* of Patriarch Gabriel V (1409–1427), regulations that still govern the Coptic rite today. See A. 'Abdallah, *L'ordinamento liturgico di Gabriele V - 88° Patriarca Copto, 1409–1427* (Studia orientalia christiana: Aegyptiaca, Cairo: Edizioni del Centro Francescano di Studi orientali cristiani 1962) 381.

15. In the traditional East-Syrian Eucharist, one of the concelebrating presybters was chosen to say the anaphora. See ch. 6, section 1 above.

16. Letter of Išo'yahb I to the bishop of Darai, AD 585, in J. Chabot, *Synodicon orientale ou recueil des synodes nestoriens* (Paris: Imprimerie nationale 1902) 429–430.

17. Ch. IV, 25, R. H. Connolly (ed.), *Anonymi auctoris Expositio officiorum ecclesiae Georgio Arbelensi vulgo adscripta*, vol. 2 (CSCO 76 = scr. syri 32, ser. 2, tom. 92, Rome: C. de Luigi 1915) 70–71 in the Latin translation.

18. The reference is to canon 3 of Išo'yahb I, Chabot, *Synodicon* (note 16 above) 430.

19. H. Kaufhold, *Die Rechtssammlung des Gabriel von Basra und ihr Verhältnis zu den anderen juristischen Sammelwerken der Nestorianer* (Münchener Universitätsschriften, Juristische Fakultät, Abhandlungen zur rechtswissenschaftlichen Grundlagenforschung, Bd. 21, Berlin: J. Schweitzer Verlag 1976) 242–243.

20. P. Bedjan (ed.), *Nomocanon Gregorii Barhebraei* (Leipzig: Harrassowitz 1898) 45–46 (=Syriac text); Latin trans. by J. A. Assemani in A. Mai, *Scriptorum veterum nova collectio* X.2 (Rome: Typis Collegii Urbani 1838) 24. The Maphrian was a sort of exarch or metropolitan who was primate of the Syrian Jacobite Church in Mesopotamia.

21. I am grateful to my student Rev. Khajag Barsamian for this information.

22. Abba Tekle-Mariam Semharay Selim, *La messe éthiopienne* (Rome: Ecole typographique "Pie X" 1937) 92.

23. I am grateful to Rev. Mathai Mattathil for this information.

24. See G. P. Badger, *The Nestorians and their Rituals* (London: J. Masters 1852) vol. 2, 238, where the modern usage is described.

Chapter 8

# THE SPIRIT OF EASTERN CHRISTIAN WORSHIP

1. THE CENTRAL PLACE OF THE LITURGY IN EASTERN PIETY

Several years ago a visitor from Western Europe is said to have asked His Holiness Alexij (d. 1970), Patriarch of Moscow and all the Russias, how he would define the Russian Orthodox Church. The late patriarch replied, "A Church that celebrates the Divine Liturgy."[1] Such a reply was surely disconcerting to the Western Christian, accustomed to consider as more characteristic of church life other, more active tasks: preaching and catechetics, foreign missions, charitable works, hospitals, schools, the social apostolate.

And yet the patriarch's reply would not have surprised the Eastern Christian. It simply indicates the overriding role played by liturgy in the life of the Christian East: the Eastern Church is before all else a Church that keeps vigil before God, celebrating the mysteries of his Son in the age-old rites passed on by the fathers in the faith.

The legendary origins of Kievan Christianity illustrate strikingly that for Eastern Christians, worship is the supreme crystallization of their faith. According to the so-called *Chronicle of Nestor* for the year 987, the Bulgars (Moslems), Germans (Latins), Jews and Greeks had all tried to persuade Prince Vladimir of Kiev to adopt their faith as the religion of Rus. When the prince summoned the notables of the realm to hear their counsel, they advised him:

> You know, oh Prince, that no man condemns his own possessions, but praises them instead. If you desire to make certain, you have servants at your disposal. Send them to inquire about the ritual of each and how he worships God.

(Note the object of their inquiry: not *creed* but *liturgy*.)

---

Revised from *Diakonia* 12 (1977) 103–120.

Vladimir took their advice and sent out emissaries. When they reached Constantinople,

> . . . the Emperor sent a message to the Patriarch to inform him that a Russian delegation had arrived to examine the Greek faith, and directed him to prepare the church and the clergy, and to array himself in his sacerdotal robes, so that the Russes might behold the glory of the God of the Greeks. When the Patriarch received these commands, he bade the clergy assemble, and they performed the customary rites. They burned incense, and the choirs sang hymns. The Emperor accompanied the Russes to the church, and placed them in a wide space, calling their attention to the beauty of the edifice, the chanting, and the pontifical services and the ministry of the deacons, while he explained to them the worship of his God.

When they arrived home, the ambassadors reported to Vladimir. The worship of the Moslems had not impressed them. As for the Germans, they had seen them

> . . . performing many ceremonies in their temples; but we beheld no glory there. Then we went to Greece, and the Greeks led us to the edifices where they worship their God, and we knew not whether we were in heaven or on earth. For on earth there is no such splendor or such beauty, and we are at a loss how to describe it. We only know that God dwells there among men, and their service is fairer than the ceremonies of other nations. For we cannot forget that beauty.[2]

From this legend we can understand why the Eastern Christian would find nothing revolutionary in the opening paragraphs of the Vatican II Constitution on the Sacred Liturgy:

> . . . it is through the liturgy . . . that "the work of our redemption is exercised." The liturgy is thus the outstanding means by which the faithful can express in their lives, and manifest to others, the mystery of Christ and the real nature of the true Church.

The Eastern Churches for the most part have remained faithful to the liturgical spirit of the golden age of the Fathers, when pagan society became christendom by the saving power of Word and Sacrament celebrated in the liturgical assembly. In a very real sense the whole life of the Church in the patristic period was "liturgical." There were no Christian schools or catechism classes, no popular missions or retreats. But there were the daily assemblies for morning and evening prayer, in which the Scriptures were abundantly read and commented. On the Lord's Day there was the vigil and eucharistic synaxis, with lessons and homilies. And there was Lent, when the bishop prepared the community's candidates for Easter baptism with long catechetical homilies such as have come down to us from John Chrysostom, Cyril of Jerusalem, and Theodore of Mopsuestia. Even the more mundane ministries were part and parcel of the liturgical assembly. Offerings for the sick and poor were brought there and given to the deacons who saw to their distribution; it was there that catechumens were instructed and baptized, penitents reconciled, the wayward corrected.

So to say that the whole life of the Church was liturgical does not mean the Church did nothing but "say mass." Contemporary compartmentalization of life into clearly defined and mutually exclusive categories, and the even more recent limitation of parish liturgical life to the Eucharist, were foreign to the early Church, whose life was liturgical in that it was a community whose every activity was *leitourgia*, a public service of the one Body of Christ.

This spirit still pervades the Eastern Churches today. Throughout all the vicissitudes of its history the Christian East has preserved a continuity of faith and worship that has sustained its faithful during the dark ages of oppression. Political circumstances have often deprived Eastern Christians of the possibility of developing the more active apostolic activities so integral to church life and organization in the West. But as long as they are free to participate in the worship of their local church, the Eastern Christians can survive. As long as the mysteries can be celebrated the Church lives, held together not by organization nor authority nor education, but by communion year after year in the regular cycle of feast and fast. This is the secret of Russian Orthodoxy's survival in the USSR. By the providence of God the Communists have left to the Church the one freedom she would herself have chosen above all to preserve. As the late Metropolitan Nikodim of Leningrad once said, "Our salvation rests on our fidelity to our cultic forms."[3]

Peter Hammond in his moving account of the Greek Church right after World War II has expressed in striking terms the hold that worship has on the Christian of the East:

Nobody who has lived and worshipped amongst Greek Christians for any length of time but has sensed in some measure the extraordinary hold which the recurring cycle of the Church's liturgy has upon the piety of the common people. Nobody who has kept great lent with the Greek Church, who has shared in the fast which lies heavy upon the whole nation for forty days; who has stood for long hours, one of an innumerable multitude who crowd the tiny Byzantine churches of Athens and overflow into the streets, while the familiar pattern of God's saving economy towards man is represented in psalm and prophecy, in lections from the Gospel, and the matchless poetry of the canons; who has known the desolation of the holy and great Friday, when every bell in Greece tolls its lament and the body of the Saviour lies shrouded in flowers in all the village churches throughout the land; who has been present at the kindling of the new fire and tasted of the joy of a world released from the bondage of sin and death—none can have lived through all this and not have realised that for the Greek Christian the Gospel is inseparably linked with the liturgy that is unfolded week by week in his parish church. Not among the Greeks only but throughout Orthodox Christendom the liturgy has remained at the very heart of the Church's life.[4]

What are some of the salient traits of this worship that is the very soul of the Christian East?

## 2. Worship of the Local Church

From a purely external, sociological point of view, what strikes one about Eastern worship is its intimate union with the culture and history of the local church. This may be why the liturgy means so much even to the simple faithful. The Easterners are not disturbed by the fact that they belong to a "National Church" any more than a Dutchman is upset to discover that he is a citizen of the Netherlands! Their church and its worship is meaningful to them because it is totally and intimately *theirs*, not because it is also yours. That their rite should be inextricably bound up with the history of their people, that they should worship God in a language and ritual that are the product of their own culture, is for them inevitable. Anything else would be incomprehensible.

Far from implying a negation of the Church's catholicity, this is the only possible means of assuring it. Paradoxically, it is only through a

multiplicity of particularisms and the resulting diversity that the
universality of the Church can reach its full expression. If one wishes
to address all humanity, one must speak in all languages. Pretentions
to universality via uniformity can lead to formalism and super-
ficiality. What is imposed on all becomes the property of none. More
than one tragic rent in the robe of Western Christianity might have
been averted were it not for Rome's steadfast refusal to allow more
latitude to legitimate local demands in matters of church polity and
liturgical practice.

Yet Roman caution is not without reason, for the history of the
Western Church since the post-patristic period is a dialectic of
extremes. Paradoxically, in the East local autonomy has produced not
anarchy but the continuity of a living tradition—a second characteristic of the worship of the Christian East.

## 3. THE CONTINUITY OF TRADITION

An attachment to tradition, to the ways handed down from time
immemorial by their fathers in the faith, is evident in every aspect of
church life in the East, but above all in worship.

The security that comes from praising God in forms that were
known to Basil the Great and John Chrysostom might be taken as a
sign of stagnation. But the liturgiologist, driven frantic trying to trace
the vagaries of liturgical development in an Eastern liturgy, can only
be amused at the accusations of immobilism thrown up against the
Eastern rites. In reality there has always been slow, almost imper-
ceptible growth and change. However, it is less easy for the historian
to observe, since it has been a natural process, not accomplished by
*fiat* from above. Growth through gradual changes that are in
themselves insignificant may be less dramatic than periods of
imposed uniformity followed by sudden, committee-programmed
reform—but it is certainly more natural.

Since the liturgical reform of the Roman Rite instituted by the
Second Vatican Council, it has become common for Western
Catholics to ask their Eastern brethren if their rites have undergone a
similar reform, whether one is projected, and if not, why? Such
questioning shows a tendency to raise a limited, Western experience

to the level of a universal principle, a general norm by which to measure the experience of others.

Contrary to what is popularly thought, the liturgical reforms of Vatican II were not a universally applicable Catholic response to the exigencies of modern life, but are rather the product of the peculiar history of the Roman Rite in the post-patristic era. Liturgical stability in the West was achieved much later than in the East. Although the whole of the West was Latin and united under the leadership of one Apostolic See, there was great liturgical diversity until the reforms decreed by the Council of Trent.

In fact, it was the growing liturgical chaos in the West that eventually provoked the sixteenth century reform of the liturgical books of the Romano-Gallican Rite and their imposition on most of the Western Church as "typical" liturgical books, to be followed *verbatim* by all. This step was necessary, given the circumstances of the time, but it resulted in a certain rigidity. Anarchy ceased, but at the price of stifling natural liturgical growth, thus forcing the piety of the people of God to express itself in so-called "non-liturgical" devotions divorced from the official prayer tradition of the Church.

This post-Tridentine liturgical situation was a Western innovation foreign to the experience of Eastern christendom. There is no such thing as a "typical" liturgical book in any Eastern Rite.[5] And no Eastern Church has ever imposed a liturgy of which neither jot nor tittle could be changed without approval from above.

This does not mean, however, that Eastern liturgy is at the mercy of individual caprice, as happened in the West when liturgical law was relaxed at Vatican II. In the East the alternative to an imposed legalism and rubricism is not anarchic individualism but spontaneous fidelity to the common tradition. Take for example the Byzantine Rite. Except for some synodal decrees and a few *novellae* of Justinian, there is no corpus of liturgical law obligatory in the Byzantine Churches.[6] Incredible as it may seem, this most splendid, complex, highly ceremonialized worship in the whole of christendom has evolved and maintained itself for the most part in a natural way, without the need of formal law. This is precisely what we mean by a *living* liturgical tradition. Of course it results in any number of loose ends, hard to reconcile practices, customs that overlap or even contradict one another—but they are the loose ends of the living, rather than the well-ordered immobility of the dead.

4. Communal Worship

The Latin Church since the Middle Ages has suffered a gradual privatization of the Eucharist into a personal devotion of the priest, who had "his" daily mass, and a monasticization of matins and vespers, formerly the morning and evening prayer of the whole Christian community. Eastern worship, being both native and traditional, has remained closer to its popular roots and more communal. It goes without saying that "private mass" is foreign to the Eastern spirit, and concelebration is practiced as a manifestation of the unity of the local church in one Eucharist, not in order to provide presbyters with the opportunity of satisfying their private devotion while avoiding the abuse of private or even solitary masses.

Even the Liturgy of the Hours has remained an integral part of the full office of parochial worship on Sundays and feasts. Rather than reduce the liturgy to a more manageable length and then multiply masses to accommodate several shifts, the Eastern Church has striven to maintain the liturgical cycle of vespers, matins and Eucharist in all its solemnity as the patrimony and responsibility of the parish community, and not a monastic preserve, much less the performance of a coterie of professional initiates like the cathedral canons that still maintain the office in some basilicas in the West.

In the East every parish has its cantors and readers whose knowledge of the complicated offices and chants is passed on from generation to generation, the precious heritage of the community. Peter Hammond's description of Greek offices illustrates this:

> . . . one of the things which commonly strikes the visitor to Greece who finds his way for the first time to a parish church is the unexpectedly prominent (some would say obtrusive) part played by the laity in the Church services. Very often long stretches of incomprehensible offices seem to be conducted entirely by laymen; the parish priest only occasionally emerging from the sanctuary, and disappearing as quickly after a brief *ekphonesis*, to leave matters wholly in the hands of two middle-aged gentlemen in double-breasted suits, supported by a nondescript collection of young men and boys.[7]

So, contrary to what one would expect, the Eastern rites for all their complex ritual splendor and magnificent vestments, their beards and brocade, clouds of incense and endless monastic chants, are far less clericalized than liturgy in the West before Vatican II.

True, there is the iconostasis or barrier that encloses and to a certain extent hides the sanctuary from the people in many Eastern traditions. But we must not reduce popular participation to seeing, because Eastern liturgy is always sung: there is no such thing as "low mass." And the deacon, standing at the head of the congregation before the central doors of the iconostasis, forms a bridge between the people and the holy of holies, "a body standing before men, but a mind knocking at the gates of heaven through prayer,"[8] in the lively image of St. John Climacus.

Furthermore, there are—at least ideally—no pews, so the congregation is not locked into the audience-stage arrangement that has become the almost exclusive liturgical disposition of the Western church. Consequently not just the sanctuary but the whole church is "liturgical space." In fact the sanctuary is ideally the preserve of the eucharistic canon. In the Byzantine tradition almost all non-eucharistic rites are celebrated in the center of the church. And the Eucharist itself is structured around a series of appearances in which the clergy come forth from the sanctuary and go through the church in two solemn processions, the "Little" and "Great Entrance," or emerge from behind the iconostasis to bless, incense, read the Scriptures, preach and bring communion to the faithful.[9]

## 5. COMMUNION OF SAINTS

Even in the atmosphere of profuse symbolism with which Eastern worship and iconography envelops one, Eastern Christians feel quite at home and not at all overwhelmed, for it is here too that they can be touched by the continuous tradition that is both communal and their own. Latin Catholics often visit church to be alone with God; they have a feeling of emptiness in a Protestant church where the sacrament is not reserved. Not so the Byzantine Christians. On entering church they do not proceed to their private prayers without first going round to visit the icons, kissing them and lighting a candle before them, thus saluting the saints and joining in their communion.[10]

In fact a sense of the "communion of saints" is one of the most profound impressions of Byzantine worship.[11] Iconographic representations of the saints cover the walls of the church: patriarchs and prophets of the Old Law join fathers and doctors of the New; Gregories and Cyrils of catholic fame rub shoulders with local saints and martyrs who may have lived in the very town where the church stands. The hymns and canticles sung in their honor are to the faithful a part of their own family history. Their legends are retold again and again, their intercession constantly implored. Integral to this mentality is the great devotion to the dead in the Christian East. Devotion to the saints and to the dead really amount to the same thing: the sense of unity with a common past that is so strong in the worship of the East.

Even apart from the liturgy, church life in the East has never become an exclusively clerical preserve. Lay theologians and preachers, permanent deacons and subdeacons, lay representation in the government of the Church are all common. And the Eastern clergyman, generally married, does not belong to a social class above the level of his flock. Go into any Greek village in the cool of a summer evening, and you will find the local *papas* having an *ouzo* with the men of his flock, a villager distinguishable from his fellows only in coiffure and dress. Access to the local bishop is equally casual. Chanceries in the East are always overflowing with the laity, peasant and merchant as well as dignitary, who have come to seek a favor, redress a grievance or to pay their respects.

This inevitably has its effect on worship, which in the East has remained a true *leitourgia* or public service of the whole community. Hence there is no question of any need for a "liturgical movement" to bring the piety of the people back to its source in the prayer of the Church. The East has never known the separation of spirituality, theology and ecclesiology from liturgy, with the consequent degeneration of piety into individualism finding its expression in private prayer, meditation, and devotions in the face of inaccessible, clericalized public rites.

Present strenuous efforts in the West to forge once again the link between individual piety and the public prayer of the Church highlight the ease with which Easterners situate their spiritual life within the cadre of liturgical prayer. If we were to ask Eastern Christians which of their devotions were "private" and which "liturgical," they would not know what we were talking about. It is all one: popular piety *is* liturgy, the very life of the local church.

## 6. WORSHIP AS ICON

This integrity and equilibrium, a sense of the balanced wholeness of things, is another quality of the Eastern liturgical experience: transcendent but not distant, hieratic but not clericalized, communal but not impersonal, traditional but not formalistic. How easy it is to shatter the equilibrium by omitting one tessera from the mosaic of integral parts! This may be because of the *iconographic* nature of worship in the East: the liturgical action is not just a "ceremony"; it is an object of contemplation, an awesome vision, full of mystery, before which one prostrates in reverential fear.

This is true not only of the rite itself but of the whole atmosphere of sacredness and mystery that surrounds its every movement and communicates a sense of reverential awe. In the creation of this spirit it would be hard to exaggerate the importance of the church and its iconography. How flat and uninspiring a Byzantine liturgy can appear when celebrated in a Western church! But to see it in a properly appointed Byzantine church is to cross the threshold to another world, or rather to this world made visible in its redeemed reality as the transfigured cosmos beyond time.

This is why icons are called windows to another world, why the most humble village church is "heaven on earth" according to St. Germanus of Constantinople, "the place where the God of Heaven dwells and moves"; where one can "lay aside all worldly care," as the Cherubic Hymn enjoins, "to receive the King of all." It is the heavenly sanctuary "where men and women, according to their capacity and desire, are caught up into the adoring worship of the redeemed cosmos; where dogmas are no barren abstractions but hymns of exulting praise."[12]

## 7. THE HEAVENLY LITURGY

Eastern Christians chanting the liturgy in this atmosphere, as clouds of incense rise with their prayers toward Christ-Pantocrator in the dome, are in the world of the Fathers of the Church. Their theology of visible creation as a symbol of the invisible, of the incarnation as the icon-restorer of the reflection of divine beauty to humankind, thus making Christian iconography possible—this is the soul of the Byzantine liturgical and aesthetic spirit. In his treatise *On the Holy Temple*, Symeon of Thessalonica (d. 1429) applies this incarnational exemplarism to the Byzantine church.

> The church, as the house of God, is an image of the whole world, for God is everywhere and above everything . . . The sanctuary is a symbol of the higher and supra-heavenly spheres, where the throne of God and his dwelling place are said to be. It is this throne that the altar represents. The heavenly hierarchies are found in many places, but here they are accompanied by priests who take their place. The bishop represents Christ, the church represents this visible world . . . Outside it are the lower regions and the world of beings that live not according to reason, and have no higher life. The sanctuary receives within itself the bishop, who represents the Godman Jesus whose almighty powers he shares. The other sacred ministers represent the apostles and especially the angels and archangels, each according to his order. I mention the apostles with the angels, bishops and priests because there is only one Church, above and below, since God came down and lived among us, doing that for which he was sent on our behalf. And it is a work which is one, as is Our Lord's sacrifice, communion, and contemplation. And it is carried out both above and here below, but with this difference: above it is done without any veils or symbols, but here it is accomplished through symbols, because we humans are burdened with the flesh that is subject to corruption.[13]

The appointments and spatial disposition of the Byzantine church also reflect this imagery. Whoever visits a Byzantine church feels at once in a place of mystery, a holy place, detached from the world and flooded with the presence of God. The great barrier of the iconostasis rises up before the sanctuary, Holy of Holies and throne of God. Through the doors of this altar-screen none but the sacred ministers dare to pass. For the Eastern Christian, the Latin's claim to gaze on the Lord, to be admitted at any moment to his presence, is indeed an extraordinary one. In the East the throne must be viewed from afar.

But this sanctuary barrier which cuts off the altar from our view is not a hindrance to popular participation in the mysteries of the liturgy, but rather an aid, an aid to the Eastern spirit of worship. For

Eastern devotion is aroused by concealment as well as by exposition, and the doors and veils of the iconostasis are not only to hide, but also to reveal. Understood in this way, the icon screen is a tangible witness to the mystery we live in the liturgy. It is not a barrier but a symbolic gateway into the kingdom of heaven, presented here below in mystery. As the well-known Russian writer Gogol says in his *Meditations on the Divine Liturgy*:

> Now the Royal Gates are solemnly opened, as though they were the gates of the Kingdom of Heaven itself opening wide, and before the eyes of the worshippers the altar, radiant, stands revealed like the habitation of the glory of God and the seat of heavenly wisdom whence flows out to us knowledge of truth and the proclamation of eternal life.[14]

In the present dispensation it is only in this way, in symbol, that we are enabled to enter "behind the veil where our forerunner Jesus Christ has entered for us" (Heb 6:20). The entrance is none the less real, for since Christ has "entered once for all through the greater and more perfect tabernacle, not made by hands" (Heb 9:11), a breach has been opened in the wall of heaven, and we are in communion with the celestial liturgy offered by the heavenly powers around the throne of God.

This view of the liturgy as a participation in the worship of heaven reaches its climax in the Byzantine rite of the "Great Entrance," when the clergy bear the sacred offerings in procession from the altar of preparation to the altar of sacrifice. The Cherubic Hymn sung during the procession expresses the symbolism in which the whole cult is immersed, enjoining the faithful to associate themselves with the heavenly choirs and share in their eternal view:

> We who mystically represent the Cherubim and sing the thrice-holy hymn to the life-giving Trinity, let us lay aside all worldly care to receive the King of all escorted unseen by the angelic corps. Alleluia, Alleluia, Alleluia!

Worshiping in this atmosphere of profuse symbolism, through which the supernatural splendor of the inaccessible divine majesty and holiness is approached, Eastern Christians witness the exaltation and sanctification of creation, the majestic appearance of God who enters then, sanctifies them, divinizes them through the transfiguring light of his heavenly grace. It is not only a matter of "receiving the sacraments," but of living habitually within a liturgical ambiance that encompasses one in body and soul, transfiguring one's faith into a concrete vision of spiritual beauty and joy.

## 8. THE SYMBOLISM OF LIGHT[15]

One of the most suggestive themes used in the Byzantine liturgy to illustrate the transfiguring nature of our life in Christ is light. The Johannine theme of light, the light of the Lamb in the City of God (Apoc 21:22–26), pervades Eastern spirituality and mysticism. The life of the spirit is an illumination by this divine light; to see God by this light is to live in Him. St. Irenaeus wrote: "To see the light is to be in the light and participate in its clarity; likewise to see God is to be in him and participate in his life-giving splendor; thus those who see God participate in his life."[16]

This symbolism of light marks the rhythm of the hours in the Byzantine Office, evoking in the faithful a nostalgia for the divine vision which they are allowed to glimpse symbolically here on earth. It is a symbolism fulfilled in the eucharistic liturgy, as we hear in the refrain chanted after communion:

> We have seen the true light, we have received the heavenly Spirit, we have found the true faith worshiping the undivided Trinity that has saved us.

The liturgical tropes of the feast of the Transfiguration bear the same message:

> You were transfigured on the mount, O Christ-God, revealing to Your disciples Your glory in so far as they could bear it. Let Your eternal light illumine us sinners too . . . O Light-giver, glory to You!

> Come, let us climb up the mountain of the Lord into the house of our God and contemplate the glory of His Transfiguration; . . . in its light let us acquire the light, and elevated by the Spirit let us hymn the consubstantial Trinity in every age.

9.  THE IMPORTANCE OF THE RESURRECTION IN THE EASTERN LITURGIES

But the liturgical texts make clear that the glory of Tabor is but a sign of the resurrection, a figure of the cosmic divinization that is to come:

> Before Your crucifixion, O Lord, having taken Your disciples onto a high mountain, You were transfigured before them . . . desiring to show them the radiance of the resurrection.

For it is faith especially in the mystery of Christ's resurrection that renders effective the Byzantine liturgy's confession of the reality of the vision of God. It is difficult to communicate the importance of this mystery in the life of the East. Even in Holy Week, when the Great Fast lies heavy on the Church and the liturgy marks the lament and desolation of the death on the cross, the note of joy is heard.[17]

> Lament not for me, O Mother, when you behold in the tomb the Son whom, without seed, you conceived in your womb, for I shall rise again and glorify myself; and since I am God I will raise up to unending glory those who with faith and love magnify you.

This joy mounts in crescendo to the moment of the resurrection at Easter matins when the church, now alight with hundreds of flickering tapers, resounds with the cry of the priest. "Christ is risen!" And a world that is reliving the joy of its release from the bondage of sin and death exults: "In truth he is risen!"

The whole liturgical life of the Byzantine East is a praise of this Risen Lord, "the light that never sets." To this saving Passover all other mysteries point; in it they find their fulfillment. The offices of every Sunday in the year are dedicated to the celebration of the resurrection. Every Saturday evening, during matins of the vigil, one of the eleven gospels of the resurrection is proclaimed, followed by this hymn:

> Having beheld the resurrection of Christ, let us adore the Holy Lord Jesus, the only sinless one. Your cross do we adore, O Christ, and your holy resurrection we praise and glorify: for you are our God and we know no other besides you; it is your name that we proclaim. Come all you faithful, let us adore Christ's holy resurrection. For lo, through the cross has joy come into all the world. Ever blessing the Lord, let us sing

his resurrection: for, having endured the cross for us, he has by his death trampled death.


## 10. COME AND SEE

This is not mere poetry. In the East, liturgy is theophany, the privileged ground of our encounter with God, in which the mysteries are truly seen, albeit with the transfigured eyes of faith. What this means to the Eastern Christian can be seen in the following reply of a Russian Orthodox *batiushka* to his Catholic confrere, who tried to tell him that what was important was the conversion of sinners, confession, the teachings of the catechism, prayer, beside which "rite" plays only a secondary role.

The Russian priest replied:

> Among you it is indeed only an accessory. Among us Orthodox (and at these words he blessed himself) it is not so. The liturgy is our common prayer, it initiates our faithful into the mystery of Christ better than all your catechism. It passes before our eyes the life of our Christ, the Russian Christ, and that can be understood only in common, at our holy rites, in the mystery of our icons. When one sins, one sins alone. But to understand the mystery of the Risen Christ, neither your books nor your sermons are of any help. For that, one must have lived with the Orthodox Church the Joyous Night (Easter). And he blessed himself again.[18]

In the same way, our words are hardly adequate to communicate the spirit of a living tradition that is not an exotic curiosity, a pleasant antiquarian hobby appropriate to the eccentric dabbler in things oriental, but a divine vision that must be lived in faith and love. To the interested reader one can only say in the words of Philip to the sceptical Nathaniel: "Come and see" (Jn 1:46).


NOTES

1. *Mensuel. Service Oecumenique de Presse et d'Information*, no. 10 (avril, 1975) 7.

2. S. H. Cross and O. P. Sherbowitz-Weltzor, *The Russian Primary Chronicle. Laurention Text* (Cambridge, Mass.: The Mediaeval Academy of America 1953) 110–11.

3. Cf. note 1.

4. P. Hammond, *The Waters of Marah. The present state of the Greek Church*, (London: Rockliff 1956) 51–52.

5. There was a definite move in this direction in Russia, however, with the reform of Nikon in 1666–1667, and even today a certain ritual rigidity is characteristic of the Russian spirit.

6. Cf. J. Darrouzès, *Recherches sur les "offikia" de l'église byzantine* (=Archives de l'Orient Chrétien. 11, Paris: Inst. Français de'Études byzantines 1970) 435–436. There is of course the *Typicon* which regulates liturgical practice, but this is more a book of usage than a book of law, and no one adheres to its prescriptions exactly.

7. *Waters of Marah* 62.

8. *Ibid.* 36.

9. T. Mathews, *The Early Churches of Constantinople: Architecture and Liturgy* (University Park and London: Penn. State University 1971) 111.

10. Cf. N. Zernov, "The Worship of the Orthodox Church and its Message," A. J. Philippou (ed.), *The Orthodox Ethos* (Studies in Orthodoxy 1, Oxford: Holywell 1964) 117.

11. Cf. T. Ware, "The Communion of Saints," *ibid.* 140–149.

12. Hammond, *Waters of Marah* 16.

13. PG 155, 337–340.

14. N. V. Gogol, *The Divine Liturgy of the Russian Orthodox Church*, trans. R. Edmonds (London: Darton, Longman and Todd 1960) 19.

15. Cf. N. Egender, "Liturgie et vie spirituelle en Orient," *Les questions liturgiques et paroissiales* 43 (1962) 206–221. Some of the material here is resumed from my pamphlet *Eastern-rite Catholicism: its Heritage and Vocation* (Paulist Press 1963) later reprinted by John XXIII Center, Fordham University.

16. *Adv. haer.* IV, 20:5, PG 7, 1035.

17. Cf. Hammond, *Waters of Marah* 20.

18. C. Bourgeois, "Chez les paysans de la Podlachie et du nord-est de la Pologne. Mai 1924—décembre 1925," *Études* 191 (1927) 585.

Chapter 9

# "THANKSGIVING FOR THE LIGHT."[1] TOWARD A THEOLOGY OF VESPERS

## 1. The Meaning of Ritual

To understand the meaning of vespers we need first to clarify some notions on the nature of liturgy or ritual celebration. For the Liturgy of the Hours is just that: liturgy, a community celebration, the public worship of the Church. This must be the framework of any discussion of the office. It is not just common prayer, nor is it "saying the breviary." It is of the essence of sacramental and liturgical life to manifest symbolically what it represents, and liturgy is by nature a "public work."[2]

Why have human beings at all times and in all religions come together to express themselves in ritual? And what are they expressing? Ritual is a set of conventions, an organized pattern of signs and gestures which the members of a community use to interpret and enact for themselves, and to express and transmit to others, their relation to reality.[3] It is a way of saying what we as a group are, in the full sense of that *are*, with our past that made us what we are, our present in which we live what we are, and the future we hope to be. Ritual, then, is ideology and experience in action, the celebration or interpretation-through-action of our human experience and how we view it.

Human societies have used ritual especially to express their religious outlook, their universal system for relating to the ultimate questions of life. A religion is different from a personal philosophy of

Revised from *Diakonia* 13 (1978) 27–50.

life in that it is a *shared* perspective, a common outlook on reality. As such it depends on *history,* on the group's collective remembrance of things past, of events that have been transformed in the memory of the community into key symbolic episodes determinative of the community's being and self-understanding.

This is the basis of ritual behavior. For it is through the interpretation of its past that a community relates to the present and copes with the future. In the process of ritual representation, past constitutive events are made present in ritual time in order to communicate their force to new generations of the social group, providing thus a continuity of identity throughout history.

In primitive, natural religious systems the past was seen as cyclic, as an ever-repeated pattern of natural seasons. Rituals were celebrations of this cycle of autumn, winter, spring, harvest—of natural death and rebirth. But even at this primitive stage men and women came to see these natural rhythms as symbols of higher realities, of death and rebirth, of the perdurance of human existence beyond natural death.

So even natural religious ritual is not just an interpretation of experience, but implies a reaching for the beyond, for an ultimate meaning in the cycle of life that seemed to be an ever-recurring circle closed by death. The discovery of history was a breakthrough in this process: life was seen to have a pattern that extended beyond the closed cycles of life and death.[4] Time acquired a new meaning, and human ritual was transformed from a way of interpreting nature into a way of interpreting history.

By the ritual celebration of events in the past that had acquired a universal symbolic value in the minds of the community as foundational events that created and constituted its very identity—by celebrating these events ritually the community made present again and mediated to its members their formative power. Of course these were usually events of salvation, of escape from calamity and death, and it was but one further step for them to become transformed in the collective memory of the group into symbols of God's care and eternal salvation.

This is what happened with Israel. What makes Israelite liturgy different from other rituals is revelation. The Jews did not have to *imagine* that their escape from Egypt was a sign of God's saving providence: He *told* them so. When they celebrated ritually this exodus in the Passover meal, they knew they were celebrating more than the universalization of a past event in the historical imagination of their poets and prophets. The covenant with God which they re-affirmed ritually was a permanent and hence ever present reality because God had said so.

Here we encounter a basic difference between Judeo-Christian worship and other cults. Biblical worship is not an attempt to contact the divine, to mediate to us the power of God's intervention in past saving events. It is the other way around. It is a worship of the already saved. We do not reach for God to appease him; he has bent down to us.

## 2. CHRISTIAN LITURGY

With Christian liturgy we take another step in our understanding of ritual. As in the Old Testament, we too celebrate a saving event. For us, too, the meaning of this event has been revealed. But that is where the parallel ends. For Old Testament ritual looked forward to a promised fulfillment; it was not only an actualization of the covenant, but the pledge of a yet unrealized messianic future. In Christianity, what all other rituals strain to achieve has, we believe, already been fulfilled once and for all by Christ. Reconciliation with the Father has been accomplished eternally in the mystery of his Son (2 Cor 5:18–19; Rom 5:10–11). The gap is bridged forever through God's initiative.

So Christian worship is not how we seek to contact God; it is a celebration of how God has touched us, has united us to himself and is ever present to us and dwelling in us. It is not a reaching out for a distant reality but a joyful celebration of a salvation that is just as real and active in the ritual celebration as it was in the historical event, though in sacramental, not natural form. It is ritual perfected by divine realism; ritual in which the symbolic action is not a memorial of the past, but a participation in the eternally present salvific Pasch of Christ.

Liturgy then is the common work of Christ and his Church. This is its glory. It is also what makes possible the extraordinary claims we have made about the nature of Christian worship. Our prayers are worthless, but in the liturgy Christ himself prays in us. For the liturgy is the efficacious sign of Christ's saving presence in his Church. His saving offering is eternally active and present before the throne of the Father. By our celebration of the divine mysteries, we are drawn into the saving action of Christ and our personal oblation of self is transformed into an act of the Body of Christ through the worship of the Body with its head. What humankind has vainly striven for throughout history in natural ritual—contact with the divine—is transformed from image to reality in Christ.

## 3. Liturgy and Spirituality

This common celebration of our salvation in Christ is the most perfect expression and realization of the spirituality of the Church. There are many "schools" of spirituality, but they are legitimate only insofar as they are rooted in the worship of the Church.[5] The purpose of the spiritual life is to "put on Christ," so that, as St. Paul says, "It is no longer I who live, but Christ who lives in me" (Gal 2:20). And this life is created, fed and renewed in the liturgy. Baptized into the mystery of his death and resurrection, we rise in him, having "put on Christ." Henceforth he dwells in us, prays in us, proclaims to us the Word of his new covenant, seals it with his sacrifice, feeds us with his body and blood, draws us to penance and conversion, glorifies the Father in us. In proclamation and preaching he explains to us his mystery; in rite and song he celebrates it with us; in sacramental grace he gives us the strength to live it.

The mystery that is Christ is the center of Christian life and it is this mystery and nothing else that the Church renews sacramentally in the liturgy so that we might be drawn into it. When we leave the assembly to return to our other tasks, we have only to assimilate what we have experienced and realize the mystery in our lives: in a word, to become other Christs. For the purpose of the liturgy is to reproduce in our lives what the Church exemplifies for us in her public worship. The spiritual life is just another word for a personal relationship with God and the liturgy is nothing less than the common expression of the Mystical Body's personal relationship with God.

In such a liturgical spirituality the Church's public worship and the spiritual life of the individual are one. All the supposed tension in spirituality between public and private, objective and subjective, liturgical and personal, is an illusion, a false dichotomy. For in her public worship it is precisely this work of spiritual formation that the Church carries on.

## 4. THE LITURGY OF THE HOURS

So liturgy is just a celebration of the Christian reality. The eternally present Christ-event is an everlasting hymn of praise and glory before the throne of the Father. Since it is our vocation to enter into this salvific event and live that Christ-life of priestly praise and glory, the Church, as his Mystical Body, associates herself with the eternal priestly prayer of her head. In so doing, she truly participates in the salvific praise of Christ, according to the theology of Vatican II:

> Christ Jesus, high priest of the new and eternal covenant, taking human nature, introduced into this earthly exile that hymn which is sung throughout all ages in the halls of heaven. He joins the entire community of mankind to Himself, associating it with His own singing of this canticle of divine praise.
>
> For He continues His priestly work through the agency of His Church, which is ceaselessly engaged in praising the Lord and interceding for the salvation of the whole world. This she does not only by celebrating the Eucharist, but also in other ways, especially by praying the divine Office . . . It is truly the voice of the bride addressing her bridgroom; it is the very prayer which Christ Himself, together with His body, addresses to the Father. Hence all who perform this service are not only fulfilling a duty of the Church, but also are sharing in the greatest honor accorded to Christ's spouse, for by offering these praises to God they are standing before God's throne in the name of the Church, their Mother.[6]

Traditionally, morning praise and evensong, with Eucharist, have been the principle ways in which the Church exercises this *leitourgia*.

## 5. MORNING AND EVENING PRAYER IN THE EARLY CHURCH[7]

There is of course nothing specifically Christian about morning and evening as times for prayer. They are the natural beginning and end of the day and were the hours of temple sacrifice and incense offering prescribed in the Old Testament (Ex 29:38–42; 30:7–8; Num 28:1–8), and the hours when the *Shema* was recited in the synagogue. It is clear from the writings of the early Fathers such as Tertullian that the Old Testament prescription was the motive for considering these two hours of prayer "obligatory" on all Christians.[8]

Originally they were times of "private prayer" or of common prayer in small groups. Our first witness to the practice of celebrating these hours in common as a normal part of public worship at the beginning of the fourth century is the famous church historian Eusebius (c. 263–339), bishop of his hometown, Caesaria in Palestine, from 313. In his *Commentary on Ps 64*, verse 9b (LXX): "You shall make the outgoings of the morning and evening rejoice," Eusebius explains that these morning and evening joys have been interpreted as hymns (*hymnologias*) and praises (*ainopoiéseis*), and then he tells why:

> For it is surely no small sign of God's power that throughout the whole world in the churches of God at the morning rising of the sun and at the evening hours, hymns, praises, and truly divine delights are offered to God. God's delights are indeed the hymns sent up everywhere on earth in his Church at the times of morning and evening. For this reason it is said somewhere, "Let my praise be sung sweetly to him" (cf. Ps. 146:1), and "Let my prayer be like incense before you" (Ps 140:2).[9]

Note that Eusebius is talking about what we would call "parish worship," not about the prayer of monks. Matins and vespers are not of monastic provenance, contrary to what is popularly thought. Morning and evening prayer was incumbent on all, laity and religious alike.

In the *Apostolic Constitutions* (II, 59), a document from the environs of Antioch around the year 380, we see that a psalm selected for its suitability to the hour of prayer formed the core of both services:

> When you teach, bishop, command and exhort the people to frequent the church regularly, morning and evening every day, and not to forsake it at all, but to assemble continually and not diminish the Church by absenting themselves and making the Body of Christ lack a member. For it is not only said for the benefit of the priests, but let each of the laity hear what was said by the Lord as spoken to himself: "He who is not with me is against me, and he who does not gather with me

scatters" (Mt 12:30) . . . Do not be neglectful of yourselves, nor rob the savior of his own members, nor divide his body, nor scatter his members, nor prefer the needs of this life to the Word of God, but assemble each day morning and evening, singing psalms and praying in the Lord's houses, in the morning saying Ps 62, and in the evening Ps 140.[10]

The services concluded with an exercise of the common priesthood of the community interceding for the needs of all mankind as well as for those of the Church, an act of the people of God as "chosen race, a royal priesthood" (1 Pet 2:9) performing its public work (*leitourgia*) for society according to the instruction of St. Paul in 1 Tim 2:

First of all, then, I urge that supplications, prayers, intercessions, and thanksgivings be made for all men, for kings and all who are in high positions, that we may lead a calm and tranquil life, godly and respectful in every way. This is good, and it is acceptable in the sight of God our savior, who desires all men to be saved and to come to the knowledge of the truth. For there is one God, and there is one mediator between God and men, the man Jesus Christ, who gave himself as a ransom for all . . . I desire then that in every place the men should pray, lifting up holy hands without anger or quarreling . . .

St. John Chrysostom applies this passage to the mediation of the Church in the intercessions of morning prayer and evensong:

What does "first of all" mean in the daily worship? The initiates know how this is done morning and evening, every day: how we pray for the whole world, for kings and for those in authority.[11]

Elsewhere Chrysostom speaks of the "great power of the prayer offered by the people together in church,"[12] a power that far surpasses the strength of our individual petitions.

Such prayers at the end of the service constituted a bridge linking the liturgical celebration with the needs of everyday life to which the congregation was about to be blessed and dismissed.

6. THE SPIRIT OF EVENING PRAYER IN THE FATHERS

Chrysostom, commenting on Psalm 140 in the daily evening office of Antioch before he became archbishop of Constantinople in 397, expresses the spirit of this vesperal psalm which came to form the core of evensong in all traditions throughout christendom:

> Many things in this psalm are suitable for the time of evening. Not for this reason, however, did the fathers choose this psalm, but rather they ordered it to be said as a salutary medicine and forgiveness of sins, so that whatever has dirtied us throughout the whole length of the day, either in the marketplace or at home or wherever we spend our time, we get rid of it in the evening through this spiritual song. For it is indeed a medicine that destroys all those things.[13]

In his *Baptismal Catechesis* VIII, 17–18, given in Antioch around 390, Chrysostom gives the same motivation for evening prayer:

> ... Let each one go to his affairs with fear and trembling, and so pass the time of day as one obliged to return here [to church] in the evening to give the master an account of the entire day and to ask pardon for failures. For it is impossible even if we are ten thousand times watchful to avoid being liable for all sorts of faults. Either we have said something inopportune, or listened to idle talk, or been disturbed by some indecent thought, or have not controlled our eyes, or have spent time in vain and idle things rather than doing what we should. And that is why every evening we must ask the master's pardon for all these faults ... Then we must pass the time of night in sobriety and thus be ready to present ourselves again at the morning praise ...[14]

For Chrysostom, then, vespers is basically a penitential service and— we might add—an efficacious one: the forgiveness sincerely asked is in fact granted.

St. Basil's explanation of vespers in question 37 of *The Longer Rules* adds thanksgiving before repentance as another basic vesperal theme:

> And when the day is ended, thanksgiving should be offered for what has been given us during the day or for what we have done rightly, and confession made of what we have failed to do—an offence committed, be it voluntary or involuntary, or perhaps unnoticed, either in word or deed or in the very heart—propitiating God in our prayers for all our failings. For the examination of past actions is a great help against falling into similar faults again. Wherefore it says: "The things you say in your hearts, be sorry for on your beds" (Ps 4:5).[15]

The collect that concludes evensong in the *Apostolic Constitutions* (VIII, 37) expresses a like spirit:

O God . . . who has made the day for the works of light and the night for
the refreshment of our infirmity . . . mercifully accept now this, our
evening thanksgiving. You who have brought us through the length of
the day and to the beginning of the night, preserve us by your Christ.
Grant us a peaceful evening and a night free from sin, and give us
everlasting life by your Christ . . . [16]

It is clear from these texts that the earliest tradition of non-
eucharistic public prayer had nothing to do with theories of the
"sanctification of time," with *kairos* and *chronos*, with a liturgy of
"time" or "history" as distinct from the "eschatological" Eucharist.
Rather, the evening office at the close of day leads us to reflect on the
hours just passed, with thanksgiving for the good they have brought
and sorrow for the evil we have done.

## 7. THE RITUALIZATION OF THE OFFICE

In the cathedral offices by the beginning of the fifth century these
bare bones of psalmody and prayer had been fleshed out with rites
and symbols that transformed the morning and evening hours into
sacraments of the mystery of Christ. In this sense the early cathedral
office can be called a "sanctification of time" in that time is
"sacramentalized" into a symbol of the time that transcends time. In
the liturgical mystery, time becomes transformed into event, an
epiphany of the kingdom of God.

All of creation is a cosmic sacrament of our saving God, and the
Church's use of such symbolism in the office is but a step in the
restoration of all things in Christ (Eph 1:10). For the Christian
everything, including the morning and evening, the day and the
night, the sun and its setting, can be a means of communion with
God: "The heavens declare the glory of God and the firmament
proclaims his handiwork" (Ps 19:1).

## 8. "GOD IS LIGHT" (1 JN 1:15)

The basic natural symbol from which this ritual elaboration springs
is, of course, light, a theme that can be traced back to the Old
Testament and even beyond, to the prominent use of sun imagery in
the paganism of the Mediterranean world.

Behind the imagery of the light and the sun in the religions of the Near East was the attempt to find meaning and hope for human life in the daily victory of light over darkness: the dawn was the harbinger of divine rescue and of eternal salvation. Indeed, the power of the light to bring hope is much older and deeper than mere human history. In responding as they did to the power of the light, the religions of the Near East gave liturgical expression to the yearnings and the stirrings of the protoplasm, the nameless need in the very stuff of life to be sustained by light.[17]

In spite of the power of the imagery of sun and light in Hellenistic Judaism (Philo), it does not seem to have especially affected the ritual of Jewish morning and evening prayer. The *Yotzer* benediction of the *Shema* recited at these hours in the synagogue does refer to light and darkness in the context of creation, but its symbolic application does not seem to have been ritualized: "Blessed are you, Lord our God, King of the universe, who form the light and create the darkness, who make peace and create all things (Isaiah 45:7), who illumine the earth and those that dwell on it with mercy, and from your goodness renew daily the work of creation . . ."[18]

Christians at any rate were quick to apply this symbolism to Christ; it is a constant New Testament theme, especially in the Johannine and deutero-Pauline literature:

Jn 1:4–9: In him was life, and the life was the light of men. The light shines in the darkness, and the darkness has not overcome it. There was a man sent from God, whose name was John. He came for testimony, to bear witness to the light, that all might believe through him. He was not the light, but came to bear witness to the light. The true light that enlightens every man was coming into the world.

Jn 8:12 (9:5): I am the light of the world; he who follows me will not walk in darkness, but will have the light of life.

12:45–6: He who sees me sees him who sent me. I have come as light into the world, that whoever believes in me may not remain in darkness. (cf. 12:35–36)

In Christ, this illumination has already been accomplished:

Col 1:12–13: . . . (give) thanks to the Father, who has qualified us to share in the inheritance of the saints of light. He has delivered us from the dominion of darkness and transferred us to the kingdom of his beloved Son, in whom we have redemption, the forgiveness of sins. (cf. 1 Thess 5:5; Heb 6:4, 10:32)

Ephesians 5 and the First Letter of John stress that this illumination has a moral and communitarian dimension:

1 Jn 1:5–7: . . . God is light and in him is no darkness at all. If we say we have fellowship with him while we walk in darkness, we lie and do not live according to the truth; but if we walk in the light, as he is in the light, we have fellowship with one another, and the blood of Jesus his son cleanses us from all sin.

2:8–11: Yet I am writing you a new commandment, which is true in him and in you, because the darkness is passing away and the light is already shining. He who says he is in the light and hates his brother abides in the darkness still. He who loves his brother abides in the light, and in it there is no cause for stumbling. But he who hates his brother is in the darkness and walks in the darkness, and does not know where he is going, because the darkness has blinded his eyes.

But perhaps the most pregnantly beautiful passage for our purposes is the description in Apocalypse 21:22–26 of the light of the Lamb in the Heavenly City of God, the New Jerusalem:

And I saw no temple in the city, for its temple is the Lord God the Almighty and the Lamb. And the city has no need of sun or moon to shine upon it, for the glory of God is its light, and its lamp is the Lamb. By its light shall the nations walk; and the kings of the earth shall bring their glory into it, and its gates shall never be shut by day—and there shall be no night there . . .

The passage is a deliberate fulfillment of the prophecy of Isaiah (60:1–3, 11, 19–20) in the prophet's vision of the restored Holy City of the Messianic times:

Arise, shine; for your light has come,
    and the glory of the Lord has risen upon you.
For behold, darkness shall cover the earth . . . but the Lord will arise
    upon you, and his glory will be seen upon you.
And the nations shall come to your light, and kings to the brightness of
    your rising . . .
Your gates shall be open continually;
    day and night they shall not be shut . . .
The sun shall be no more your light by day,
    nor for brightness shall the moon give light to you by night;
But the Lord will be your everlasting light,
    and your God will be your glory.
Your sun shall no more go down, nor your moon withdraw itself;

for the Lord will be your everlasting light,
  and your days of mourning shall be ended . . .

It was not long before this symbolism passed into the poetry and
hymnody of Christian worship. A venerable hymn is cited in part in
Ephesians 5:14. Clement of Alexandria (d. 215) in his *Protrepticus*
9,84:2 gives the full text:

Awake, O sleeper, and rise from the dead,
and Christ shall give you light,
  the sun of the resurrection,
    begotten before the morning star (Ps 109)
  who gives life by his own very rays.[19]

This light Christ gives is salvation and it is received in baptism. The
Letter to the Hebrews, in a passage strikingly reminiscent of the three
stages of initiation, speaks of "those who have . . . been enlightened,
who have tasted the heavenly gift, and have become partakers of the
Holy Spirit and have tasted the goodness of the work of God and the
power of the age to come . . . " (6:4–6).[20] And in the early Church,
baptism was called *"photisma,"* illumination; those to be baptised
were *"illuminandi, photizomenoi."* Ancient prayers for them can still be
found in the Byzantine Liturgy of the Presanctified Gifts for the final
weeks of Great Lent.

It is not surprising, then, that in the evening office, celebrated at
the setting of the sun and the onset of darkness, the hour of
lamplighting, Christians were drawn to see the evening lamp as a
symbol of Christ the light of the world, the lamp of the Heavenly City
where there is no darkness or night but only day, and to render
thanks to God for it.

The evening service began with the lighting of the lamps needed to
provide light for the service. In our age of abundant electricity "it is
difficult for us to appreciate the wonder of flickering oil lamps
piercing the settling darkness of the night. But pre-Edisonian cultures
greeted artificial light with a sense of grateful welcome."[21]

Pagans were accustomed to greet the light with the exclamation
"*Chaire, phôs agathon* (Hail, good light)!", or "*Chaire, phôs philon* (Hail,
friendly light)!". And Clement of Alexandria recommends that we
greet the true God with "Hail, light!"[22] So even before the development of evensong into a liturgical office held in church, Christian

domestic piety had inherited from paganism the *lucernarium,* the practice of greeting the evening lamp with prayer and praise.[23]

St. Gregory of Nyssa (d. 394), brother of St. Basil the Great, describes in his *Life of St. Macrina* the death of their sister in 379, at the hour of lamplighting.

> And when evening had arrived and the lamp was brought in, she opened her eyes that had been closed till then and looked at the light, and made clear that she wished to say the thanksgiving for the light, but since her voice failed her, she fulfilled the offering with her heart and with the movement of her hands, while her lips moved in harmony with the inner impulse.[24]

Earlier sources from the Western Churches give us the Christian interpretation of this light symbolism in evening prayer long before it had become a public service. St. Cyprian (d. 258), for example, interprets evening prayer thus:

> Likewise at the setting of the sun and the passing of the day it is necessary to pray. For since Christ is the true sun and the true day, when we pray as the sun and the day of the world recede and ask that the light may come upon us again, we are asking for the coming of Christ, which provides us with the grace of eternal light.[25]

And the *Apostolic Tradition* of Hippolytus of Rome (ca. 215) describes an early Christian domestic *lucernarium* that included a prayer of "Thanksgiving for the Light":

> When the bishop is present, and evening has come, a deacon brings in a lamp; and standing in the midst of all the faithful who are present (the bishop) shall give thanks . . . And he shall pray thus, saying: "We give you thanks Lord, through your Son Jesus Christ our Lord, through whom you have shone upon us and revealed to us the inextinguishable light. So when we have completed the length of the day and have come to the beginning of the night, and have satisfied ourselves with the light of day which you created for our satisfying; and since now through your grace we do not lack the light of evening, we praise and glorify you through your Son Jesus Christ our Lord, through whom be glory and power and honour to you with the holy Spirit, both now and always and to the ages of ages. Amen."[26]

By the end of the fourth century elements from the domestic ritual and symbolism of the evening lamp appear in cathedral vespers in

Cappadocia and Palestine, though not in Antioch.[27] In Jerusalem, the famous pilgrim-nun, Egeria, writing about 384, describes the lighting of the evening lamp from the ever-burning light in the cave of the Holy Sepulchre, an obvious symbol of risen Christ, light of the world:

> ... at four o'clock they have *lychnicon*, as they call it, or in our language, *lucernare*. All the people congregate once more in the Anastasis and the lamps and candles are all lit, which makes it very bright. The fire is brought not from outside, but from the cave—inside the screen—where a lamp is always burning night and day. For some time they have the *lucernare* psalms and antiphons; then they send for the bishop, who enters and sits in the chief seat ... [28]

In Cappadocia, too, St. Gregory of Nyssa in the *Life of St. Macrina* already cited, refers to the *lucernarium* as a public service: "The voice of the singers calling to the thanksgiving for the light also called me forth to the church."[29] St. Basil (d. 379) speaking of the same lamplighting hymn of thanks, cites the ancient *Phos hilaron* (*Svete tikhij*) which still forms the core of the light service of Byzantine vespers.

> O radiant Light, O Sun divine
> Of God the Father's deathless face,
> O Image of the light sublime
> That fills the heav'nly dwelling place.
>
> Lord Jesus Christ, as daylight fades,
> As shine the lights of eventide,
> We praise the Father with the Son,
> The Spirit blest and with them one.
>
> O Son of God, the source of life,
> Praise is your due by night and day.
> Unsullied lips must raise the strain
> Of your proclaimed and splendid name.[30]

Basil says that the hymn was ancient even in his time—so old that he did not even know who wrote it.

> It seemed fitting to our fathers not to receive the gift of the evening light in silence, but to give thanks immediately upon its appearance. We can't say who was the father of the words of the thanksgiving for the light. But the people utter the ancient formula, and those that say "We praise

the Father, and the Son and the Holy Spirit of God" were never thought impious by anyone.[31]

This *epilychnios eucharistia,* one of the earliest extant Christian hymns, is a praise to Christ who is the true light shining in the darkness of the world and illuminating—i.e. saving—all men and women.

This is the second basic element of the rite of vespers in every tradition: thanksgiving for the light, in which the Church uses the lamplighting at sunset to remind us of the Johannine vision of the Lamb who is the eternal lamp of the Heavenly Jerusalem, the sun that never sets.

## 9. "LET MY PRAYER RISE LIKE INCENSE . . . " (Ps. 140:2)

A further element of the vesperal ritual is the oblation of incense, inspired undoubtedly by Ps 140:2, "Let my prayer rise like incense before you, my hands like the evening sacrifice," and by the Old Testament evening oblation of incense at the lighting of the lamps (Ex 30:8): "When Aaron sets up the lamps in the evening he shall burn it, a perpetual incense before the Lord throughout your generations." This offering is first mentioned at Christian vespers by Theodoret in his *Questions on Exodus* 28, written sometime after 453. Commenting on Ex 30:7-8 in relation to Christian worship, Theodoret says "We perform the liturgy reserved to the interior of the tabernacle [i.e. the offering of incense]. For it is the incense and the light of the lamps that we offer to God, as well as the service of the mysteries of the holy table."[32] In the Eastern traditions the vesperal offering of incense accompanies Psalm 140 and has a penitential meaning: it is a symbol of our self-offering of repentance rising with our prayers and our uplifted hands.

Other songs, readings, and prayers that have been added to the basic skeleton do not change the fundamental thrust of the evening rite. So from what we have seen it is not difficult to disengage the primitive constitutive elements that still comprise our Byzantine vespers and the spirit that animates them. Thanksgiving and forgiveness were the two basic motifs expressed by our witnesses to evensong in early Christian literature. In today's rite, after the monastic meditation of continuous psalmody,[33] the cathedral service opens with the vesperal Psalm 140, accompanied by the offering of incense.

The theme of repentance for the sins of the day focuses on this evening psalm, the core of vespers which Chrysostom interprets as an efficacious act of perfect contrition. In time this penitential prayer came to be ritualized by the addition of a rite of incense. The "evening thanks" finds expression in the ancient *Phos hilaron* (*Svete tikhij*) of thanksgiving for Christ, light of the world, symbolized by the evening lamp. Other lesser themes also appear in the service: preparation for the coming night, vigilance and expectancy for the coming new day when we shall rise again to praise God, etc. As at every Christian synaxis, the assembly concludes with general intercessions for salvation and for the basic needs of daily life to which the members are about to depart.[34]

## 10. The Office as a Proclamation of the Paschal Mystery

Note the limpid simplicity of the early Church's liturgical theology reflected in the basic structure and spirit of evensong. Like all prayer in both the Old and New Testaments, it is a glorification of God that wells up from the joyful proclamation of his saving deeds: "The Almighty has done great things for me! Holy is his name!" (Lk 1:49). This is the core of biblical prayer: remembrance, praise and thanksgiving—which can then flow into petition for the continuance of this saving care in our present time of need. Remembrance, *anamnesis*, is also at the heart of all ritual celebration, for celebrations are celebrations *of* something: through symbol and gesture and text we render present—proclaim—once again the reality we feast.

In the early liturgical tradition this reality is one unique event, the paschal mystery in its totality, the mystery of Christ and of our salvation in him. This is the meaning of baptism; it is the meaning of Eucharist; it is the meaning of the office as well. The *anamnesis* of the Christ-event is the well-spring of all Christian prayer. This is still reflected in the proper of the Byzantine Office found in the daily cycle of the *Oktoichos*: The texts are all focused squarely on the paschal mystery of salvation. Here for example are some of the refrains of the Byzantine Office for Saturday vespers, tone 3:[35]

We bow down in worship before your precious Cross, O Christ, and we praise and glorify your Resurrection: for it is by your wounds that we have been healed.

We praise the Saviour, incarnate of a Virgin: for he was crucified for us and rose on the third day, giving us the great mercy.

The Christ, having descended among those who were in Hell, proclaimed, saying: "Take courage, I have conquered. I am the Resurrection and I shall lead you away, after having destroyed the gates of death."

Your life-giving Resurrection, O Lord, has illuminated the whole world, and your own creation, which had been corrupted, has been called back. Therefore, freed from the curse of Adam, we cry: "O Lord almighty, glory to you."

It is incorrect, then, to view the office as primarily "historical" rather than "eschatological." Theologically the coming of Christ is one indivisible event, though it can intersect with human history at different points in time. The *eschaton*, the final fulfillment of history, has already occurred in Christ. The time of the kingdom, the beginning of the final days, is already begun.

In *all* true Christian worship the basic emphasis must *always* be on this eschatological element; on salvation history, yes, but as one indivisible, eternally present reality which is the Kingdom of God realized in its fulness in the Passover of Christ.

Hence the Liturgy of the Hours, like all Christian liturgy, is an eschatological proclamation of the salvation received in Christ, and a glorification and thanksgiving to God for that gift. In this original and primitive sense the Liturgy of the Hours—indeed, all liturgy—is beyond time. For the Christian there is really no sacred space, no sacred persons or times: all are redeemed in Christ, for whom only God is holy and those to whom he has given his sanctification, his saints—i.e. his people.

By a curious reversal of the ritual process, the later development of the Christian calendar and its proper tended to turn the offices into historical commemorations of individual events in salvation history, thus permitting a decomposition of the mystery into its component parts. We do not have time to go into this very complex question of how the Christian community came to give more attention to the historical dimension of its liturgical *anamnesis*. Nor is it our intention to denigrate it. But it was an innovation that must not be allowed to obscure the original purity of the meaning of primitive Christian morning and evening prayer, which was not an "historical commemoration" nor a "liturgy of time" as opposed to the "eschatological," "beyond-time" service of the Eucharist. Both were and are a praise of the same God for the same reason: Christ.

Christians by faith had the supreme joy of knowing that they lived a new life in Christ, a life of love shared with all of the same faith. What could have been more normal, then, than for those who were able to gather at daybreak to turn the first thoughts of the day to this mystery of their salvation and to praise and glorify God for it? And at the close of day they came together again to ask forgiveness for the failings of the day and to praise God once more for his mighty deeds. In this way the natural rhythm of time was turned into a hymn of praise to God and a proclamation before the world of faith in his salvation in Christ.

11. THE OFFICE AS A CELEBRATION OF OUR LIFE IN CHRIST

The Liturgy of the Hours, then, is a sanctification of the day by turning to God at its beginning and end to do what all liturgy always does: to celebrate and manifest in ritual moments what is and must be the constant stance of our every minute of the day: our priestly offering, in Christ, of self, to the praise and glory of the Father in thanks for his saving gift in Christ.

For Christian ritual is distinguished not only by its eschatological fulfillment and its sacramental realism; it is also distinct in that it is but the external expression of what is present within us: our salvation is an interior reality implying a whole way of life.[36] Hence true Christian ritual is the opposite of magical rituals, which concentrate on the working of *things*. Christian ritual is *personalistic*: the purpose of Eucharist is not to change bread and wine, but to change you and me.[37] And so our liturgy must be an expression of the covenant in our hearts, a celebration of what we are—otherwise it is an empty show.

Hence in the liturgy there is a constant dialectic between celebration and life. For if we do not live what we celebrate, our liturgy is a meaningless expression of what we are not.

Nothing is clearer in the New Testament, especially in St. Paul, than this fact: the true cult of the Christian is interior; it is the life of self-oblation in charity; a life, like Christ's, that is lived in loving service—in short, a life of self-giving. Paul tells the Corinthians (1 Cor 11:17–34) that their Eucharist is in fact no Eucharist at all because the mystery of communion—i.e. unity in Christ—which Eucharist expresses was not lived in their lives.[38]

That mystery is a mystery of self-oblation, a giving of self for others, in obedience to the will of the Father, who has shown us, in Christ, that this is the only life worthy of human persons. This is what St. Paul means in Rom 12:1: "I implore you by God's mercy to offer your very selves to him: a living sacrifice, consecrated and fit for his acceptance; *this is your authentic worship.*"

In the present dispensation there is of course only one acceptable sacrifice, that of Christ. But his offering needs to be "filled up." We must fill up what is wanting in the sacrifice of Christ (Col 1:24). This does not mean that Christ's salvific work was defective. Rather, it remains incomplete until all men and women have freely entered into Christ's offering, making their lives, too, a Christian oblation. This offering is pleasing in the sight of God only because Christ has made us his Body, so that our offering is joined to his and transformed by it.

We make this offering in every act of our Christian lives. We do it when our faith is expressed in charity, as in Heb 13:15–16:

> Through Jesus . . . let us continually offer up to God the sacrifice of praise, that is the tribute of lips which acknowledge his name, and never forget to show kindness and to share what you have with others; *for such are the sacrifices which God approves.*

We also offer liturgy when we proclaim our faith. In Phil 2:17 Paul speaks of "that liturgical sacrifice which is your faith." In Rom 1:9 he says "I worship God with my person, proclaiming the Gospel of his Son," and 15:16, "My priestly service is the announcing of the good news of God."

This is why we are all priests: as Christians it is of the very essence of our lives to *offer*. And all we have to offer is ourselves, in witness to our faith, professing it before others and living it through love. 1 Pet 2:2 says: "You are a chosen race, a royal priesthood, a dedicated nation, a people claimed by God for his own, to proclaim the triumphs of him who has called you out of darkness into his marvellous light."

## 12. Liturgy and Life

Hence for the New Testament there is no separtion between liturgy and life. Our Christian life *is* our liturgy. That is why the New Testament uses liturgical and priestly vocabulary for two things only: 1) for Christ and his offering; 2) for all of us and the offering of our lives. For the Christian, then, worship, sacrifice, liturgy, are a life of faith and fraternal love—i.e. surrender to God and service of others. And these two, faith and charity, are really one. For by faith we see the world as the place where God's love is active and given to each person in a unique way; and hence we see each one as lovable. To say "yes" to God and "no" to man is impossible for the Christian. "If anyone says 'I love God', and hates his brother, he is a liar" (1 John 4:20). Worship, then, is not a department of life; it is life itself.

And all true Christian liturgy is a celebration of that reality. Thus the offices at the beginning and end of the day are just ritual moments symbolic of the whole of time. As such they, are a proclamation of faith to the world and partake of our mission to witness to Christ and his salvation. They are also a praise and thanksgiving for this gift of salvation in Christ. Lastly, they are our priestly prayer, as God's priestly people, for our needs and those of the entire world. That is what liturgy means. That is what vespers means. As a matter of fact, that is what life means.

## Notes

1. "*Epilychnios eucharistia*," the name given evening prayer in St. Gregory of Nyssa's *Life of Macrina*, sister of St. Basil the Great, as well as in Basil's *On the Holy Spirit*, both cited below. Similarly, in the West, Gregory of Tours called vespers "*gratia vespertina*" ("evening thanks"), *De miraculis S. Juliani* 20, PL 71, 813.

2. Of course the office and other liturgical prayers may be used for private prayer and meditation. When thus used, at the proper hour, by one who is prevented from joining in the community celebration, the office takes on a value that goes beyond that of our purely individual prayer. Furthermore, the original sense of the word *leitourgia*—public service—does not imply a community activity, in spite of what is often said. Individuals performed public services for, or in the name of, the

community, and these were called "liturgies." Of course the Christian understanding of liturgy is not determined by etymology, but even in the New Testament the term is used for various aspects of Christian *life*. Hence *historically* the word liturgy reflects the same ambiguous richness as our English word *service*: it can mean a church service or any activity devoted to the service of God and neighbor. Today, however, we use the term liturgy to refer to public community worship, an expression of the unity of the Body of Christ as such, and liturgical prayer said privately should not be considered liturgy in this restricted sense of the term.

3. Victor Turner, "Ritual, Tribal and Catholic," *Worship* 50 (1976) 504–526, gives some reflections of a Catholic anthropologist on the nature of ritual. Some of Turner's ideas are incorporated here.

4. L. Deiss, *God's Word and God's People*, (Collegeville: Liturgical Press 1976) ch. 1, describes this process in the religious history of the Jews.

5. See G. Braso, *Liturgy and Spirituality*, (Collegeville: Liturgical Press 1976) for a discussion of the liturgical spirituality of the Church.

6. *Constitution on the Sacred Liturgy*, 83–85, trans. W. M. Abbott, *The Documents of Vatican II* (New York: America Press 1966) 163–164.

7. The best summary treatment of this subject in English is found in two articles of J. Mateos, "The Origins of the Divine Office," *Worship* 41 (1967) 477–485, and "The Morning and Evening Office," *Worship* 42 (1968) 31–47. What Mateos says concerning the Egyptian monastic office needs to be complemented by my study, "Praise in the Desert: The Coptic Monastic Office Yesterday and Today," *Worship* 56 (1982) 513–536. For a full treatment, see part I of my new book, *The Liturgy of the Hours in the Christian East: Origins, Meaning Place in the Life of the Church* (Cochin [India]: KCM Press 1984).

8. Tertullian, *De oratione* 25, 5, CCL 1, 272–273; also Chrysostom, *In ps. 140*, PG 55, 430; Cassian, *De inst. coenob.* II, 3. CSEL 17, 19. Cf. Mateos, "The Origins," 479, and "Quelques anciens documents sur l'office du soir," *OCP* 35 (1969) 370–71.

9. PG 23, 640.

10. F. X. Funk, *Didascalia et Constitutiones Apostolorum* (Paderborn: F. Schoeningh 1905) I, 171.

11. *In 1 Tim.* 2, *hom, 6*, PG 62, 640.

12. *De prophetarum obscuritate* II, 5, PG 56, 182.

13. *In ps. 140*, PG 55, 427.

14. A. Wenger (ed.), Jean Chrysostome, *Huit catéchèses baptismales inédites* (SC 50, Paris: Cerf 1957) 257.

15. PG 31, 1014.

16. Funk I, 544.

17. J. Pelikan, *The Light of the World. A Basic Image in Early Christian Thought* (New York: Harper and Brothers 1962) 13.

18. Cf. W. O. E. Oesterley, *The Jewish Background of the Christian Liturgy* (Gloucester, Mass.: Peter Smith 1965) 48. Of course Jewish tradition offers fruitful parallels in the ritual of the Hanukkah lights, and especially in the ritual of the lighting of the Sabbath lights Friday evening and of the Havdalah lamp at the end of the Sabbath. But I know of no ritual parallel in the *daily* domestic or synagogue rituals of the Jews in the first centuries A.D. In modern Jewish services daily evening prayer praises God for the natural darkness as well as for the light, without any reference to or symbolising of the evening lamp: "Praised are you, O Lord, for the evening dusk" *Weekday Prayer Book* (New York: Rabbinical Assembly of America 1974) 141. For the other services mentioned, see 172, 211, and *Gates of Prayer. The New Union Prayerbook* (New York: Central Conference of American Rabbis 1975) 31ff, 117, 142–143, 158, 176, 189, 204,

219, 244, 260, 269, 397, 633ff, 637–44. See also the references to the Sabbath and Havdalah lamp blessings in Jewish sources from around the end of the second century A.D. and later: *Mishna* VIII, 5–7 and *Tosephta* VI, 6–8, *Tractate Berakoth*, trans. A. Lukyn Williams (Translations of Early Documents, series III: Rabbinic Texts London: SPCK 1921) 68–71. The parallel between the blessing of the Havdalah lamp and spices (incense) before the ritual meal, and the Christian *lucernarium* before the agape, has been noted by Winkler in the study cited below in note 23.

19. Ed. O. Stählin, *Clemens Alexandrinus* 1 (GCS, Leipzig: J. C. Hinrichs 1905) 63.

20. See T. Camelot, *Spiritualité du baptême* (Lex orandi 30, Paris: Cerf 1963) ch. 4.

21. A. Ciferni, "The Lucernarium," *Liturgical Prayer* 5 (Winter 1976–77) 32–33.

22. *Protrepticus* 11, 114:1, ed. Stählin, 80. Cf. F.J. Dölger, "*Chaire hieron phôs* als antike Lichtbegrüssing bei Nikarchos und Jesus als heiliges Licht bei Klemens von Alexandrien," *AC* 6 (1940) 147–151.

23. On the early Christian *lucernarium* and its pagan parallels, in addition to the works cited in notes 17 and 22, see the numerous writings on the symbol of light by F.J. Dölger: *Die Sonne der Gerechtigkeit und der Schwarze* (LF 2 [14], Münster: Aschendorff 1918); *Sol salutis. Gebet und Gesang im christlichen Altertum, mit besonderer Rücksicht auf die Ostung in Gebet und Liturgie* (LF 4/5 [16/17], Münster: Aschendorff 1920); "Sonne und Sonnenstrahl als Gleichnis in der Logostheologie des christlichen Altertums," *AC* 1 (1929) 271–290; "Konstantin der Grosse und der Manichäismus. Sonne und Christus im Manichäismus, "*AC* 2 (1930) 301–314; several brief notes in *AC* 3 (1932) 76–79, 282; "Lumen Christi," *AC* 5 (1936) 1–43 (French trans. by M. Zemb, Paris: Cerf 1958); "Sonnengleichnis in einer Weihnachtspredikt des Bischofs Zeno von Verona. Christus als wahre und ewige Sonne," *AC* 6 (1940) 1–56. See also J. Mateos, "Quelques anciens documents sur l'office du soir," *OCP* 35 (1969) 348–351; A. Tripolitis, "*Phôs hilaron*. Ancient Hymn and Modern Enigma," *Vigiliae Christianae* 24 (1970) 190ff; A. Quacquarelli, *Retorica e liturgia antinicena* (Ricerche patristiche 1, Rome: Desclée 1960) ch. 7: "*Lux perpetua* e l'inno lucernare," 153–180. G. Winkler favors a domestic Jewish origin of the Christian lucernarium in her study "Über die Kathedralvesper in den verschiedenen Riten des Ostens und Westens," *ALW* 16 (1974) 60ff.

24. Ch. 22; P. Maraval (ed.), Grégoire de Nysse, *Vie de sainte Macrine* (SC 178, Paris: Cerf 1971) 212.

25. *De dominica oratione* 35, CSEL 3/1, 293.

26. Ch. 25; trans. G. J. Cuming, *Hippolytus. A Text for Students* (Grove Liturgical Study 8, Bramcote: Grove Books 1976) 23.

27. See Mateos, "Quelques anciens documents," 351.

28. Ch. 24:4; trans. J. Wilkinson, *Egeria's Travels* (London: SPCK 1971) 123–4.

29. Ch. 25, ed. Maraval, 226.

30. I cite the beautiful contemporary adaptation by W. G. Storey, *Morning Praise and Evensong* (Notre Dame: Fides 1973) 73.

31. *On the Holy Spirit* 29:73, PG 32, 205. In the Byzantine tradition the hymn is attributed—wrongly—to Athenogenes, an error based on a misreading of Basil. See Tripolitis, "*Phôs hilaron*" 191–3. I give further bibliography in R. Taft, "The Byzantine Office in the *Prayerbook* of New Skete: Evaluation of a Proposed Reform," *OCP* 48 (1982) 367 nos. 153–6; see also nos. 83, 97.

32. PG 80, 284.

33. Under the influence of urban monasticism there was added to the beginning of cathedral vespers the continuous psalmody of the monastic tradition. This psalmody formed a sort of common spiritual reading and meditation of the assembled community of monks or nuns. In parish celebrations most of this psalmody is omitted.

On the history of this monastic addition to Byzantine vespers, see J. Mateos, "La synaxe monastique des vêpres byzantines," *OCP* 36 (1970) 248–272. On monastic and cathedral offices and their relationship in the early Church, see my book *The Liturgy of the Hours in the Christian East* (above, note 7) and the literature cited there.

34. On the intercessions that conclude Christian synaxes see Mateos, "Quelques anciens documents" 351–9, 362–7, and R. Taft, *The Great Entrance* (OCA 200, Rome: PIO 1978$^2$) 313ff.

35. Translation adapted from *The Office of Vespers in the Byzantine Rite* (London: Darton, Longman and Todd 1965) 42–43.

36. See S. Lyonnet, "La nature du culte dans le Nouveau Testament," Y. Congar et al., *La liturgie après Vatican II* (Unam sanctum 66, Paris: Cerf 1967) 357–384; J. Mateos, *Beyond Conventional Christianity* (Manila: East Asian Pastoral Institute 1974) esp. ch. 2; and ch. 1 above.

37. The expression is borrowed from Joseph Powers, S.J.

38. See J. Murphy-O'Connor, "Eucharist and Community in First Corinthians," *Worship* 50 (1967) 370–385; 51 (1977) 56–59.

Chapter 10

# THE STRUCTURAL ANALYSIS OF LITURGICAL UNITS: AN ESSAY IN METHODOLOGY

With an admirable boldness Francophone authors will throw into the agora an inchoative theory to be gnawed on by the critics before retrieving what remains and polishing it up for a second edition. They cover their flank by calling their sallies *esquisses, jalons, essais.* The following pages are no more than that. They do not propose *the* method for studying liturgy, nor even *an* organic, complete methodology. They are simply some reflections on methods I have found fruitful in my own work. In the present state of the methodological question among the practitioners of our craft, perhaps no more can be expected.[1]

I call the method "structural" rather than "structuralist" deliberately. It owes nothing genetically to the structuralist school, but is rather my own elaboration of procedures learned by apprenticeship in what can be legitimately called the "Mateos school" of oriental liturgiology,[2] methods which are themselves an extension of Anton Baumstark's system of "comparative liturgy" later perfected by H. Engberding and others of Baumstark's school.[3]

The comparative method does, however, have something in common with structuralism: both are ways of rendering intelligible through systematizing. There is no communication without clarity, no clarity without understanding, no understanding without organization—and organization means system. Structural linguistics, for example, attempts to evolve unified systems, "intelligibility frameworks," as I call them, to uncover the structure and basic laws of how language works. That is why grammar school teachers are able to teach what a verb is, and why on a much more sophisticated level experts can reverse the process from system building to language

Adapted from *Worship* 52 (1978) 314–329.

reconstruction and rebuild extinct linguistic forms or even whole languages from their extant fragments. What Lévi-Strauss calls the "surface structure" may vary from language to language, but the "deep structure" is common—and commonality is the basis of all generalization, and the prerequisite of all system.

Lévi-Strauss has applied this type of analysis to the study of myth, and I believe it can be applied, *mutatis mutandis*, to the study of liturgy. Liturgies also have a common "deep structure"; they also operate and evolve according to certain common "laws." Moreover, both methods are "comparative," seeking to find the deep commonality underlying all individual differences that permits systematization. Finally, both systems manifest the same characteristics:[4] (1) economy of explanation; (2) unity of solution; (3) the ability to reconstruct the whole from its remaining fragments; (4) the ability to reconstruct later from earlier stages of development.

There are, however, some differences. The structuralist is seeking meaning; I am seeking primarily the structure itself. For in the history of liturgical *development*, structure outlives meaning. Elements are preserved even when their meaning is lost (conservatism), or when they have become detached from their original limited place and purpose, acquiring new and broader meanings in the process (universalization). And elements are introduced which have no apparent relationship to others (arbitrariness).

In the history of liturgical *explanation*, however, there has been a contrary shift from structure to symbolic interpretation. Most medieval liturgical commentators attended only to meaning, and their interpretations often did violence to structure. In the Reformation period structure was bent to serve theology. *Legem credendi lex statuat supplicandi*[5] was turned around, and theology determined rather than interpreted liturgical text and form. Recently more respect has been paid to history and text, but not to structure, at least among Western liturgists. In my own work I attempt to reverse this process, insisting with the structuralists on the importance of imminent analysis of the structure itself before relating it to other disciplines such as history, sociology—or even theology. These disciplines are essential for explaining the how and the whys, but prior structural analysis is necessary to recover the what.

The purpose of this method is understanding. The "structure" is simply a model that reveals how the object "works." Of course this analysis is not carried on in a vacuum. There must be a constant dialectic between structural analysis and historical research. I describe the analysis first because it is conceptually prior, if not always so in execution.

Indeed for me structural analysis is basically an aid not only to understanding, but also to historical reconstruction. Karl Popper and other philosophers of science have proposed that knowledge in a field advances not by the accumulation of new data but by the invention of new systems; not by hypothesis verification but by hypothesis negation.[6] Repetition of the same experiment under the same conditions to get the same results may be reassuring, but it does not increase our understanding one whit. What does increase it is a new intelligibility framework, as when Einstein turned Newtonian physics on its head.

If our understanding of liturgy is to advance, we too must constantly seek to bend and negate our frameworks, create new systems that will yield new understanding.[7] I am convinced that one cannot do this while ignoring history. It has become popular in recent years to accuse liturgiologists of being *just* historians (presumably an insult) and even to make the remarkable assertion that, in liturgy, the historical work has already been done. But history is talked down only by those ignorant of it. And those that think its work already done have misunderstood the nature and uses of the craft.

If there is anything that the philosophers have taught us in recent years, it is that everything, including the "exact" or natural sciences, has its history, and that so-called "scientific laws" are hypothetical constructs, products of the human mind. They do not leap out of reality before the eyes of every observer. Rather, they are *perceived structures* that change not because reality changes, but because perception does. And so history is a science not of past happenings, but of present understanding.[8] As someone has said, history is not events, but events that have become ideas—and ideas are of the present. The past does not change, but we do, which is why the work of history is always of the present, and never done.

Liturgical history, therefore, does not deal with the past, but with tradition, which is a *genetic vision of the present*, a present conditioned by its understanding of its roots. And the purpose of this history is not to recover the past (which is impossible), much less to imitate it (which would be fatuous), but to *understand liturgy* which, because it has a history, can only be understood in motion, just as the only way to understand a top is to spin it.[9]

How does structural analysis fit into all this as method? In my initial work in liturgical history it soon became apparent to me that hypothesis formation must come early in the study of any problem if one is to get anywhere. Knowledge is not the accumulation of data but the perception of relationships that permit data to be organized into intelligible patterns. The sooner one can perceive enough pattern to arrive at a working hypothesis, the quicker things will go. This is true even if the hypothesis turns out wrong. Columbus knew the world was round before he set sail—and if it hadn't been, he'd have found out soon enough. More than once I have sailed forth merrily to prove a thesis that further research and testing showed to be the opposite of the truth. No matter. Testing it is what led to the right answer, which is where I wanted to get all along.

Now in this process of hypothesis formation, I have found the structural analysis of liturgical units to be the most useful first step after the gathering of initial data. That is, I have found it preferable to identify, isolate, and hypothetically reconstruct individual liturgical structures, then trace their history as such, rather than attempt to study complete rites as a unity in each historical period. For it has been my constant observation that liturgies do not grow evenly, like living organisms. Rather, their individual elements possess a life of their own.

Instead of trying further to describe or justify this procedure conceptually, I shall simply give some examples. Taking litanies and antiphonal psalmody first, I shall try to show how I would use comparative structural analysis to reconstruct hypothetically the origin and history of those units. Then in the following chapter I shall apply the same method to solving an actual historical problem, the original shape of the Byzantine liturgy.

## 1. LITANIES

A variety of prayer forms for the intercessions or "common prayers" that traditionally concluded all Christian synaxes are still found—sometimes in muddled or debased form—in our present liturgies.

The basic primitive unit is the diaconal invitation to prayer (*Oremus*), followed by silent prayer, and concluded by a collect:

> *Deacon*: Let us pray.
> (Silent prayer).
> *Presbyter or bishop*: Collect.

It was customary, at least in some places and/or seasons, for the congregation to kneel or prostrate themselves for the period of silent prayer, then rise for the collect. We see this described for the Egyptian monastic office at the end of the fourth century by Cassian, for example.[10] In the Roman prayers this was sometimes made explicit by diaconal commands to kneel, then rise:

> *Deacon*: *Oremus*.
> *Flectamus genua*.
> (Silent prayer).
> *Levate*.
> *Priest*: Collect.

Occasionally the *Oremus* was expanded to express the intentions to be prayed for: "Oremus pro pontifice nostro N., ut Deus eum custodiat. . . ."[11]

The so-called "little litany" (*mikra synapté*) that abounds in the Byzantine tradition is a faithful remnant of this structure: (1) *Oremus*, (2) command to rise, (4) collect—to which has been added, in some instances, a commemoration of the Mother of God (3):

> *Deacon*: (1) Again and again in peace let us pray to the Lord.
> (2) Help, save, pity and preserve us, O God, by your grace.
> (3) Commemorating our most holy, most pure, most blessed and glorious Lady, the Theotokos. . . .
> *Priest*: (4) Collect.

Mateos has shown that the second member (2) is a reworking of the old command to rise (*Levate*).[12] The commemoration of the Theotokos (3) is a later addition to only some instances of the *synapté*.[13]

In the Roman and Alexandrine traditions, it was customary to repeat this basic unit (in whole or in part) for the several intentions being prayed for.[14]

Note also the literary form: the celebrant addresses prayer to God, in the name of the congregation, as minister. Or the congregation as a "priestly people" prays to God as a unit, though here this is done in silence. When the deacon speaks, he addresses not God but the congregation: "Let *us* pray."

In the fourth century sources of the non-Egyptian Eastern traditions, a new development appears: the litany. Different as it may at first seem, it is just an expansion of the primitive unit (*Oremus-*collect) still preserved in the more conservative Roman tradition. For a litany does no more than fill in with a series of expressed diaconal petitions what in the older system was a period of silent prayer. And there is abundant evidence from the *Apostolic Constitutions*, Chrysostom's homilies in Antioch and Constantinople, the *Testamentum Domini*, and Byzantine sources, that the people knelt during the litany, the last member of which included the command to rise (*Levate*).[15] The literary form remains the same: the deacon addresses the people ("For . . . let us pray to the Lord"), but in their response, if expressed, the faithful address themselves to God (*Kyrie eleison*), as does the celebrant in the concluding oration.

A further expansion can be found, for example, in the (reconstructed) prayers of the faithful in the Byzantine tradition. While the deacon was filling in the former period of silent prayer by recommending petitions to the people, the celebrant said silently an oration *pro clero* in which he prayed for the grace to do what he was about to do, that is, say the collect in the name of the people.[16] If the litany concluded a service, or was for a category about to be dismissed, the collect was followed by a greeting ("Peace to all"), diaconal command ("Bow down your heads to the Lord") and "Prayer of Inclination" or final blessing over the bowed heads of the people.[17]

The initial and indeed sufficient purpose of such analysis is simply intelligibility. But this understanding of structures can have broader implications. Not only can it provide paradigms for the reading of obscure texts and the reconstitution of debased remnants into their original shape; it can also help one identify an organic rhythm and theology of community prayer, ministerial roles, and so on, underlying the ancient structures and their literary forms.

## 2. ANTIPHONAL PSALMODY

Psalmody is another area in which this analysis can be exemplified.[18] It is generally believed that "antiphonal psalmody" means the alternation of psalm verses by the congregation or community divided into two choirs. Such alternative monastic psalmody is as a matter of fact described by some early writers such as Basil the Great.[19] But that is not antiphonal psalmody. From an analysis of the historical sources and from comparative liturgy, it appears that antiphonal psalmody was a form of cathedral (that is, nonmonastic) psalmody that evolved out of the earlier responsorial method of psalm execution.[20] The responsory consisted in having the psalm verses chanted by a soloist, the people responding to each verse with a single, set psalm verse called the response. This verse was first intoned by the soloist so that the people would know what to respond with:

*Soloist*: response
*People*: response
*Soloist*: verse 1
*People*: response
etc.

In the antiphonal elaboration of this pristine biblical form, the people are divided into two choir and respond alternately with a refrain or antiphon. The refrain is more often than not an ecclesiastical (that is, nonbiblical) composition, and the psalm ends with the *Gloria Patri*. In responsorial psalmody the response is always a psalm verse, and the psalmody does not end with the doxology.

These are the basics; within this framework all sorts of variants can be observed. Sometimes there are two soloists who alternate the psalm verses and each choir responds to its own soloist. Often a different refrain is used by each choir. If the refrain is too long to be repeated in is entirety after each verse, only its final clause, called *akroteleution* in Greek nomenclature, is used. At the beginning and end of the psalmody soloists and choirs come together to form a unit. After the *Gloria Patri* that signals the end of the psalm, a variant refrain is often substituted, called in Greek *perissé* or "appendix."[21]

Here, for example, is one form of antiphonal psalmody found in early Byzantine documents.[22]

Soloists together:  refrain (3 times)

Readers and people:  refrain (3 times)

Soloist 1:  verse 1

Choir 1:  clause (*akroteleution*)

Soloist 2:  verse 2

Choir 2:  clause

etc.

Soloist 1:  *Gloria Patri*

Choir 1:  clause or refrain

Soloists together:  refrain or *perissé*

Readers and people:  refrain or *perissé*

In almost all traditions antiphonal psalmody has decomposed, and what we are left with is the débris of the original unit. But an understanding of its original form can assist us to reconstruct the unit from its remains. One step in the decomposition process is for the choir to take over the role of the soloist. Another is for the unit itself to be abbreviated. In the Roman office this was done by suppressing the refrain except at the beginning and end of the psalm, leaving the choirs to alternate just the psalm verses (hence the present confusion between antiphonal and alternate psalmody in much Western liturgical writing). In the Eastern traditions it was more common for the two choirs to become one, and for the refrain to suffocate most or all of the scriptural element.[23] We see this, for example, in the Trisagion of the Byzantine liturgy, presently sung as follows:

1. Holy God, holy, mighty, holy, immortal, have mercy on us (3 times).
2. Glory be to the Father . . . both now and always . . .
3. Holy, immortal, have mercy on us.
4. Holy God, holy, mighty, holy, immortal, have mercy on us.

What we have here is the beginning (1) and end (2–4) of a former antiphonal psalm, including the *akroteleution* (3), with the psalm verses and their refrains entirely suppressed.[24]

Note the popular nature of this psalmody. The people respond with a fixed refrain, easily manageable. And the scriptural element, sung clearly and intelligibly by one soloist, does not succumb to choral muffling. Failure to understand these original forms has resulted in confusion between alternate psalmody, which is monastic, and antiphonal, which is popular; in the execution—often unintelligibly—of the psalm verses by choir instead of soloist, and so forth. It also results frequently in a misreading of the historical sources, especially for the liturgy of hours.

## 3. Structural Analysis and the Comparative Study of Liturgical History

Structural analysis joined to a knowledge of comparative liturgy is also of help in perceiving how liturgical units and clusters of units are articulated, how they grow, and how they decompose. I have found this sort of analysis useful in unscrambling the confused and disordered state of many extant liturgical pieces, and in reconstructing their original shape.

Liturgiologists are sometimes accused of archaism, of the "older is better" syndrome. This accusation is unjustified. The purpose of tracing things back is not to reach the most temporally remote recoverable forms and then hold them up for imitation but, once again, understanding. One seeks to go back to that point at which the unit under study emerges in its pristine integrity, before decomposition set in. Decomposition is usually provoked by later additions. Overloaded rites like overloaded circuits eventually blow a fuse. Something has to be unplugged, and in liturgical load reducing the integrity of units is rarely respected, especially if their original form is no longer understood, or if they are no longer executed as they were originally intended to be. Observing how this happens to liturgical structures tells us something not only about the past, but also about the very dynamics of liturgical growth and change.

Let us take an example from the Eucharist. In attempting to understand the history of how the eucharistic ritual in the various traditions has evolved in the prereformation period, I have developed the following intelligibility framework—what Lonergan would call, perhaps, a "heuristic structure"—as a model for understanding and organizing the disparate data which the sources yield. This of course cannot be a rigid mold. It is simply one more tool to assist in the interpretation of the data of research. The uncovering of data that contradict the framework and cannot be explained as aberrant deviations leads one to bend the framework, and understanding moves forward another step.

Initially, then, I would divide the *structural* history of the eucharistic rite into several periods:

1. In the period of initial formation, the "first stratum" of what Dix called the classical "shape of the liturgy" emerges by the middle of the second century in the *Apology* of Justin (I, 65, 67):[25]

readings
preaching
common prayers
kiss of peace
transfer of gifts
anaphora
(fraction)
communion
(dismissal)

2. After the peace of Constantine in 313, we enter a new period of structural development and enrichment, but also of unification and standardization. Enrichment was centrifugal, leading to greater diversity among families; unification was centripetal, leading to greater standardization within families. Mutual borrowing from family to family counterbalanced both these forces.

3. In a further stage of liturgical history, ritual families continued to evolve, but thenceforth as already formed and hence identifiably distinct entities with a relatively independent life of their own.

Now in spite of the great diversity in the history of the several liturgical families, common patterns of growth can be observed. For if one compares the liturgical developments in the second and third periods to Justin's "first stratum" of the eucharistic service, one sees that ligurgical evolution respected this primitive outline in the second period of liturgical growth, and violated it in the third.

The second period, the period of the unification of rites, saw a filling in of the basic common outline of the Eucharist at the three "soft points" of the service: (1) before the readings, (2) between the word service and the eucharistic prayer, and (3) at the communion and dismissal that follow this prayer. In the primitive liturgy these were points of action without words: (1) the entrance into church; (2) the kiss of peace and transfer of gifts; (3) the fraction, communion, and dismissal rites.

As ceremonial and text rush in to fill the vacuum at the three action points of the liturgy, thus overlaying the primitive shape with a "second stratum" of introit, preanaphoral, and communion rites, a contrary movement if provoked. The liturgy, thus filled out, appears overburdened and must be cut back. What characterizes this next step is the abandonment of the former respect for the primitive shape. For it is universally verifiable that the elements thus reduced or suppressed are never the later additions, but elements of the original core: the Old Testament lessons, the responsorial psalmody between the readings, the prayers after the readings, the kiss of peace, and so forth.[26]

Only an analysis of the liturgical sources from each epoch and each area of liturgical influence or center of diffusion can provide the historical details of when and whence these later additions were introduced. In the next chapter I attempt to show how this structural analysis of units can assist in the interpretation of historical sources, and in the identification and reconstruction of pristine liturgical forms. We shall see there a basic repetition of the same basic structure at all three traditional "action points" of the eucharistic liturgy: a ritual action (introit, transfer or preparation of gifts, communion), covered by an antiphonal chant, and concluded by a collect. But this is also what we find in the Roman rite, the Armenian rite, the East-Syrian rite, etc., once we strip away later accretions to the basic unit. This illustrates, I think, not only the usefulness of a structural approach in isolating the original shape and purpose of our by now rather cluttered liturgical rites, but also shows the underlying commonality of our several liturgical traditions, which in liturgiology, as in linguistics, makes comparative structural analysis possible.

I have not attempted to draw out any of the broader implications of this sort of analysis. But it can in some instances lead to a radical reinterpretation of the original meaning and purpose of liturgical units, as can be seen, I believe, in my study of the Byzantine preanaphoral rites.[27] The import of such a reinterpretation for liturgical understanding and hence for liturgical renewal is obvious. And in any case, it is a process that I believe one must go through as a prelude to hermeneutics or even to exegesis: it is impossible to interpret unless one knows what it is one is interpreting.

NOTES

1. A good discussion of the shifts in understanding of liturgiology and its purposes, with ample bibliography, can be found in A. Häussling, "Die kritische Funktion der Liturgiewissenschaft," in *Liturgie und Gesellschaft*, ed. H.-B. Meyer (Innsbruck: Tyrolia 1970) 103–130. See also Häussling's remarks in *ALW* 17–18 (1975–76) 409.

2. Juan Mateos is professor of Eastern Liturgy at the Pontifical Oriental Institute, Rome. Representative studies of this "school" can be found, for example, in the monograph series OCA published by the same institute (cf. nos. 156, 165, 166, 185, 187, 191, 193, 200), and in numerous articles in *OCP* and other journals by Arranz, Jammo, Janeras, Mateos, Taft, Van de Paverd, Winkler.

3. Baumstark's theory of comparative liturgy, elaborated in earlier studies, was first enunciated in his *Vom geschichtlichen Werden der Liturgie* (Ecclesia orans 10, Freiburg/ Breisgau: Herder 1923) and later more fully in *Comparative Liturgy* (Westminster, Maryland: Newman 1958). Engberding's major modification of Baumstark's principles resulted from his classic study, *Das eucharistische Hochgebet der Basileiosliturgie. Textgeschichtliche Untersuchungen und kritische Ausgabe* (Theologie des christlichen Ostens. Texte und Untersuchungen, Heft 1; Münster: Aschendorff 1931). Other studies of this school can be found in the series LQF (formerly LF) and in the periodical *OC*. For Baumstark's vita and bibliography, see Th. Klauser, "Anton Baumstark (1872–1948)," *Ephemerides Liturgicae* 63 (1949) 184–207; *OC* 37 (1953) 2–3.

4. Claude Lévi-Strauss; *Structural Anthropology* (New York: Basic Books 1963) 211.

5. This usually misquoted, almost always misinterpreted clause, taken out of context, has become an aphorism to express the notion—true if properly understood—that liturgy is a norm of faith. We use it here in this vulgarly accepted meaning. For its original context in the *Capitula Celestini* (it probably came from Prosper of Aquitaine, d. *ca* 463), see Mansi, 4, 461. As for its original meaning, see the discussion in M. Righetti, *Manuale di storia liturgica* I (Milano: Ancora 1964[3]) 35–36, and especially Karl Federer, *Liturgie und Glaube, Eine theologiegeschichtliche Untersuchung* (Paradosis IV, Fribourg Switzerland: Paulusverlag 1950).

6. See especially K. Popper, *Logik der Forschung* (Vienna 1935); E. tr.: *The Logic of Scientific Discovery* (New York: Hutchinson 1959); also *Conjectures and Refutations. The Growth of Scientific Knowledge* (London: Routledge and Kegan Paul 1963).

7. For an example of this see G. Kretschmar, "Recent Research on Christian Initiation," *Studia Liturgica* 12 (1977) 87–106, which challenges some of the current principles for the understanding of initiation—for example, that the fourth century catecheses represent its "classic" form; that baptism-confirmation-eucharist formed one original, three-stage rite that decomposed in the Middle Ages. What Kretschmar's study shows, once again, is not that such notions are wrong, but that they, too, are "intelligibility frameworks," ways of organizing data into understandable patterns, and not *per se* evident conclusions that fall from the tree like Newton's apple. What makes it possible to challenge and bend the framework a bit, thus advancing our under-

standing, is not some abstract process of reflection on the "theology of initiation," but new reflection on and consequent new organization of the data of history. Any "theology of initiation" that is not based on the concrete historical tradition of baptism is a delusion and a waste of time.

8. This does not mean that one is free to interpret the past in the light of present concerns, as communist historians and other sectarian ideologists do. On the contrary, the historian must "free himself from the pre-suppositions of the present in order to understand the past in its own terms." (B. Tierney, "Infallibility and the Medieval Canonists: A Discussion with Alfons Stickler," *Catholic Historical Review* 61 [1975] 271.) It is precisely in liberating ourselves from the weight of contemporary clichés and prejudices, that we can see present things in their origins and growth, and hence with a new, more objective perception.

9. In this regard, note the comments of Kretschmar (note 7 above, p. 87) on the value of theology as a practical science that determines human action: "This is particularly true and relevant where liturgiology is concerned. Even contributions to historical research, especially the far-reaching theories, are in most cases intended to clear up some contemporary problem, to explain, justify or alter the Church's practice of worship, or at least to deepen the theology of worship. It would be easy to exemplify this from many of the recent studies on the history of the baptismal liturgy."

Of course we must not expect history to tell us what present practice or doctrine should be. That would be to confuse history with theology. But history can free us from the temptation to absolutize past or present by opening up to us the changing patterns—and hence relativity—of much in our practice and doctrine. Studies of the history of baptism will not tell us whether or not we should baptize infants, but they certainly will show us that the question is to be solved by conscious pastoral decisions, and not by adhering to some absolute passed down out of a misty but inviolate past.

10. *De inst. coen.* II, 7, 1–2, ed. J.-C. Guy (SC 109, Paris: Cerf 1965) 70–73.

11. See G. G. Willis, "The Solemn Prayers of Good Friday," *Essays in Early Roman Liturgy* (Alcuin Club Collections 46; London: SPCK 1964) 1–48.

12. J. Mateos, *La célébration de la Parole dans la liturgie byzantine. Étude historique,* (OCA 191, Rome: P10 1971) 31–33; 165–166.

13. Mateos, *Célébration,* 31. For the *synapté* without this commemoration, see F. E. Brightman, *Liturgies Eastern and Western* (Oxford: Clarendon 1896) 375–376, 397.

14. See note 11 above and Brightman, *Liturgies Eastern and Western,* 121–122, 158ff, 170ff, 223ff.

15. *Ap. Const.* VIII, 10–11; ed. Funk I, 488–495; Chrysostom, *In ep. 2 ad Cor. hom.* 2, 8 and *hom. 18,* 3, PG 61, 404 and 527 (=Antioch); *In acta apost. hom* 24, 4, PG 60, 190 (=Constantinople); *Test. domini* I, 35; ed. Rahmani, 82–89. For the Byzantine sources see R. Taft, *The Great Entrance. A History of the Transfer of Gifts and other Preanaphoral Rites of the Liturgy of St. John Chrysostom,* (OCA 200, Rome: P10 1975) 325–326. Cf. J. Mateos, "Quelques anciens documents sur l'office du soir," *OCP* 35 (1969) 354ff; *Célébration,* 163ff; F. van de Paverd, *Zur Geschichte der Messliturgie in Antiocheia und Konstantinopel gegen Ende des 4. Jahrhunderts. Analyse der Quellen bei Johannes Chrysostomus* (OCA 187, Rome: P10 1970) 139, 148–149, 153–154, 157–160, 176, 197, 199–200, 205–206, 218, 220, 462–463.

16. The prayer referred to is the "First Prayer of the Faithful," (Brightman, 375–376). Cf. Mateos, *Célébration,* 57–61, 160–161, 168–173.

17. See Mateos, *Célébration,* 57ff, 169ff; "Quelques anciens documents," 354–356, 363–369; van de Paverd, *Messliturgie,* 464, 467, and "Inklinationsgebet," "Segen," in the Index; Chrysostom (in Constantinople), *In ep. ad. Col. hom. 3,* 4, PG 62, 322–323;

Egeria, *Journal* 24–25, ed. H. Pétré (SC 21, Paris: Cerf 1948) 190–194, 198–200; *Ap. Const.* VIII, 6–9 *passim* and 37, 4–7, ed. Funk I, 478–487, 546–547; Narsai, *Homily 17,* ed. R. H. Connolly, *The Liturgical Homilies of Narsai* (Texts and Studies 8/1; Cambridge: University Press 1909) 2; and various liturgies in Brightman, *Liturgies Eastern and Western,* 40, 84 (?), 266–267, 429–430.

18. For a correct analysis of antiphonal psalmody, see, for example, Mateos, *Célébration,* 7–26; Baumstark, *Nocturna laus. Typen frühchristlicher Vigilienfeier und ihr Fortleben im römischen und monastischen Ritus,* aus dem Nachlass hrsg. von O. Heiming (LQF 32, Münster: Aschendorff 1957) 124ff; H. Leeb, *Die Psalmodie bei Ambrosius* (Wiener Beiträge zur Theologie 18; Vienna: Herder 1967); Taft, *Great Entrance,* 86ff.

19. *Ep. 207,* 3, PG 32, 764; cf. J. Mateos, "L'office monastique à la fin du IV^e siècle: Antioche, Palestine, Cappadoce," *OC* 47 (1963) 83–84.

20. Baumstark, *Nocturna laus* 124.

21. Cf. Mateos, *Célébration* 13–26; Taft, *Great Entrance* 86ff. For the Greek nomenclature consult the excellent "Index liturgique" at the end of Mateos, *Le Typican de la Grande Eglise,* vol. 2 (OCA 166, Rome: P10 1963).

22. Reconstruction of Mateos (*Célébration,* 17) from C. Høeg and G. Zuntz, *Prophetologium* (Monumenta musicae byzantinae: Lectionaria, vol. I, fasc. 1; Copenhagen: E. Munksgaard 1939) 39–41. Cf. Taft, *Great Entrance* 86–87.

23. See Taft, *Great Entrance* 112ff.

24. Mateos, *Célébration* 106–114.

25. PG 6, 428–429. Justin does not mention the fraction or dismissal, but they were surely part of the original "shape."

26. Cf. Baumstark, *Comparative Liturgy* 23ff.

27. *The Great Entrance.*

Chapter 11

# HOW LITURGIES GROW.
# THE EVOLUTION OF THE
# BYZANTINE DIVINE LITURGY

In this chapter I shall try to locate the evolution of the Byzantine eucharistic liturgy within the larger context of liturgical history, using it as a "model" or "case study" with which to illustrate some of the general methodological principles enuntiated in the previous chapter.

As we saw there, after the peace of Constantine in 313, when Christian worship became the public ceremonial of a Church freed from civil restraints and fast becoming an important social force, liturgical development quickened. It is in this period that we first hear of the rite of Byzantium. Indeed, this rite can be said to characterize this stage of liturgical history. For it is the rite of the new capital of Constantine, the founding of which in 315 inaugurates the new era of Constantinian or imperial christendom.

This is the period of the unification of rites, when worship, like church government, not only evolved new forms, but also let the weaker variants of the species die out, as the Church developed, via the creation of intermediate unities, into a federation of federations of local churches, with ever-increasing unity of practice within each federation, and ever-increasing diversity of practice from federation to federation. In other words what was once one loose collection of individual local churches each with its own liturgical uses, evolved into a series of intermediate structures or federations (later called patriarchates) grouped around certain major sees. This process stimulated a corresponding unification and standardizing of church practice, liturgical and otherwise. Hence, the process of formation of rites is not one of diversification, as is usually held, but of unification. And what one finds in extant rites today is not a synthesis of all that

Revised from *OCP* 43 (1977) 355–378.

went before, but rather the result of a selective evolution: the survival of the fittest—of the fittest, not necessarily of the best.

In the medieval period these rites continue to evolve, but now as identifiably distinct liturgical families. For as Anton Baumstark wrote:

> It seems to be of the nature of Liturgy to relate itself to concrete situations of times and places. No sooner had the vast liturgical domains come into being than they began to be divided up into smaller territories whose several forms of worship were adapted to local needs.[1]

Now what one sees happening in the period of the unification of rites is a filling in of the basic, common framework of the Eucharist at what I have called the "soft points" of the service, the three points of "action without words" in the primitive structure: (1) the entrance into church, (2) the kiss of peace and transfer of gifts, and (3) the fraction, communion, and dismissal rites. What could be more natural than to develop the ceremonial of these actions, cover them with chants, and add to them suitable prayers? For one of the most common phenomena in later liturgical development is the steadfast refusal to let a gesture speak for itself.

This process often took the form of the permanent addition to the service of rites and ceremonies which in origin had an exclusively local scope in the festive or stational rites of a particular time and place. When added to the eucharistic rite as permanent, integral parts, they inevitably lose their original connection to the religious topography of their place of origin—and hence, too, their original scope and meaning—and assume a life independent of their past. This too is a common occurrence in liturgical history. It is especially noticeable in the rites derived from cities where liturgy was stational: Rome, Jerusalem, and Constantinople, the three most important centers of liturgical diffusion in the period after Chalcedon (451).

But as the liturgy thus acquires a "second stratum" of introit, preanaphoral, communion, and dismissal rites, a contrary movement is provoked. The liturgy thus filled out appears overburdened, and must be cut back. But in this pruning it is never the later, secondary, often questionable additions that are reduced or suppressed, but elements of the primitive "shape."

## 1. THE BYZANTINE DIVINE LITURGY: GENERAL TRAITS

For our purposes here, I shall limit myself to the period extending from the end of the fourth century until the beginning of the sixteenth. From the end of the fourth because the writings of John Chrysostom, bishop of Constantinople from 397–404, are our first witness to the liturgical uses of Constantine's new capital; to the beginning of the sixteenth because the first printed edition of our liturgy appeared in 1526, and it was the printing press rather than the intervention of bishop, synod, or liturgical commission, that was responsible for the final unification of liturgical usage in the Byzantine East.

Of course one must not picture this unification in rigid, Tridentine categories, for in the East there is no such thing as a "typical" liturgical book, i.e. an official liturgical text obligatory on all. Nor did the advent of printing mark the end of growth and local adaptation. But since then the developments are so easy to trace that liturgical history ceases to be a scholarly problem and so becomes relatively uninteresting except as a mirror of local customs, minor variations on an already well-known theme.

The Byzantine Divine Liturgy can be characterized as the eucharistic service of the Great Church—of Hagia Sophia, the cathedral church of Constantinople—as formed into an initial synthesis in the capital by the tenth century, and then modified by later monastic influence. This is not a truism, to say that the Byzantine Eucharist is the rite of Constantinople. There is nothing "Roman" about much of the Roman rite, and nothing "Byzantine" about much of the present Byzantine Divine Office, which comes from the monasteries of Palestine, and replaced the Office of the Great Church after Constantinople fell to the Latins in the Fourth Crusade (1204).

To the Westerner onlooker, perhaps the most striking quality of the rite that has evolved from the Eucharist of the Great Church is its opulent ritualization, a ceremonial splendour heightened by its marked contrast to the sterile verbalism of so much contemporary Western liturgy, where worship often seems just words. The Byzantine ritual is structured around a series of appearances of the sacred ministers from behind the iconastasis or sanctuary barrier.

The most important of the appearances are the two solemn introits. The minor introit or "Little Entrance" of the Word service, after the opening rite of the enarxis, is a procession with the Gospel, said to symbolize Christ's coming to us in the Word. The other, major or "Great Entrance" at the beginning of the eucharistic part of the service, right after the intercessory prayers following the readings, is a procession bearing to the altar the gifts of bread and wine prepared before the beginning of the liturgy. It is said to prefigure Christ's coming to us in the sacrament of his body and blood. Both these foreshadowings are fulfilled in two later appearances, the procession of the deacon with the Gospel lectionary to the ambo for the reading; and the procession of the celebrant to distribute in communion the consecrated gifts, after they have been blessed in the eucharistic prayer.

Most of the ritual is taken up with such comings and goings. But liturgy is not ceremonial. It is prayer. And so these ceremonies are the ritual expression of a text. In the present-day Byzantine rite the liturgical formulae comprise two distinct levels. While the deacon stands outside the doors of the iconostasis chanting the litanies and leading the people in prayer, within the sanctuary a parallel service is proceeding. Through the open doors of the icon screen the altar is distantly visible, brilliantly lighted and enveloped in clouds of incense, impressing upon the worshiper a sense of mystery and sacredness. Before this altar, within the holy of holies, stands the celebrant, his back to the people as he faces East, reciting in silence the priestly prayers. When the priest has to bless or address the people he comes out. Inside he is talking to God.

This ritual pattern is the result of centuries of slow evolution, in which many rites, at first added for a specific purpose, later lost their original scope, then decomposed under the pressure of later changes and additions, acquiring in the process new mystagogic interpretations often far removed from their actual historical roots.

## 2. THE ENARXIS

There are many ways in which one can approach the history of how this came about. My own approach is structural and historical, that is, I try to identify and isolate individual liturgical structures or units, then trace their history as such, rather than attempt to study the entire rite as a unity in each historical period. For as I said in chapter 10, liturgies do not grow evenly like a healthy living organism. Rather, their individual structures possess a life of their own. More like cancer than native cells, they can appear like aggressors, showing riotous growth at a time when all else lies dormant. Let us see how this happened in the Byzantine tradition.

I shall prescind from the elaborate Rite of the Prothesis or preparation of bread and wine that precedes the liturgy. With the exception of the Prothesis Prayer or prayer of offering, it began to evolve only in the eighth century, largely as a result of monastic influence.

More important is the enarxis that introduces the Liturgy of the Word. Today the reading of the epistle is preceded by an office of three antiphons, each with its litany and collect. The minor introit takes place during the singing of the third antiphon. This entrance is also accompanied by a collect, the Prayer of the Entrance, said outside the central doors of the iconostasis before the procession enters to the altar. There follow various troparia or refrains, and then the Trisagion chant with its accompanying prayer, giving us the following structure:

Initial blessing
Litany and prayer I
Antiphon I
Litany and prayer II
Antiphon II
Litany and prayer III
Antiphon III with added troparia (refrains), entrance procession, entrance prayer
Trisagion prayer and chant
Procession to the throne
Greeting: "Peace to all".

During the Trisagion the celebrants proceed to the throne behind the altar for the readings. With this procession to the throne we rejoin the primitive introit of the liturgy as described in the homilies of Chrysostom at the end of the fourth century: the clergy enter the church together with the people, and proceed directly to the throne in the apse. There the bishop greets the people with "Peace to all", then sits down for the readings; no antiphons, no litanies, no prayers, nothing. But by the time of our earliest manuscript of the Byzantine liturgy, the eighth century codex *Barberini 336*,[2] we already have our enarxis almost as it is today. Where did it come from?

First of all, we can see at a glance that the enarxis is made of up later, secondary additions to the liturgy, for its formulae are all common to the liturgies of Chrysostom and Basil, which are independent only from the prayer over the catechumens.[3] Now any time we see common elements in two liturgies, it is obvious that they went from one formulary to the other, or were introduced to both simultaneously from some third source after they had begun to share a common history as variant liturgical formularies of the same local church, to whose liturgical shape the both were thenceforth made to conform.

### a) The litany:

Let us look at the liturgical units of this enarxis.[4] We can dispense immediately with the opening blessing; it does not appear until the eleventh century.[5] The initial litany is also out of place. In our primitive shape such intercessions occur only after the readings, thus safeguarding the priority of the divine action in the order of service: only after God speaks to us his Word do we respond in psalmody and prayer. As a matter of fact our litany was once found just before the transfer of gifts. Its remains are still visible there in the vulgate recension of the Slavonic books.[6]

But following a tendency observable in almost all liturgical traditions, these intercessions were either suppressed or moved up to the beginning of the Liturgy of the Word. Thus, in the tenth and eleventh century sources of our liturgy we find this litany in its original place before the transfer of gifts, and also after the Little Entrance, just before the enarxis was added. By the end of the eleventh century it is found also before the antiphons, i.e. at the new beginning. In the twelfth century it disappears from its original place in the prayers of the faithful; in the thirteenth it disappears before the Trisagion, remaining only where we still find it today.[7]

So our litany is really the original litany of the faithful of the Byzantine mass. The two abbreviated litanies that accompany the prayers of antiphons II and III are probably just a development of the original *oremus* of the two collects they now accompany.

*b) The antiphons:*

What about these three antiphons and their collects? Where did they come from, and when were they added to the liturgy? The when is easy: some time between 630 and 730 A.D. There is no mention of them in the *Mystagogy* of Maximus Confessor written about 630.[8] As he describes it, the liturgy begins with the entrance into church of the people with the bishop, followed immediately by the readings. Now until at least the eleventh century the bishop was not present in church for the enarxis but entered only at the Little Entrance.[9] Obviously, then, there was no enarxis in the time of Maximus. But just one century later our next Byzantine liturgical commentary, the *Historia ecclesiastica* of Patriarch St. Germanus I (d. *ca.* 730), does mention the antiphons.[10] So they first appear at the beginning of the eighth century.

But this does not mean that they are a permanent fixture at that time. Liturgies tend to be snobbish. They take their time about accepting newcomers as permanent members. Even as late as the tenth century the three antiphons had not yet won a permanent place as a fixed part of every mass.[11]

Our main source for the history of how they did win it is the tenth century Typicon of the Great Church edited by Juan Mateos, S.J. of the Pontifical Oriental Institute in Rome.[12] This crucial document has provided the key to almost the whole history of the Byzantine liturgy in the post-Justinian era. A typicon is not used in the actual celebration of the liturgy, but provides the directions for the correct use of the books that are, indicating the proper of mass and office, and giving, like the old *ordines romani*, detailed rubrics for special celebrations that occur in the liturgical cycle.

Now in the tenth century typicon of Hagia Sophia we see that the liturgy of New Rome, like that of Old Rome, was highly stational in character. On many days in the church calendar the liturgy was celebrated not just anywhere, but in some specially designated church. This church was the "station" of the day, and on more solemn feasts the crowd would gather with the clergy at some other sanctuary and process solemnly from there to the stational church for the liturgy. During the procession an antiphonal psalm would be chanted. Upon arrival at the station, the end of the antiphon would be signalled by intoning the *Gloria patri* that announces the conclusion of antiphonal psalmody in almost every tradition, followed by the final repetition of the antiphon or refrain, called the περισσὴ or "appendix". Sometimes a variant refrain would be substituted at the *perisse*.

The clergy recited the introit prayer before the doors of the nave—not before the doors of the sanctuary chancel as now—and then entered the church, followed by the people. Proceeding past the great ambo in the center of the nave, they went along the solea or walled-in processional way that extended from the sanctuary to the ambo,[13] and took their places at the synthronon in the apse.

All this is almost the same as the opening of the contemporary Roman stational mass described in the *Ordo romanus primus* about 750 A.D. even to the entrance along a walled-in processional way, the so-called *schola cantorum* which Mathews has shown to be an exact parallel to the old Byzantine solea.[14] To the best of my knowledge this surprising similarity between two liturgies presently so different in structure and ethos has never been noticed by the students of liturgy. It is but one more indication of the commonality of much in early liturgy, showing again the validity of the comparative method of liturgiology first formulated by Anton Baumstark (d. 1948) half a century ago.[15]

I have already noted that the three base-traditions—Rome, Constantinople, Jerusalem—out of which have come the only two universal rites of Christendom, the Roman and the Byzantine, were all distinguished by their stational character. It is not an exaggeration to say that practically every addition to the Byzantine Eucharist from Justinian until the post-iconoclastic period had its origin in the stational rites of Constantinople. The antiphons will be our first example.

The old typicon tells us that on some feasts, on the way to the stational church, the stational procession would stop either in the forum or in some church along the processional route for a rogation. On some days this prayer-service included an office of three antiphons. After this rogation the procession would continue on to the stational church, to the accompaniment of the usual processional antiphon.

But evidently the office of three antiphons was very popular, because it soon became customary to celebrate it in church before the liturgy on days when there was no stational procession. Here we see an example of a liturgical unit gradually detaching itself from the service in which it originated and becoming an integral part of another service.

Note however that these three antiphons celebrated in church before nonstational liturgies were a combination of the three rogation antiphons with a fourth antiphon, the processional antiphon to the church. For example, in the typicon for New Year's Day— September 1, at that time—there are two liturgies prescribed, one in the Church of the Theotokos in Chalkoprateia, one in Hagia Sophia.[16] The one in Chalkoprateia was stational, preceded by an office of three antiphons in the forum, followed by the procession to Chalkoprateia for mass to the accompaniment of another, fourth antiphon. But the liturgy in Hagia Sophia in memory of St. Stephen the Stylite begins right there with an office of three antiphons. And at the third antiphon two refrains, that of the saint, and that of the fourth processional antiphon from the stational service of Chalkoprateia, are both sung. What they have done is simply fuse together the third antiphon of the devotional service with the introit antiphon, probably because three antiphons, not four, was the customary liturgical unit in the office of the Great Church. So the rogational office of three antiphons and the introit antiphon are two different things, which explains why today we have four orations— three antiphon prayers plus an introit prayer—with only three antiphons.

Up until the tenth century the three antiphons were not a necessary part of every liturgy. Even after this date the patriarch still does not enter the church until the third antiphon,[17] because this is the old introit of the liturgy, as we saw above. And even today vigil masses in the Byzantine rite, in which mass is preceded by vespers, have no antiphons at all but begin with the Trisagion. It is said that in such masses, vespers replace the Liturgy of the Word. They replace nothing, but are joined to the mass at its old beginning, the Trisagion, thus illustrating Baumstark's law that older usages are preserved in more solemn seasons and rites.[18]

Today the three antiphons have been reduced to a few scraps of their original form, and the troparia after the third antiphon have been so multiplied as to take on an independent existence detached from the psalmody which they were originally destined to serve as refrains. This exemplifies another common development in liturgical history: the process whereby eccelsiastical compositions multiply and eventually suffocate the scriptural element of a liturgical chant, forcing, in turn, the decomposition of the original liturgical unit, so that what we are left with is simply débris, bits and scraps of this and that, a verse here, a refrain there, that evince no recognizable form or unity until they are painstakingly reconstituted into their original structures by piecing together the remaining scraps, then filling in the blanks, sort of like doing a jig-saw puzzle with only a tenth of the pieces[19]. This is why the study of liturgical units and their mutual articulation within larger ritual structures is so crucial in the reconstruction of pristine liturgical forms.

### c) The Trisagion:

We see another example of this in our next piece, the Trisagion. Today it is chanted as follows:

> Holy God, holy, mighty, holy, immortal, have mercy on us
> (three times).
> Glory be to the Father . . . now and always and unto ages of
> ages, amen.
> Holy, immortal, have mercy on us.
> Holy God, holy, mighty, holy, immortal, have mercy on us.

From what we said above in chapter 10, section 2, about the structure of Byzantine antiphonal psalmody, it seems that we have here the *incipit* and *finale* of an antiphonal psalm, i.e. the opening triple repetition of the complete refrain, then the concluding doxology, the ἀκροτελεύτιον, and final repetition of the refrain (*perisse*), with the intervening psalm verses suppressed.[20] Now we first hear of the Trisagion in the fifth century, when it was apparently used as a processional antiphon during stational services in Constantinople.[21] Early in the sixth century we see it at the beginning of mass. This chant, then, is the remains of the original, invariable introit antiphon of our mass, to which at a later date first one, then three variable antiphons were appended.

So at the beginning of the fifth century our liturgy opened with the entrance of the clergy and people into church without ceremony or, apparently, accompanying chant. By the sixth century this introit had been ritualized by the addition of an element from the stational processions, an antiphonal psalm with the Trisagion as its fixed refrain. About a century later, undoubtedly as a result of further developments in the stational rites, all but the refrain of this antiphon was suppressed in favor of a more recent stational antiphon that provided more variety for this rapidly expanding rite.

Why wasn't the original fixed refrain just suppressed, or retained as an occasional variant? Probably because of its immense popularity as testified to by the legends of its origins in divine revelation, because it had become a liturgical element common throughout the whole East, and because of the role it played in the Monophysite controversy.

### d) *The ektene:*

One further element that entered the liturgy from the stational services is the ektene or litany that immediately follows the Gospel. It is sometimes referred to in modern versions as the "ecumenic" or "universal" prayer for all needs—i.e. the *oratio fidelium* of the Byzantine mass. It is no such thing, as should be obvious from its position *before* the dismissal of the catechumens. Common prayer with their participation was excluded, which is why they were first dismissed, and not because they mustn't receive communion, as is often thought. They were also dismissed at non-eucharistic services, where there was no risk of them going to communion. In our tenth century typicon this ektene or penitential litany was chanted after the Gospel in stational rogation services, and rubrics prescribe the same practice after the Gospel of the Liturgy of the Word on certain days of the year.[22] This can be taken perhaps as a remnant of a previous stage of evolution when this litany was gradually gaining a foothold in the mass, where it appears for the first time in the eighth century codex *Barberini 336.*

## 3. REGRESSIVE TRAITS

Meanwhile the regressive evolution whereby primitive elements were suppressed in favor of later additions is proceeding. By the eighth century the Old Testament reading,[23] the prayers over the penitents,[24] and elements of the psalmody have been suppressed,[25] and the prayer of blessing that concluded the Liturgy of the Word in the time of Chrysostom has been displaced.[26] By the eleventh century the litany of the faithful has shifted forward.

The disappearane from the Liturgy of the Word of its final blessing illustrates another common liturgical development in this period: the gradual blurring of the clear division between the Liturgies of Word and Eucharist. The present prayers of the faithful of the Liturgy of Basil are another example of this. They are really prayers of preparation for the Eucharist, and certainly are not original to the Liturgy of the Word. In the same process, the kiss of peace, formerly the conclusion of the Word service,[27] becomes detached from the concluding prayers of the synaxis and moved to before the anaphora by the addition of later ritual elements between the *pax* and the end of the Liturgy of the Word.

## 4. THE PREANAPHORA

These later elements are the preanaphoral rites that now precede the eucharistic prayer.[28] They comprise:

> The Cherubic Hymn
> Prayer of the Cherubic Hymn ("No one is worthy . . . ")
> Incensation
> Transfer and deposition of gifts
> *Orate fratres* dialogue
> Litany and Prayer of the Proskomide
> Kiss of Peace
> Nicene Creed

The persistent attempt to interpret Eastern preanaphoral rites in Western terms of "offertory" have vitiated all understanding of what we are dealing with here. The primitive nucleus common to the Eastern and Western preanaphora was the simple, unritualized transfer of gifts to the altar by the deacons. In some Western liturgies this did evolve later into rites of offering. Attempts to read Eastern evidence in the same way have proved fruitless. My own analysis of the formulae of the preanaphora in the Eastern traditions has forced me to conclude that the "offertory" paradigm is not the model to be used in interpreting these rites. Ideas of offering do find expression, especially in later prayers, but they are not the dominant theme. And in the Liturgy of St. John Chrysostom they find no place whatever in the primitive layer of the rite. In the earliest sources of this liturgy, we find only three elements:

1) the transfer, deposition, and covering of the gifts by the deacons
2) an oration said by the priest
3) the Cherubic Hymn sung by the people during the whole liturgical action.

It is probable that the deposition of gifts included an incensation of the altar, and that the prayer was preceded by a *lavabo* and by a brief dialogue between the presiding bishop and his concelebrating presbyters, similar to the Roman *Orate fratres*.

From this original simplicity the nature and scope of the Byzantine preanaphoral rites emerge. They form a twofold preparation for the anaphora:

1) the material preparation of altar and gifts
2) the spiritual preparation of the ministers by prayer, and of the people by a chant evoking the dispositions appropriate to the imminent eucharistic offering.

*a) The Great-Entrance Procession:*

The material preparation of the gifts in the Byzantine tradition has become highly ritualized into the Great Entrance procession, in which today even the presbyters take part. But this must not be allowed to obscure its humble origins in the transfer of gifts by the deacons, originally a material act of no ritual import whatever. Formerly the Great Entrance was a true entrance into the church from outside, for the deacons had to fetch the gifts from the sacristy or skeuophylakion, which in Constantinople was not an auxiliary chamber inside the church, but a separate edifice like the baptistry and campanile of so many Italian churches.[29] Hence, the Byzantine Liturgy of the Eucharist, like the Liturgy of the Word, once began with an introit into the church. In both cases the entrance later degenerated into a non-functional procession around the inside of the church that ends where it begins, in the sanctuary. Here we have a perfect example of rites which perdure, supported by newly acquired symbolic meanings, long after they have become detached from their original practical purpose.[30]

*b) Preparation of the Ministers:*

While the deacons were bringing in the gifts, the presiding minister washed his hands, requested the prayers of his fellow ministers, then together with them said the following Prayer of the Proskomide:

> O Lord God almighty, who alone are holy, who alone accept the sacrifices of praise from those that call upon you with a whole heart, accept also the prayer of us sinners, and bring us to your holy altar, and enable us to present to you these gifts and spiritual sacrifices for our own sins and for the faults of the people, and make us worthy to find favor in your sight, so that our sacrifice may be acceptable to you and so that the good spirit of your grace may rest upon us and upon these present gifts and upon all your people.

The prayer asks for three things:

1) that the ministers be conducted to the altar,
2) that they be enabled to offer there the Eucharist,
3) that they be made worthy so that this offering will be acceptable, and the Spirit come.

It is not a prayer of offering but a prayer of preparation for the true offering, the anaphora. It is a prayer of *accessus ad altare* in which the ministers pray God to make them worthy of the ministry they are about to perform. It exists only in function of what is to follow, a pattern also seen in the two prayers of the faithful. In the first, the ministers pray for the grace to intercede for their people, i.e. for the grace to say the intercessory collect that immediately follows.

But since our preanaphoral oration is entitled "Prayer of the Offering" (Εὐχὴ τῆς προσκομιδῆς) it is almost always misinterpreted and mistranslated—understandably so. Actually, this is not the title of the prayer, but of the whole eucharistic rite of which this prayer was but the first formula, a fact that was later obscured by the addition of numerous other elements to the preanaphora before this title.[31]

*c) The Entrance Chant:*

While all this is going on, the people are chanting the Cherubicon,[32] a refrain that was a ded to the liturgy under Justin II in 573–4 A.D.. Today this troparion stands alone, but from what we know of the history of liturgical chant this cannot have been its original form. In the early centuries a free-standing liturgical song, i.e. a non-scriptural composition sung independently, was a rarity, at least after the second century, when reaction to heretical Gnostic *psalmoi idiotikoi*—private, i.e. non-scriptural, compositions—apparently tended to limit liturgical chant to some form of biblical psalmody. At any rate before the sixth century there is no evidence that ecclesiastical songs ever had an independent existence in the eucharistic liturgy except in the anaphora, even if the Divine Office knew such hymns as the *Phôs hilaron*.[33] In the Eucharist such compositions served only as refrains to be repeated after the verses of a psalm. And in fact the historical evidence seems to indicate that the Cherubicon was added to or replaced an earlier antiphonal psalm at the transfer of gifts, Ps 23(24):7–10 with alleluia as refrain.

So the Byzantine liturgy had an introit antiphon not only with its first entrance, just like the Roman *antiphona ad introitum*; it also had one with its second entrance, like the Roman *antiphona ad offertorium*. The later degeneration of the psalmody has obscured its original form, but the parallel in both cases is exact.

The object of the chant, however, has often been viewed too narrowly, because the misinterpretation of one word has appeared to restrict its meaning to the entrance of the gifts. The chant reads as follows:

> We who mystically represent the Cherubim and sing the thrice-holy hymn to the life-giving Trinity, let us lay aside all worldly care to receive the King of All escorted unseen by the angelic hosts. Alleluia.

The phrase "to receive the King of All" is usually taken to mean "to welcome Christ entering now in the procession under the symbols of bread and wine". But ὑποδέχομαι means *receive in communion*, as can be seen not only from Byzantine liturgical terminology but also in the *Protheoria* (1085–95), the earliest Byzantine commentary to interpret the phrase.[34] So the chant does not refer only to the procession, but is an introduction to the whole eucharistic action from anaphora to communion. It instructs the faithful that they who are about to sing the thrice-holy hymn of the Cherubim (the *Sanctus* of the anaphora) must lay aside all worldly care (*Sursum corda*) to prepare to receive Christ (in communion).

A study of numerous other Eastern hymns for the transfer of gifts has confirmed this conclusion: they are not offertory chants, nor merely processional antiphons, but are introductions to the whole eucharistic service, and serve to instill in the faithful the sentiments appropriate to the action about to begin. Thus understood, the Great-Entrance chant assumes a broader, more balanced liturgical role, tempering the exaggerated symbolic importance assigned in the later medieval period to the Great-Entrance procession itself. At the entrance we indeed welcome the gifts, symbol of Christ—but only with a view to their consecration and reception in communion.

### d) Creed and Pax:[35]

I do not intend to trace the origins of the numerous other, lesser formulae that have been added to the preanaphora since the Middle Ages, but two older elements must be mentioned. The first, the creed, stands somewhat outside the scope of these rites. It was added during the Monophysite crisis in the sixth century, and drew with it some lesser formulae that have obsured the second rite, the kiss of peace. This fraternal greeting, an original member of the primitive shape, has since the eleventh century been exchanged only by the clergy. As we mentioned previously, its original purpose was to conclude the service of the Word.

### 5. COMMUNION RITES

The third "soft point" of the eucharistic rite includes the rites and prayers that follow the consecration of the gifts:

Litany and prayer
Our Father
Prayer of Inclination
Prayer of Elevation
Elevation: "Holy things for the holy".

Chant: "One is holy . . . "
κοινωνικὸν (*communio*)
Manual acts (fraction, etc.)
Communion
Blessing with gifts: "O God, save your people and bless your
    inheritance."
Chant: "We have seen the true light . . . "
Gifts returned to altar, incensed.
"Always, now and forever, and unto ages of ages."
Chant: "Amen. May our mouth be filled . . . "
Gifts returned to altar of preparation.
Litany and Prayer of Thanksgiving.

It may seem strange to skip over what is clearly the most important
prayer of the whole rite, the eucharistic prayer itself, but the
anaphora has undergone little *ritual* evolution, and the *textual*
modifications it exhibits would require a close analysis of the Greek
text that is hardly feasible here. So I shall pass directly to the
communion rites after mentioning that the anaphora of Chrysostom
shows clear signs of reworking in several places. The mere fact that
there is no command to repeat ("Do this in memory of me"), and that
the commemoration of the dead precedes that of the living,[36] is
extraordinary and most problematic.

a) *The Litany and Prayer before Communion*:

After the doxology that concludes the anaphora, there is a long
litany comprising two distinct sets of petitions. A similar litany is
found with the Prayer of the Proskomide, just before the anaphora. A
textual comparison of this litany with the parallel litanies in the
Liturgy of James and the Armenian liturgy shows, I believe, that the
second series of petitions, the so-called αἰτήσεις ("demands") in
Byzantine terminology, is a later addition, from the Divine Office.[37]

I have not yet made up my mind as to which of the two prayers
that now come before and after the Our Father is older, but it is most
probable that only one of them is original at this point of the liturgy.
The Our Father itself is not found in the eucharistic liturgy of even
such late fourth-century documents as the *Apostolic Constitutions* VIII,
13 or *Homily 16*, 21–22 of Theodore of Mopsuestia.[38] Our first
positive evidence of it before communion in a eucharistic liturgy
seens to by Cyril of Jerusalem (*ca.* 348), *Mystagogic Cathechesis 5*, 11–

18.[39] Somewhat later Augustine claims that "almost the whole Church now concludes" the eucharistic prayer with the Our Father.[40] Chrysostom witnesses to it in the Eucharist at Constantinople at the turn of the century (397–404),[41] but it could not have been there for long. Previous to its introduction into the rites of preparation before communion, the Byzantine Eucharist may have followed the structure seen in the *Apostolic Constitutions* VIII, 13, 3–14: anaphora, litany, prayer, "Holy things for the holy."[42]

Mateos thinks that the Prayer of Inclination after the Our Father in the Chrysostom formulary of today's Byzantine Divine Liturgy was originally the final prayer of the faithful which, as we saw above, was also a concluding Prayer of Inclination.[43] Against this is the weight of comparative liturgy: some Prayer of Inclination is witnessed to for the Constantinopolitan Eucharist by Chrysostom,[44] there is a parallel formula in the mass described by Theodore of Mopsuestia,[45] and the text of the present Byzantine prayer is not unlike that of the prayer before "Holy things for the holy!" in *Apostolic Constitutions* VIII, 13, 10.[46]

So all we can say with certainty is that the Our Father is a later addition, and that previous to its introduction the litany just before communion may have been followed by only one prayer. As for the Elevation Prayer that now follows the Prayer of Inclination, it is common to the liturgies of both Chrysostom and Basil, and we know that it is a later addition.[47]

*b) The Communion Antiphon:*

More problematic are the three chants that now accompany communion. At present they are a complete structural mess, which of course betrays their youth: primitive liturgy was tidy if nothing else. Let us see if we can reconstruct their original shape. Presently the communion rites look like this. After the Our Father, Prayer of Inclination, and Prayer of Elevation, we see:

1. *Deacon:* "Let us be attentive!"
2. *Priest:* "Holy things for the holy."
3. *People:* "One [is] holy, one Lord, Jesus Christ, to the glory of God the Father. Amen."
4. *People:* koinônikon *(communio),* variable psalm verse with triple alleluia.

5. Manual acts (fraction, etc.).

6. Communion, with accompanying formulae.

7. *Priest*: (blessing people with chalice): "O God, save your people and bless your inheritance."

8. *People*: "We have seen the true light, we have received the heavenly spirit, we have found the true faith, worshiping the undivided Trinity, that has saved us." (During this chant the gifts are returned to the altar, prepared for removal, and incensed, with accompanying formulae.)

9. *Priest*: (silently) "Blessed is our God (aloud) always, now and ever, and unto ages of ages."

10. *People*: "Amen. May our mouth be filled with your praise, O Lord, because you have made us worthy to partake of your holy, immortal and most pure mysteries, so that we may sing your glory, meditating all day on your justice, alleluia, alleluia, alleluia." (During this chant the gifts are removed to the prothesis or place of preparation.)

11. Litany and prayer of thanksgiving after communion.

An initial analysis of the three chants in question (nos. 4, 8, 10) would lead one to suspect that the present overloaded ritual structure is the result of later additions that followed the degeneration of an original unit. In the first place, we saw that freestanding ecclesiastical chants such as 8 and 10 are unknown in the eucharistic rite outside the anaphora before the sixth century (*circa*). Such texts, had no independent existence, but served rather as refrains (antiphons) for the psalms.

From comparative liturgy we know that most rites had antiphonal psalmody at the three "soft points" of the service: the introit, the offertory or preanaphora, and the communion.[48] Furthermore, it has already been established that the Byzantine Eucharist once had an antiphonal psalm at the lesser and probably also at the major introit (preanaphora).[49] So there is a strong presumption in favor of the same at communion.

Hence it would seem that the remainder of the original unit is to be found in the single psalm verse with alleluia that still bears the title "*koinônikon*" (4), exact parallel of the Latin term *communio* (=*antiphona ad communionem*). Almost certainly, this was once a complete psalm.

A bit of rummaging about in the historical evidence will support this hypothesis, and fill in the missing pieces. According to the *Chronicon paschale* for A.D. 624, in that year under Patriarch Sergius I of Constantinople (610–638) a refain was added to the *koinônikon*.

From this source, it is evident that in the seventh century the *koinônikon* included more than one verse of a psalm:

> In this year [624] in the month of Artemesius—May according to the Romans—on the 12th indiction, under Patriarch Sergius of Constantinople, it was decided that after all have received the Holy Mysteries, when the clergy are about to return to the skeuophylakion the precious ripidia, patens and chalices, and other sacred vessels; and after the distribution of communion from the side tables everything is brought back to the holy altar; and finally, after the chanting of the final verse of the koinonikon; this troparion be sung: "May our mouth be filled with your praise, O Lord . . . .[50]

From this it is clear that:

1) the *koinônikon* was not just one psalm verse with alleluia as refrain, but an entire psalm;
2) the refrain "May our mouth be filled with your praise . . . " was added as a variant *perisse* or concluding refrain to be chanted after the doxology of the psalm;
3) the phrase "Always, now and ever, and unto ages of ages" that the priest now sings to introduce this refrain is simply the remains of that same doxology.

And in fact a study of the manuscript tradition reveals that the intervening material we find today between the communion verse (4) and the remains of the doxology (9) is a later addition not found in any source earlier than the twelfth century, including the clause "Blessed is our God" that has been appended to the finale of the doxology ("Always, now and ever . . . ") to give it some sense (9). So what we have is the débris of what was once a complete unit of psalmody. What remains is its beginning and end, with a lot of later freefloating bits and pieces added after the original unit had come unstuck in the degenerative process already observed with regard to the original antiphonal psalmody at the Little and Great Entrances. Any time such scraps of verse and chant pop up in liturgy, they are either the débris of a degenerated liturgical unit, or detached elements added in the later period when folks had forgotten what psalmody was all about.

But was this psalmic unit originally antiphonal, as would appear from the presence of the doxology and concluding *perisse* troparion? The use of non-scriptural refrains at the *koinônikon* in the tenth century Typicon of the Great Church and in later usage—e.g. "Receive the Body of Christ" and "At your Mystical Supper"—would seem to confirm this view.[51] For in Byzantine usage the concluding doxology and such non-biblical refrains are characteristic of antiphonal psalmody.[52] In responsorial psalmody the response was a verse of Scripture—usually a psalm verse—or alleluia.[53]

But Thomas H. Schattauer's exhaustive analysis of the entire corpus of *koinônika* or communion verses in the tenth century Typicon shows that these verses are the original responses to the communion psalm, which therefore must have once been a responsory and not an antiphon.[54] This agrees with our earliest historical evidence for psalmody at communion in Cyril of Jerusalem, *Mystagogic Catechesis* 5, 20,[55] the *Apostolic Constitutions* VIII, 13, 16–17,[56] and John Chrysostom's exposition of Ps 144.[57] From Chrysostom's description it is clear that the psalm sung during communion at Antioch was responsorial, and although Cyril's text is not explicit, later hagiopolite sources confirm the same for Jerusalem, as Helmut Leeb has shown.[58] This must have been true also for the *Apostolic Constitutions* from the environs of Antioch though not from the metropolis itself,[59] since all these late fourth century sources antedate the introduction of antiphonal psalmody into the eucharistic liturgy at the introit and preanaphora.[60]

So we can only conclude that the Byzantine *koinônikon* was originally a responsorial psalm later "antiphonalized" by the introduction of a concluding doxology and *perisse*, and by the substitution of ecclesiastical compositions for the *responsorium* on certain days. The appearance of such hybrid structures in later liturgical development should not surprise us. Leeb has shown that the same thing occurred with the communion responsory in the Eucharist of Jerusalem.[61]

The Prayer of Thanksgiving after communion is parallel to the *postcommunio* of the Roman mass. The accompanying litany, like similar developments elsewhere in the Byzantine and other traditions, is just an expanded *oremus* as explained in ch. 10.

So one sees at communion a repetition of the same basic structure that emerged in the analysis of the other two "action points" of the liturgy, the two entrances: the structure comprises a ritual action, covered by the chanting of psalmody, and concluded by a collect—just as in the Roman Rite.

## 6. The Dismissal

The conclusion of the liturgy is clear enough. It goes as follows:

"Let us depart in peace."
"In the name of the Lord."
Prayer Behind the Ambo
Ps. 112:2 ("Blessed be the name of the Lord . . . ") thrice.
Prayer in the Skeuophylakion
Blessing
Apolysis

The original final blessing prayer, the so-called "Prayer behind the Ambo (ὀπισθάμβωνος), was probably said from the great ambo in the center of the nave as the clergy processed down the solea or processional path on their way out of the church to the skeuophylakion at the end of the service. One more prayer, the "Prayer in the Skeuophylakion," was said in the skeuophylakion at the consummation of the left-over gifts, thus rounding off the liturgy just as it began, with a prayer over the gifts in the sacristy.

What follows this prayer in today's rite is the traditional ending of the Byzantine monastic office, which was added to the mass as a second conclusion, in the Middle Ages, because of a more recent tendancy in Byzantine liturgical development to shape all the services so that their beginning and end look more or less alike. The Romans are doing somewhat the same thing today. The only difference is that they have chosen as their model the Liturgy of the Word, whereas the Byzantines, under monastic influence, opted for the Palestinian monastic office that came to hold sway throughout the Byzantine East after the fall of Constantinople to the Latins in the Fourth Crusade (1204).

We need not discuss the details of when and whence the later additions were introduced.[62] What we have seen should be sufficient to indicate how structural analysis of units can assist in the interpretation of historical sources, and in the identification and reconstruction of pristine liturgical forms, in this case the post-fourth century additions to the Byzantine Divine Liturgy.

Notes

1. *Comparative Liturgy* (Westminster Md.: Newman 1958) 18–19.

2. For the literature on this and other sources of the Byzantine liturgy, see R. Taft, *The Great Entrance* (OCA 200, Rome: PIO 1978²) "Introduction" and "Index of Manuscripts."

3. Some ancient Italian mss fill in the enarxis of the Chrysostom formulary with prayers from other Greek liturgies. A. Jacob has traced the origins of this local peculiarity, which formerly had led liturgical historians to suppose that the Chrysostom formulary was once different from that of Basil in its entirety. See A. Jacob, *Histoire du formulaire grec de la Liturgie de S. Jean Chrysostome* (unpublished doctoral dissertation, Louvain 1968); "La tradition manuscrite de la Liturgie de S. Jean Chrysostome (VIIIᵉ–XIIᵉ siècles)," *Eucharisties d'Orient et d'Occident* (Lex orandi 47, Paris: Cerf 1970) II, 109–138; "L'evoluzione dei libri liturgici bizantini in Calabria e in Sicilia dall'VIII al XVI secolo, con particolare riguardo ai riti eucaristici," *Calabria bizantina. Vita religiosa e strutture amministrative* (Atti del primo e del secondo incontro di Studi Bizantini, Reggio Calabria: Edizioni Parallelo 38, 1974) 47–69; cf. Taft, *Great Entrance* xxxi–xxxii.

4. For a complete and reliable history of the Byzantine Liturgy of the Word, see J. Mateos, *La célébration de la parole dans la liturgie byzantine* (OCA 191, Rome: PIO 1971). Mateos' study is complemented in certain details by the later work of Jacob in the ms tradition (see previous note).

5. To the best of my knowledge it first appears in the *Codex S. Simeonis Siracusani* (ca. 1030) preserved in the Latin version of Ambrose Pelargus: *Divina ac sacra Liturgia sancti Ioannis Chrysostomi. Interprete Ambrosio Pelargo Niddano, O.P. . . .* (Worms: Sebastianus Wagner 1541) f. Blv. On this source see Taft, *Great Entrance* xxvii–xxviii.

6. See A. Strittmatter, "Notes on the Byzantine Synapte," *Traditio* 10 (1954) 51–108; "A Peculiarity of the Slavic Liturgy found in Greek Euchologies," *Late Classical and Medieval Studies in Honor of Albert Mathias Friend, Jr.*, ed. K. Weitzmann (Princeton, N.J.: Princeton University Press 1955) 197–203.

7. *Loc. cit.* and Mateos, *Célébration* 29–31.

8. Ch. 9, PG 91, 688–689.

9. Mateos' treatment of the pontifical liturgy (*Célébration* 40–41) needs to be corrected somewhat, as a result of later research. See Taft, *Great Entrance* 267–269; review of C. Strube, *Die westliche Eingangsseite der Kirchen von Konstantinopel . . . OCP* 42 (1976) 300; and especially "The Pontifical Liturgy of the Great Church according to a Twelfth-Century Diataxis in Codex *British Museum Add. 34060*," *OCP* 46 (1980) 105ff.

10. N. Borgia (ed.), *Il commentario liturgico di S. Germano Patriarca Costantinopolitano e la versione latina di Anastasio Bibliotecario* (Studi liturgici 1, Grottaferrata: Badia Greca 1912) 21.

11. The history of the antiphons is reconstructed in detail by Mateos, *Célébration* 34–71.

12. J. Mateos (ed.), *Le Typicon de la Grande Eglise. Ms. Sainte-Croix No. 40. Introduction, texte critique et notes*, 2 vols. (OCA 165–166, Rome: PIO 1962–1963).

13. On the solea and other aspects of the liturgical disposition of the early Byzantine church building, see T. Mathews, *The Early Churches of Constantinople: Architecture and Liturgy* (University Park and London: Penn. State University 1971) under "solea" in the index; S. G. Xydis, "The Chancel Barrier, Solea and Ambo of Hagia Sophia," *The*

*Art Bulletin* 29 (1947) 1–24. Mateos (*Typicon* II, 321) wrongly identifies the early solea with the sanctuary platform, which is the solea in current Byzantine liturgical nomenclature. Cf. Taft, *Great Entrance* 79.

14. M. Andrieu, *Les "Ordines romani" du haut moyen âge* II: *Les textes* (*Ordines I–XIII*) (Spicilegium sacrum Lovaniense, études et documents, fasc. 23, Louvain: Université Catholique 1960) 74ff; T. Mathews, "An Early Roman Chancel Arrangement and its Liturgical Functions," *Rivista di archeologia cristiana* 38 (1962) 73–95; G. G. Willis, "Roman Stational Liturgy," *Further Essays in Early Roman Liturgy* (Alcuin Club Collections 50, London: SPCK 1968) 3–87: J. A. Jungmann, *Missarum sollemnia* I, part I.8.

15. See his *Vom geschichtlichen Werden der Liturgie* (Ecclesia orans 10, Freiburg/B.: Herder 1923) and *Comparative Liturgy*.

16. Mateos, *Typicon* I, 2–11; *Célébration* 37ff.

17. See Taft, "The Pontifical Liturgy of the Great Church" 105–106.

18. "Das Gesetz der Erhaltung des Alten in liturgisch hochwertiger Zeit," *Jahrbuch für Liturgiewissenschaft* 7 (1927) 1–23; *Comparative Liturgy* 26ff.

19. See Taft, *Great Entrance* 112ff.

20. The *akroteleution* is the final clausula of the refrain, and was repeated after the verses of the psalm; the *perisse* ("appendix") is the final repetition(s) of the refrain after the doxology that signals the end of the psalm. See Mateos, *Célébration* 16ff.

21. *Ibid.* 99–100, 112ff.

22. Mateos, *Typicon* II, 293.

23. Mateos, *Célébration* 131.

24. This prayer is mentioned by John Chrysostom in Constantinople (397–404) but there is no trace of it in Byzantine liturgical mss, the earliest of which is from the 8th century. On the witness of Chrysostom, see F. van de Paverd, *Zur Geschichte der Messliturgie in Antiocheia und Konstantinopel gegen Ende des vierten Jahrhunderts* (OCA 187, Rome: PIO 1970) 453ff, 467.

25. E.g. at the Trisagion and *prokeimenon* (Mateos, *Célébration* 106ff, 133–134) as well as the *koinônikon*, which will be treated below.

26. Chrysostom seems to indicate the presence of this prayer in the Constantinopolitan liturgy at the end of the 4th century (van de Paverd, *Messliturgie* 464, 467) but is is not found in the liturgical mss.

27. See Taft, *Great Entrance* 50–51, 375–378.

28. On the history of these rites see *ibid.*

29. Mathews, *Early Churches* 13–18, 84–85, 87, 89, 158ff, 178.

30. On the development of Byzantine liturgical symbolism see R. Taft, "The Liturgy of the Great Church: An Initial Synthesis of Structure and Interpretation on the Eve of Iconoclasm," *DOP* 34–35 (1980–1981) 45–75.

31. See Taft, *Great Entrance* 352–355.

32. For a complete study of this chant see *ibid.* ch. 2.

33. Cf. A. Baumstark, "Psalmenvortrag und Kirchendichtung des Orients," *Gottesminne, Monatsschrift für religiöse Dichtkunst* 7 (Hamm 1912–1913) 305, 428, 540–558, 887–902; H. Leeb, *Die Gesänge im Gemeindegottesdienst von Jerusalem (vom. 5 bis 8. Jahrhundert)* (Wiener Beiträge zur Theologie 28, Vienna: Herder 1970) 41, 104. On the *Phôs hilaron* see R. Taft, *The Liturgy of the Hours in the Christian East: Origins, Meaning, Place in the Life of the Church* (Cochin [India]: KCM Press 1984) ch. 3.

34. The passage from the *Protheoria* is in PG 140, 441. The whole question is discussed in Taft, *Great Entrance* 62–68. On the date of the *Protheoria* see J. Darrouzès, "Nicolas d'Andida et les azymes," *Revue des études byzantines* 32 (1974) 199–203.

35. See Taft, *Great Entrance* ch. 11.

36. See G. Winkler, "Die Interzessionen der Chrysostomusanaphora in ihrer geschichtlichen Entwicklung," *OCP* (1970) 302–303, and "Einige Randbemerkungen zu den Interzessionen in Antiochien und Konstantinopel im 4. Jahrhundert," *Ostkirchliche Studien* 20 (1971) 55–61. F. van de Paverd resumes the debate in "Anaphoral Intercessions, Epiclesis and Communion-rites in John Chrysostom," *OCP* 49 (1983) 303–339 (cf. esp. 331ff), complementing and revising some of the conclusions in his *Messliturgie*.

37. For the arguments, see Taft, *Great Entrance* ch. 9. Van de Paverd's article "Anaphoral Intercessions, Epiclesis and Communion-rites" (esp. 332ff) also provides valuable new information on the original form of the litany after the anaphora in the liturgy of Constantinople.

38. F. X. Funk, *Didascalia et Constitutiones Apostolorum* (Paderborn: F. Schoeningh 1905) I, 514–516; R. Tonneau and R. Devreesse, *Les homélies catéchétiques de Théodore de Mopsueste* (Studi e testi 145, Vatican: Bibliotheca Apostolica Vaticana 1949) 563–565.

39. Cyrille de Jérusalem, *Catéchèses mystagogiques*, ed. A. Piédagnel, trans. P. Paris (SC 126, Paris: Cerf 1966) 160–169.

40. *Ep. 149*, 16, CSEL 44, 362.

41. *De capto Eutropio* 5, PG 52, 396; cf. van de Paverd, *Messliturgie* 526–527.

42. Ed. Funk I, 514–516.

43. *Célébration* 60, 169ff, 180–181.

44. Van de Paverd, *Messliturgie* 527–528.

45. *Hom 16*, 22, ed. Tonneau-Devreesse 565.

46. Ed. Funk I, 516.

47. See A. Jacob, *Histoire du formulaire grec* 60–61 and part I *passim*.

48. Taft, *Great Entrance* 84.

49. *Ibid.* 83–108; Mateos, *Célébration* 34–44, 106–114.

50. PG 92, 1001.

51. See T. Schattauer, "The Koinonicon of the Byzantine Liturgy: An Historical Study," *OCP* 49 (1983) 91–129 for a thorough study of the *koinônika* in the Typicon. The two non-scriptural refrains are discussed on pp. 100–101, 109–110 (nos. 3 and 19).

52. See Mateos, *Célébration* 16; Taft, *Great Entrance* 86–88.

53. Mateos, *Célébration* 7–13.

54. "The Koinonicon" 115ff.

55. Ed. Piédagnel 168–170.

56. Ed. Funk I, 518.

57. PG 55, 464; cf. van de Paverd, *Messliturgie* 395; Schattauer, "The Koinonicon" 116–117.

58. *Die Gesänge im Gemeindegottesdienst von Jerusalem* 128.

59. Van de Paverd, *Messliturgie* 106, 156, 164, 185–186.

60. Antiphonal psalmody is first heard of in 347–348 in Antioch, in Theodoret of Cyrus, *Hist. eccl.* II, 24:8–11, L. Parmentier (ed.), *Theodoret Kirchengeschichte*, revised by

F. Scheidweiler (GCS, Berlin: Akademie-Verlag 1954[2]) 154–155. The preanaphoral chant first appears in 5-6th century sources (cf. Taft, *Great Entrance* 40, 53, 65–66). The introit chant appears in Roman and Byzantine stational liturgies in the same period (Jungmann, *Missarum sollemnia* I, part III.8; Mateos, *Célébration* 112ff).

61. *Die Gesänge im Gemeindegottesdienst von Jerusalem* 128–132.

62. In a forthcoming volume on the anaphora, communion, postcommunion and final rites of the Byzantine liturgy I hope to be able to clarify some of this history.

# INDEX

Abbott, W.M., 147
'Abdallah, A., 108
*accessus ad altare*, 180; see preanaphoral
    rites
Acts of John, apocryphal, 76
Afanas'ev, N., 89, 98
*akroteleution*, 157–8, 176, 190
Alexandrine(s), 19–23, 26, 28
Alexij, Patriarch of Moscow, 111
aliturgical days, 56, 64–9
Allatius, Leo, 69, 79
Ambrose, 63, 76
anamnesis, 2–3, 6–10, 15, 18, 20–1, 25,
    29, 54, 56, 58, 127ff, 142–4;
    eucharistic, 29; in the hours, 127ff,
    142–4; basis of Christian liturgy
    and prayer, 142–4
Anastasius of Sinai, 37
Andrieu, M., 98, 108, 190
anointing of the sick, concelebration of,
    84
antiphons, antiphonal psalmody:
    meaning, execution, structure,
    reconstruction of, 157–9, 173–4,
    181, 185–7, 191; Byzantine, 158,
    171, 173–6, 181, 185–7; refrains
    (antiphons) of, 181, 184–7, 190
Antiochene(s), 20–3, 26, 28
*Apostolic Constitutions*, 38, 64, 97, 132,
    147, 156, 163–4, 183–4, 187
*Apostolic Tradition* of Hippolytus, 22, 97,
    139, 148
Arianism, 20–2, 29
Arnaldez, R., 28
Arranz, M., 162
Arseniev, N., 59
Arsenius, Abbot, 59
asceticism, mortification, 50–3, 57; see
    fasting and penance
Assemani, J.A., 109
Athanasius of Alexandria, 63, 76–7
Athanasius III Petelarus, Patriarch of
    Constantinople, 103
Aucher, J.B., 77
Augustine, 29, 63, 76, 184

Avraam of Smolensk, 71
Aznavourian, Z., 80

Badger, G.P., 109
Baldovin, J., 24
Balsaman, Theodore, 72
baptism, 51–3, 56, 58, 130; as
    illumination, 135, 142, 162–3; Lent
    prepares for, 53, 113
baptismal catecheses and typology, 19–
    21, 23, 53, 113
Bar Hebraeus, Gregory, 67, 106, 109
Barr, J., 12
Barsamian, Kh., 80, 109
Basil the Great, 35, 63–4, 76, 79, 87, 97,
    115, 134, 139–41, 146–7; Byzantine
    Liturgy of, 172, 178, 184, 189
Barnabus, 86, 97
Basset, R., 77
Baumstark, A., 16, 27, 151, 162, 164,
    174–5, 190
Baynes, N.H., 76
Bedjan, P., 109
Benedict, 69
Benoit, A., 28
Betz, J., 29
Bohl, H., 80
Borgia, N., 189
Bornert, R., 28–9
Botte, B., 27, 29, 97
Boulard, E., 28
Bourgeois, C., 126
Bouyer, L., 97
Brackmann, H., 84, 96–7
Braso, G., 147
Brightman, F.E., 96, 163–4
Brown, R., 1, 6
Browne, P., 80
Byzantine Divine Liturgy (Eucharist):
    anaphoral intercessions, 183–91;
    antiphons and their prayers, 158,
    171, 173–6, 186; Cherubicon, 122,
    178–82; communion rites, 103–4,
    106, 182–7, 192; concelebration,
    83–4, 96–7, 103–4; creed, 178, 182;